What People Are Saying About

BJ Mann has the unique ability to turn a painful situation into one where the parties can grow and maintain respect. Her compassion, combined with her mediation skills, allow her clients to work through the negotiations in an efficient and fair manner. Her thoughtful, experienced process achieves the best possible result for both parties, and prepares them to move on with their lives in a positive way.
   —David B. Cook, Esq.

As a neutral scribing attorney for BJ Mann, I find that the couples who come to me have been comprehensively and professionally facilitated/served, have benefited from managing their anxiety over the process with BJ's help, and are well prepared to move forward into the next phase of their lives with dignity and confidence.
   —Sharon DiMuro, Esq.

BJ was wonderful. She made a difficult experience much easier through her compassion, her wisdom, and her expertise. Ending a marriage is never easy, but she kept us on track, helped both of us to feel that our concerns were being heard and addressed, and guided us through the bewildering maze of details that we would never have known about if not for her. She's incredibly kind, patient, and understanding. I've recommended her to several people already and will continue to do so.
   —Karyn Dolan, former client

BJ Mann has dedicated herself as a mediator and quickly rose to become a highly insightful and respected practitioner. She has brought to this role a sensitivity and empathy from her personal experience, a precise organizational skill from her previous professional life, and a generosity and compassion to the great benefit of her clients. BJ's multi-faceted disciplined approach to her work has attracted thousands of grateful clients who have trusted her to gently guide them through difficult times. BJ's knack of concisely explaining the dimensions of divorce and its impact upon families, from finances to relationships, will make eager and informed readers of those who open this book.
   —Gail Ferraioli, Clarity Mediations

I've worked with BJ Mann and her mediation clients as a financial expert for many years. Her clients uniformly praise her mediation skills, knowledge, and ability to help them navigate through challenging, emotionally charged situations.
   —Kristen Jenks, CFA, Lumina Partners, LLC

Library of Congress Cataloging-in-Publication Data available.

ISBN 978-0-692-99456-6

Cover and book design by Lori Capron Galan
Author photo by Ben Ferro

Printed in the United States of America
First printing 2018

This book is dedicated to...

...my husband, Turk, who is the very best part of my post-divorce life. Turk has been part of my mediation journey and career from the beginning. My first mediation teacher, Mara Fain, introduced us sixteen years ago. From that time, to launching my practice, to the loving and tireless support he gives me every day, Turk is the wind beneath my wings in every way. It is because of his generous spirit and energy that I am able to sustain my mediation practice and my balance. I could not be the mediator I am today without him.

...the notion that a couple can transform from husband and wife to mom and dad, and the vision that former spouses can maintain a positive relationship without regretting the past.

Table of Contents

Foreword

Respect and dignity are the keys to a successful divorce negotiation, but these two elements were largely absent from divorce law practice until fairly recently. Today, we can thank mediators like BJ Mann for changing the way couples can approach divorce, and for bringing civility and compassion to the process.

As an attorney, I come from a background of adversarial, contested divorce law and was originally opposed to the concept of divorce mediation. My training as an attorney taught me that divorce was a zero-sum competition that could be won on behalf of one party. Attorneys considered it a victory when assets could be divided unequally or unreasonable levels of support could be bargained or won in court. Family homes and access to the children were prizes to be won and denied to the other party.

Mediators came at the issues from a different point of view. They focused on the family and what it needed to continue serving the needs of the parents and children, even if they were going to be living in separate households.

Attorneys did not respect mediators. They thought them to be naïve, untrained and focused only on reaching superficial agreement regardless of whether the settlement was practical or fair. Mediators thought that attorneys were unnecessarily combative and turned unhappy couples into angry warriors, all at the expense of the children.

Mediators typically advised their clients to stay away from attorneys, and attorneys typically advised their clients to stay away from mediators. Each group thought that the other would ruin their process.

In Rochester, New York, the differences between divorce mediation and legal process seemed to be diverging until two changes occurred. Mediators became better informed on the law and financial information, and attorneys started to realize that even divorcing couples shared common interests for the future.

Mediators formed professional organizations and developed comprehensive training for themselves in areas of dispute resolution, legal concepts, and the tax and other implications of various financial holdings. Attorneys started to learn about the benefits of "alternative" dispute resolution, which included mediation and collaborative law in addition to litigation.

For the last dozen years of my practice, I learned and later became an instructor in Collaborative Law. Collaborative Law taught attorneys the dynamics of settlement and what was needed to bring about a fair settlement for their clients. In Collaborative Law, the parties meet in a series of conferences with their attorneys present and often with a financial or child specialist to advise the parties on important decisions. Full financial disclosure is shared before any decisions are made.

By using some of the techniques developed by mediation, attorneys were able to provide better service to their clients. By learning more about the legal system and probable outcomes in court, mediators were also able to improve the outcomes for their clients.

BJ has been a leader in the Rochester community in delivering the most professional level of divorce mediation. She has also been a strong force for the training that is needed to resolve some of the most difficult situations.

BJ has not only shown remarkable sensitivity to the people that she encounters, but has looked behind positions to help people address their real needs. She has learned as much of the law in this area as many attorneys and knows that courts can be unpredictable.

BJ practices a combination of expertise and compassion that has made her a leader in her field and recognized as one of the best mediators in the Rochester area.

I have had the pleasure of sitting in on some of BJ's mediation sessions. I have seen her deal with some of the most difficult matrimonial situations with couples who are reeling from the pain and turmoil of their family situation. I have seen her mix of wisdom, compassion, and strength in dealing with people who are bewildered by their situation and may be defensive, angry, damaged and frightened. Her focus is on reaching settlements, but she is not willing to allow a settlement that is reached out of ignorance, fear or weakness.

Any dispute can be resolved. The issue is whether it is resolved in such a way that it is sustainable and recognizes the needs of all parties and treats them with respect and dignity. It is only from this recognition that people are able to find common settlements.

Every divorce is different, just as every marriage is different. People entering into this frightening period of their lives need to question what kind of process they want to resolve their disputes. What level of decision-making will they retain for themselves, and how much will they cede to surrogates or professionals? People in crisis tend to be somewhat shortsighted in their needs and actions. The manner in which a resolution is sought may be remembered by the parties and their children long after the particulars of a settlement are forgotten.

BJ has provided her wisdom, compassion, and strength as a mediator, as a mentor to new mediators, and as a leader in the mediation community. She has now written this book, which should be a guide to couples entering into the difficult period of redefining their families, and a text book to both new and experienced mediators. These pages hold the wisdom of years of experience.

—Michael Hagelberg

Michael Hagelberg practiced law in Rochester, New York for more than thirty-five years. He is a former president of the M. K. Gandhi Institute for Nonviolence and a facilitator in Restorative Justice Conferences for the Center for Dispute Settlement. Michael volunteers for the Curbside Market of Foodlink, bringing fresh fruit and vegetables to food deserts in Rochester, and he serves as a tutor in Rochester city schools.

Introduction

The Better Way... or the Bitter Way

Over the many years I have helped clients end their marriages, I am frequently the only one in the room holding the possibility of their future happiness.

Regardless of why the marriage is ending, there is always sadness and mourning. It's not what couples imagined when they walked down their wedding aisle.

Divorce is the end of a vision and a dream. That's why it can feel like a death in the family for so many people.

With this in mind, I have good news for you. Through others' stories and by meeting with couples for post-divorce mediation, I've learned that, within about two years following the divorce, each person begins to thrive.

Thriving looks different to different people. For some, it is the relief of not having tension in the home and not having to consult on simple decisions like what's for dinner. One client finally got the puppy dog she'd been yearning for her whole life. She recounts how that little dog brought joy and laughter back into her home to her and her three young teenagers.

For others, new relationships are more solid because they are forged in honesty and choice. People do learn a lot about relationships when they go through a divorce. They wisely use that information to understand the qualities they want in a partner.

In this book, I provide the information you need to choose the kind of process you want to use to end your marriage, as well as the facts, formulae, and procedures involved in separating your lives from one another. I am a mediator, so I do emphasize the benefits of an uncontested divorce and mediation throughout this book. But if you choose to follow the path of a contested divorce, the facts of splitting your assets and debts, determining spousal and child support, and custody issues are all the same. You will find this book useful no matter which way you decide to go.

I've divided this book into several parts:

- **What is Divorce?** I start with the definitions you need to know: contested versus uncontested divorce, mediation versus attorneys and court, and what goes on in mediation. I also provide you with ways to have that first discussion with your spouse in which you both acknowledge that your marriage is ending—and insights about how to proceed if it's over for one of you, but not the other.

- **The Legal Divorce.** Here I talk about the legal facts of divorce and what it will mean for you and your family. I provide definitions and information about legal terms and what impact your choices will have.
- **The Economic Divorce.** This is the nuts-and-bolts, facts-and-figures section, where you'll find all the formulae required by the guidelines to divide your assets and debts and determine spousal and child support. While many of the examples rely on New York State laws, the concepts are useful wherever you reside.
- **The Children's Divorce.** Child custody issues are critical, but sorting out the legal logistics is only the beginning of the road for children who now live in two residences—or who see one of their parents much less often than the other. I provide all the insights I can about the ups and downs of joint, shared, and sole custody, and the emotions children feel when their home life splits down the middle.
- **The Emotional Divorce.** Once your divorce is final, how do you go forward? I share with you the insights collected from more than 2,000 clients who have passed through my office.

You also will see tips highlighted throughout this book: **Better** *and* **Bitter**. At many points in the process, you come to a crossroad where you can choose to take the high road—the *Better Way*—or create complications out of anger, resentment, or a desire to hurt or punish your spouse—the *Bitter Way*. Nearly everyone going

---

Five Things Divorced People Learned from Marriage [1]

A Wall Street Journal article recently listed the results of a 25-year study of couples who married in 1986. The couples who divorced named five things they would do differently when they approach a new relationship:

- They would give their new partner more affirmations: compliments, cuddling, kissing, holding hands, and saying "I love you."
- They would discuss money more, setting ground rules for spending and expectations about saving.
- They would put the past aside, including baggage they brought with them into the relationship that had little or nothing to do with their partner.
- They would blame the relationship for their problems, not one another. Instead of saying, "You make things so difficult," they would say, "We're both so tired lately. What can we do to get along better?"
- They would communicate more openly, and learn to argue in ways that produce solutions.

[1] Bernstein, Elizabeth. "Divorcé's Guide to Marriage." *Wall Street Journal*, July 24, 2012, accessed Nov. 19, 2017. www.wsj.com/articles/SB10000872396390444025204577544951717564114

through divorce has moments like this, and I want to bring them to your attention to help you make the best decision for you. Keep an eye out for these; they may help you avoid some of the most common obstacles to progress.

My Divorce Journey

I would not have found the career of divorce mediation if my marriage had not ended more than twenty years ago. I can still feel how collapsed I was when my marriage of twenty-five years ended. I referred to myself as a "puddle on the floor." And yet, after the first rough year, my resiliency kicked in, and I became committed to helping others cross this bridge.

The ugly wrapping paper of my divorce brought me the beautiful gifts of my new career, meaning, and purpose. Today I am an Accredited Member of the New York State Council of Divorce Mediation and an Advanced Practitioner Mediator for the Association for Conflict Resolution (ACR), the highest credentials offered by these organizations. I would not have been motivated to pursue this profession had I not been through my divorce and found my passion for helping others not only survive the end of their marriages, but thrive as well.

> *"Tell me. What is it you plan to do with your one wild and precious life?"*
> —Mary Oliver

I am actually grateful—now—that my ex-husband and I had the courage to end our marriage and admit that we were not intended to grow old together. But in the moment, that was very difficult.

A Strong Path Forward

This book will help you take the right steps toward ending your marriage in the most gentle, cooperative, and equitable way possible. It also will help you find your way forward, taking the strong path toward healing and building your new, independent life.

You'll find answers here to all of your questions about ending your marriage, the materials and information you need to gather whether you use mediation or another process, the decisions you need to make, and a positive way forward that you can begin the day you decide your marriage must end.

I know you picked up this book because you're considering the hardest decision you may ever make. Before we get started, I want to share several important strategies that helped me and may help you, even in this early stage of your journey.

- **Find an impartial sounding board.** This is a time when old wounds get triggered. You want to avoid having them infect you like a virus, pushing you backwards. Finding a counselor or a skilled listener, like a pastor, is so important. In this setting you can express your feelings without feeling vulnerable. Friends and relatives may not have the same level of listening skills, patience, or objectivity.

- **Exercise.** Set a goal of exercise for at least thirty minutes every day. This is a proven strategy to reset your emotional well-being. For thirty minutes a day, you and your body know that you are important and that you intend to be healthy.
- **Meditate.** It's easy to roll your eyes at the thought of meditating. Trust me, I did for years. It turns out there really is no wrong way to meditate. Sit down in a special spot every day for ten minutes. Even if during nine of those minutes you are thinking about your to-do list, the idea that you are "meditating" and sitting still becomes a pattern. Day after day, it makes a difference. Do not judge the experience. Just do it.
- **Claim your wellness.** There is an expression in twelve-step recovery programs that states: "Actions first, then beliefs." Build on your progress. Declare that you exercise and meditate. Report that you are feeling better. Do not diminish your progress by minimizing your resiliency.
- **The struggle is optional.** Life is full of challenges and there are good times, sad times, bad times. The key is acceptance and curiosity. Yes, change feels scary, and yet there is often a silver lining. The struggle and resistance are optional. Volumes have been written about how the way you view things matters. **It is your choice to resist or accept.** A wonderful book, *It's Easier Than You Think: The Buddhist Way to Happiness* by Sylvia Boorstein, expands on this idea.

Whether you say that "beautiful gifts can come in ugly wrapping paper," or "everything happens for a reason," life is a journey. Sometimes there are hills and mountains and sometimes there are beautiful fields, but either way, we cannot see beyond the horizon.

Acceptance does not mean that you will not feel grief and sadness, but that you can have faith in the future. Have faith that what's around the corner for you is positive.

Let's get started.

PART 1
What is Divorce?

Chapter 1

What is Divorce Mediation?

"A journey of a thousand miles begins with a single step."
–Lao-tzu

Dear Readers: Let me say from the outset that I want you to choose the right method for you and your spouse as you approach the end of your marriage. This book emphasizes mediation because I am a mediator, and because I have seen so many couples benefit from the efficiency and affordability of a mediated divorce. The contents of this book apply to any process you use, whether you negotiate in the privacy of a mediator's office, engage two attorneys who haggle over the details in a conference room, or face a judge in a courtroom.

Some people approach the process of divorce with great fear because of the dramatizations they've seen on television. Whether you're a fan of the syndicated TV series *Divorce Court* or you've seen lots of movies that feature long courtroom battles over custody, you may think that these are the only options for you and your family.

Nothing could be further from the truth. You have a number of choices when you approach your own divorce. There's rarely a need to appear in a courtroom, and you can come away with a congenial relationship between you and your ex-spouse.

Essentially, there are two basic categories of divorce: uncontested and contested. In an uncontested divorce, the spouses come to agreement on the terms of their divorce, and they do not need a court to divide their assets or make decisions about child custody or support. Divorce mediation is always an option for uncontested divorces. You can also use attorneys for an uncontested divorce. An uncontested divorce moves through the system fairly quickly and at a lower cost than a contested divorce, which involves an attorney for each side.

In a contested divorce, the spouses cannot agree on the terms. They may disagree about getting divorced at all, about the division of their assets and debts, or about the custody of their children (or many other things). Each spouse hires his or her own attorney, and the attorneys meet, both with and without the spouses, to negotiate the details. The process can take a long time with a significant cost for the attorneys' billable hours.

Most contested divorces do not reach a courtroom, but some do—often when one spouse wants to punish the other, and children can become pawns in this battle. We'll talk more about what this entails when we discuss child custody and support in Chapter 6, but I can tell you now that when your divorce comes before a judge, you relinquish the final decision-making ability about your future. Whatever decision the judge makes, you must abide by it, even though it may involve access to your children. This makes a courtroom divorce a battle of last resort, to be used only if you and your spouse truly cannot negotiate any other way.

In most cases, an attorney will file the final documents with the court system. In an uncontested divorce, a neutral or "scribe" attorney can complete the paperwork based on a mediated Memorandum of Understanding (MOU). In a contested divorce, both attorneys are involved in completing and filing the divorce documents.

Mediation and the Uncontested Divorce

When you hear the word "mediation," what do you think of? Most people connect it to making peace, compromising, or resolving a conflict with the help of an objective third party. Mediation is used worldwide to work through many topics such as international problems, labor disputes, church conflicts, eldercare, and family issues.

> **Better**
>
> *Even high-conflict clients can use mediation. It's a myth that only cooperative couples are successful in mediation.*

Increasingly, people are also connecting mediation to divorce mediation, which is the focus of my practice. Divorce mediation is a settlement process for couples who want to end their relationship without using the court system. It gives you and your spouse the option to stay in charge of your futures in an atmosphere of cooperation and mutual respect and to hear what each other says directly.

Divorce mediation provides an opportunity for couples to end their marriages in an efficient, affordable, and gentle manner. Most couples are not on the same psychological page about ending their marriage. Each person is scared and often hurt or angry. However, when you both are well-informed, you are able to make decisions, and you often can repair a portion of the relationship that allows you to go forward.

During the mediation process, the two of you review all the information, work through your issues, evaluate your options, and choose how to move forward.

Then those decisions are written into a durable, lasting, and fair agreement custom-made for both you and your family. The mediation enhances your opportunity to feel valued, respected, and understood.

The MOU itself is not binding or enforceable. When completed, the MOU is ready to be processed into the legal system. Clients can use one neutral attorney to process the papers, or each person can have their own separate attorney review the MOU and either file the papers or have a neutral attorney process the agreement. Again, the decision is yours.

I have to admit being a mediator is both an art and a science. A mediator needs to listen, facilitate, inform, and also understand "divorce math" while all the time remaining neutral. It is a balancing process that requires skills and ongoing training. I am proud to have earned the professional designation of Advanced Practitioner Mediator after a rigorous process of review and observation.

With the assistance of a trained divorce mediator, you will be guided to answer questions that are custom-made for your family, your finances, and your future. I'm going to talk about my own practice from this point, but I hope this will help you determine what to ask any mediator or attorney you interview to help you with your divorce.

I make sure that you and your spouse are both well-informed. For example, my process takes you both through a series of orderly steps to create an agreement that you both consider to be fair and reasonable. I help you understand all of the issues in this book, gather and analyze the necessary information, and communicate effectively with each other.

Here's how the process works: It begins with a consultation for both of you together, where the mediation process is discussed and homework provided to make the process efficient. After the consult, you meet with me for a series of sessions. The number of sessions can vary, though many mediations require no more than two or three. To keep the process moving forward, the focus is on making the decisions needed to bring this phase of your relationship to a close.

You will sign a mediation contract with me that provides guidelines for a successful mediation. The contract details my qualifications and the role of the mediator in your divorce, my fees, the roles attorneys may play in the process, and my agreement to treat your mediation as an entirely confidential process. It also outlines your responsibility to disclose all of your financial records, and your agreement that you and your spouse will not hide assets or debts from one another during the mediation process.

Each of you is expected to gather and bring all information and paperwork concerning financial and other issues to the sessions as needed.

If you and your spouse have children, they are the first priority. We work together to create a parenting plan. We also work through how each of you will be able to afford a comparable household for your children.

Better

When you separate your finances and share them evenly, the effect is like having one tablecloth and putting it over two tables.

Then we talk about finances and arrangements concerning the marital residence, retirement assets, debts, health insurance, life insurance, and taxes, as well as any other relevant issues. Together, you will find a pathway to separate your finances and become two households.

Better

Sometimes I suggest to clients to "buy the balcony seats." I encourage them to look at their situation as if they were up in the balcony looking down at the drama on center stage. It creates a pause and often a new perspective.

I am often asked whether divorce mediation is the same as couples' therapy. While it's true that there are similarities, each has a different focus. Usually, couples' therapy focuses on issues with the goal of continuing your relationship. In divorce mediation, the focus is on resolving the practical and financial issues and on being Mom and Dad rather than husband and wife.

Even so, the magic of mediation is that it can balance the emotional and practical issues. The opportunity for healing and understanding makes mediation very effective and the agreements more durable. The clients are not rushed through the process; I make sure the pace supports the needs of both people.

Going through a divorce is a difficult emotional, practical, and financial process. As a guide, I have helped many couples cross the scary bridge from marriage to independence. Together, we navigate the maze to efficiently and affordably bring your marriage or partnership to a close.

How to Begin the End of Your Marriage

The phone rings, and the caller speaks.

"I'm calling to get more information about the divorce mediation process. My husband just told me he wants to end our marriage, and I don't know what to do. We both agree we need to end our marriage. What are the next steps?"

Whether by phone or by email, the first inquiry to start the process to end a marriage is always poignant. Over the years of my practice, I have valued these first connections as a way to bring reassurance, calm, and order to what is often a difficult and emotional conversation.

Clients later reflect that making that first call of inquiry is one of the biggest hurdles in ending the marriage. As one client said, "It makes it seem so real."

When clients begin making decisions regarding ending their marriage, they often feel as if they are entering a deep, dark woods with no path, flashlight, or map.

Many express a wish that they could understand all of the things they need to discuss in order to prepare and not be surprised.

On one hand, knowing everything that needs to be discussed is useful. On the other hand, I caution my clients not to try to figure out everything before we get started. Kitchen table negotiations often end up emotional and scary. I encourage clients to think about things, but not to negotiate anything yet. I am your guide to help you cross the bridge from marriage to independence, and it is actually more efficient and gentler to let me guide the discussion.

> **Bitter**
>
> *Kitchen table negotiations often end up emotional and scary. I encourage clients to think about things, but not to negotiate anything.*

What is most reassuring to potential clients is that the first step in my practice is a relaxed consultation. In answering the initial inquiry, I emphasize that the consult is just for gathering information:

- In my practice, there is no fee for the initial consult.
- No decisions have to be made during this first session.
- There is nothing that has to be prepared before coming to the session.
- There is no obligation.

So while "relaxed" may not be quite the way they would describe this first step, potential clients who arrive for their initial, 30-45 minute consultation are able to hear and absorb information about the divorce mediation process without any strings attached.

My job in the divorce mediation process is to guide you through the conversations you need to have to create an MOU. Along the way, I provide useful information about the divorce process. Your focus during the process is to consider your options as well as each other's needs and requests to make your decisions together.

After gathering some brief details, I go over the elements that you will need to think about to create a comprehensive agreement. We do not discuss details in the initial consult, but I review the concepts of a parenting plan, sharing money between each person (child support and/or spousal maintenance), sharing retirement funds, options for the home, life insurance, health insurance, and other relevant issues.

Sometimes the discussion during the initial consult digresses into other very important top-

Better

The Memorandum of Understanding is a blueprint for the future. You don't need to have everything in the blueprint finalized before you sign the agreement. Once it is signed, you can begin to follow and develop it as needed.

ics. It is an opportunity for clients to share their worries and concerns. Here is a sampling of what else might be discussed:

- How and when to tell the children.
- When to begin living separately.
- What needs to be done to get a spouse's name off the mortgage, and options for refinancing.
- Exploring options when you and your spouse are not on the same page about ending the marriage. In some cases, I may suggest a marriage counselor (see page 21).
- If your debt situation suggests that a bankruptcy attorney should be consulted.
- Names of financial planners and resources who can calculate the value of a business and/or pensions.
- Books, websites and support groups that may be useful based on your specific situation.

There are areas in which advance preparation really makes the divorce mediation process more efficient. If this information is not gathered before starting the mediation process, you will need to pull it together during the process before the MOU can be completed.

1. Identifying Assets and Debts

- The fair market value of the marital home (and any other properties you may own).
- The balance on all retirement funds (401(k), IRAs, pensions).
- The value of assets owned by either person, like savings, mutual funds, stocks, a businesses.
- The value of your vehicles (unless leasing), boats, RVs, etc.
- The balances on debts, including credit cards, mortgage, student loans, vehicle loans, etc.

2. Preparing Budgets for Both People

It is essential for you to have an appreciation for how much living separately is going to cost. Think of it as if you have two tables but just one tablecloth. When you discuss sharing money (either child support or spousal maintenance or both), the costs of meeting the needs of both people must be considered:

- Separate housing, insurance, car payments, food, utilities, pet care (more on this in Chapter 5).
- Children's expenses such as clothes, child care, and extracurricular activities (this is explained in detail in Chapter 8).

How Long Does the Divorce Mediation Process Take?

Lots of variables go into how long the process will take. I will not rush you, but I do help my clients stay focused. Once I have gathered information, I can make a good estimate of how long the mediation process will take. Issues that affect the length of time are:

- Do you have children? If so, what are their ages?
- Do you own a house?
- Are you and your spouse currently living together, or separately?
- What is your debt situation?
- What are your individual work situations? Do you work for an employer, or are you self-employed?
- How well are you able to communicate with each other?

Unlike a retainer agreement with an attorney, no money is required in advance. I am paid at the end of each session. When you work with divorce attorneys, you and your spouse will each sign a retainer agreement with the attorney, and you will each pay your attorney a sum of money upfront (the retainer). This may not be all the money you will pay your attorney—often the retainer needs to be supplemented by additional funds during the process.

The work we will do together is kept completely confidential. The only document you will sign in my office is our agreement to work together. All of the legal documents required to file your divorce are signed later, in the office of a neutral attorney or with your own separate attorney.

Once you have selected me as your mediator, each divorce mediation session is usually scheduled as a two-hour meeting. When clients have children, the mediation process generally takes 2-3 sessions. If there are no children, the process usually takes 1-2 sessions. Mediation is typically not a long process; sometimes, however, more sessions are needed for various reasons.

Once the process is completed, we have a final session where you both review the MOU I have drafted to make any changes and clarifications. Clients can then have the MOU reviewed by separate attorneys or other resources. If there are further changes or edits, I make those changes as well.

Including the time to draft the agreement, the mediation process typically takes about 8-12 billable hours. In the initial consult, we discuss my hourly rate and how the sliding scale and any discounts apply.

I know that throughout the mediation process, couples find information to be very comforting. I encourage folks to call me, seven days a week, if you have any follow-up questions or need other resources. Most important, I hold all aspects of my relationship with my clients as confidential, including the fact that you are clients. Whether I am working with an individual or a couple, I divulge nothing to anyone other than the client unless both clients agree to a disclosure to a third party.

At the end of almost every consult, you will leave knowing more than when you came in. You will likely be more relaxed and have a pathway that makes sense to start the journey. My clients are often reassured in knowing there is a process that is affordable, gentle, and efficient, and that they have met a divorce mediator who can guide them across the bridge from marriage to independence.

Getting to the Agreement: The Master List

Divorce is complicated. The following is a comprehensive list of issues that need to be discussed so that the final divorce papers are thorough and complete. Not all items on the list will be relevant to you. This list is the same whether you use mediation or work with attorneys.

Keep in mind that other issues might arise that are not listed here. Every couple's situation is unique, so if you don't see a topic here that you want to discuss, make a note to talk about it during your consultation.

Going through your divorce with the guidance of an experienced divorce mediator allows you to settle all of your issues quickly, peacefully, and privately.

Better
If this list seems insurmountable, don't panic—not all items pertain to your situation.

Parenting and Schedule

- ☐ Telling the children about living separately
- ☐ Children's "Bill of Rights" when parents divorce
- ☐ The daily parenting plan: When the day begins and ends
- ☐ Timeline for living separately
- ☐ Holidays: When they begin and end, and when they are shared
- ☐ Vacation: How many days annually, and how selected
- ☐ Who will be with the kids when the other parent is not available (right of first refusal)
- ☐ Sick days: Who will care for the children
- ☐ Hospitalization of child or parent: How it will be handled
- ☐ Childcare: How to select a provider and location
- ☐ Selection of schools: Where the child will attend
- ☐ Transportation: How are the children transported to each parent's home, to school, and to extracurricular activities
- ☐ Introducing children to significant others as you begin new relationships

Legal Custody of Children

- ☐ Joint, shared, or sole custody
- ☐ Designation and implication of primary residential parent
- ☐ Decision-making: Which are joint decisions and which are made by each parent individually
- ☐ Children's birth certificates, passports, and other legal documents
- ☐ Permission to travel with the children
- ☐ Access to the children when not parenting
- ☐ Expectations regarding religious education and customs
- ☐ Death of either parent
- ☐ Relocation of a parent
- ☐ Substance abuse or addictions
- ☐ Surnames and parent designation of Mom and Dad
- ☐ Pet custody and expenses

Child Support

- ☐ Calculating child support in divorce
- ☐ Child support enforcement unit
- ☐ New York State Child Support Guidelines
- ☐ Proration: Percentage of income of each parent compared to total family income
- ☐ When child support begins

- ☐ How child support will be paid
- ☐ Documentation of income
- ☐ Self-employed parent versus a W-2 employee parent
- ☐ Child care, health insurance, and uninsured medical expenses
- ☐ Other expenses for kids such as extra-curricular expenses and milestone events
- ☐ Pre-college private school costs: Tuition, room/board, books, other expenses
- ☐ College-related costs: Tuition, room/board, books, other expenses
- ☐ Frequency and circumstances for review/modification of child support

The House

- ☐ Calculating equity
- ☐ How to share the equity
- ☐ Removing names from or keeping names on mortgages and titles
- ☐ Homeowner's insurance
- ☐ Whether to sell the house
- ☐ Funding the house if refinanced
- ☐ Funding the house while you're selling it
- ☐ Sole occupancy of house
- ☐ When to live separately
- ☐ If someone dies while house is jointly titled and mortgaged

Other Assets

- ☐ Documentation of all assets
- ☐ Retirement funds, stocks, mutual funds, etc.: How to distribute
- ☐ Defined pensions: How to divide and value
- ☐ Cars, boats, campers: Titles, registrations, and loans
- ☐ Household Items: How to distribute and value
- ☐ Define separate property
- ☐ Valuation dates
- ☐ College funds (such as 529 plans)
- ☐ Value of business

Debts

- ☐ Credit cards
- ☐ Student loans

- ☐ Retirement or pension loans
- ☐ Car loans
- ☐ Bankruptcy
- ☐ Effect of divorce on credit and your credit report
- ☐ Shared or separate liability

Spousal Maintenance (Alimony)

- ☐ Temporary spousal maintenance vs. post-divorce maintenance
- ☐ How much and for how long
- ☐ Spousal maintenance guidelines
- ☐ Tax implications
- ☐ Conditions of terminating or modifying

Miscellaneous

- ☐ Changing your last name
- ☐ Health insurance for the adults
- ☐ Life insurance: Beneficiary amount and designation, for how long
- ☐ Taxes: Head of household, dependency allowances, child tax credit, and other tax filing status issues
- ☐ Future tax audits and liability
- ☐ Wills, health care proxy, and power of attorney updates
- ☐ Religious annulment
- ☐ Resolving and updating future changes to the separation agreement, and enforcement
- ☐ Social Security

Mediation and Divorce Process

- ☐ Legal separation or no-fault divorce: What's the difference
- ☐ Do fault grounds still exist?
- ☐ Designation of the plaintiff and defendant in the legal paperwork
- ☐ Fees and resources to process the MOU into the legal system
- ☐ Attorney review
- ☐ How to pay mediation and divorce fees

How to Choose a Divorce Mediator

Mediators are not all the same, so you need to consider the qualities you hope to find in the mediator you eventually choose. Here are some questions to help you make the best choice for you:

1. **Does your mediator have financial experience?** Divorce has a lot of economic issues, so experience with financial and business issues can be a big plus. Inquire about your mediator's background and comfort with the economics of divorce.

2. **Does your mediator have training and credentials?** Divorce mediation is an unregulated field, and while there are excellent training programs and accrediting organizations, there is no specific training requirement. This means that some mediators may have limited experience and mediate only a few cases. You need a mediator with a proven level of experience, so look for one who has made the effort to become trained, earn advanced professional accreditation, and works full-time as a mediator. For example, the New York State Council for Divorce Mediation and the Association for Conflict Resolution (ACR) require many hours of training, face-to-face practice, and experience before a mediator can earn accreditation. Ask your mediator about his or her credentials.

3. **Is your mediator a part-time consultant or a full-time practitioner?** Has he or she had hundreds or thousands of cases, or just a few? Most couples would prefer to work with someone who has a lot of experience so their issues are not unusual to the mediator. I have a large practice and have helped more than 2,000 clients. While I am always learning, there are not many issues that I have not encountered over the years. If you own multiple businesses, have real estate in many states, have tricky issues with your children, or have unusual assets or mountains of debt, I have dealt with other couples like you. I attend conferences and take continuing education courses, and I also keep abreast of changing rules and laws to be sure I give you the most current information.

4. **Does your mediator have a network of resources?** Chances are that while you're working toward your MOU, you may need referrals to resources that can make your path easier. An experienced mediator will have a network of counselors, including financial planners, banks, attorneys, tax accountants, child care and eldercare organizations, real estate agents, mortgage brokers, apartment rental agencies, and many others, all of whom can help you start your new life.

5. **What is your mediator's style?** Every mediator chooses a style that fits the way they view their practice. Some are directive, telling you exactly what you should do. Some are facilitative, moving you toward your goal with your full par-

ticipation to complete the process as quickly and efficiently as possible. Some use appreciative inquiry, asking questions in a way that can help you see a positive outcome in your future. Some use a method called non-violent communication, working to make every conversation constructive and minimizing conflict. Others prefer the transformative method, working with the couple to change the way they communicate with one another. Like many mediators, I use a combination of methods as needed. If your mediator promotes only one style, it may not be a match for you.

As you can probably imagine, some people work very well with a mediator who has a certain style, while others simply drive you nuts. This is why the consultation is important, so you can decide for yourself if the mediator's style is right for you.

6. **Does your mediator try to give you legal advice?** Most mediators are not attorneys. Even an attorney working as a mediator is precluded from giving you legal advice and needs to remain neutral within the mediation process.

7. **Has your mediator been divorced?** Someone who shares your personal experience with the emotional, practical, and financial side of divorce can help guide you through the havoc these factors can play. This is not to say that a person who is happily married cannot be a good mediator—many certainly are. You may benefit, however, from working with a mediator who has been where you are, who can empathize with you in a difficult and emotional time, and who can demonstrate that there is life after divorce. Do not hesitate to inquire about this; this is a valid question to ask a mediator.

Ten Reasons to Use Divorce Mediation

Is mediation really a better option than litigation? Here are the reasons I share with my clients to help them make the best decision for themselves, their resources, and their families.

1. **Divorce mediation puts your children first.** Creating a parenting plan (a.k.a. Custody Agreement) in mediation is a collaborative process with a common goal in mind: to do what is best for your children.

A mediator can help educate both spouses in a neutral manner and keep the focus on the children's needs, while engaging parents in a more sensitive and less inflammatory process. Litigated divorces or those requiring a trial can be very damaging to children.

Custody trials usually require your children to be interviewed and interact with several experts. Your children may even be required to appear at court. The animosity between parents can increase significantly while embroiled in an adversarial process, which can expose children to increased conflict, verbal attacks, and tension. This can result in stress, confusion, and long-lasting damage for your children.

Bitter

Experts say the number one factor that hurts children is parental conflict.

2. **Divorce mediation is less costly.** You and your spouse will typically pay one mediation professional who is dedicated to helping you both reach a resolution. You will pay for meetings and for her time drafting the MOU. Processing the papers into the legal system is an additional fee, paid to a review or neutral attorney; there are also court fees. The total is still substantially less than litigation.

Using attorneys and/or the court system, the divorcing couple pays two attorney fees, not only for discussions but also for drafting of motion papers back and forth and court appearances. Lengthy divorce battles and trials require significant financial resources.

3. **Divorce mediation takes less time.** In mediation, you and your spouse set your own timetable for resolving issues. It is not unusual for mediation to take 2-3 sessions. In litigation, you may have to wait months for court dates or a time when two lawyers and a judge can coordinate their calendars to resolve issues.

4. **Divorce mediation is a less adversarial process.** Mediation emphasizes cooperative problem solving and addresses the needs of all involved. The mediator can help raise points that an attorney may not want to raise for strategic reasons.

Bitter

Don't have a win-lose mentality. Divorce mediation promotes a win-win outcome.

The mediator helps the parties view issues from a neutral standpoint and with a focus on resolving the dispute, rather than validating one party's position and seeking to "win." A mediator can minimize side arguments and avoid the adversarial positioning between attorneys, while concentrating everyone's efforts towards a mutually satisfactory conclusion.

That said, using divorce mediation doesn't mean you give up the right to litigate or to go to court. Many clients consult with their attorney during mediation to supplement the process. If you and your spouse can't resolve your issues in mediation, you may opt out of mediation, retain attorneys, and have a judge resolve issues if necessary.

5. **You have better discussions and outcomes.** A good mediator will help you and your ex develop new skills for communicating with one another. When you and your ex are no longer arguing over the past, it's a lot easier to focus on how to move forward. Over time, this will considerably reduce the stress on both of you.

Better

If my clients reach an impasse, I offer to have a litigating attorney who doesn't know either party provide a glimpse of what the likely judicial outcome would be. Clients are grateful for this information, which is shared with them together in my office.

You and your mediator choose the topics that you want to discuss and settle. Even in mediated divorces, the courts have final jurisdiction (although most agreements are approved as written). Important decisions about you (and your children, if you have them) are not left in the hands of strangers. You and your spouse control how quickly or slowly decisions are made, when the divorce petition is filed, and what the terms of the divorce will be. In litigation, attorneys set court dates, and judges make decisions with limited time and information.

Finally, you and your ex may be more willing to abide by a mediated settlement since the terms aren't imposed upon you by a judge.

6. You get more personal attention. You work directly with your mediator. She will propose and get a consensus on the resolution process. She will help you create a menu of options and help you negotiate. Then she'll help you refine and understand the implications of your decisions and arrive at a final agreement.

Some judges are overworked and understaffed with too many cases. Judges often do not have the time or opportunity to get to know each family and, by necessity, must speak to the lawyers more than the people actually going through the divorce.

7. Evening and weekend appointments are often offered. In today's world, it's highly likely that both you and your spouse have jobs. Taking time off from a job for meetings concerning your divorce can add more stress to an already difficult situation.

Better

There is no downside to trying mediation. If it works, you'll save a lot of money. If it doesn't work, you haven't invested a lot of funds.

Most mediators offer evening and weekend appointments as well as daytime meetings. This gives you the flexibility you need to maintain personal and professional obligations, yet move forward with the divorce.

8. Divorce mediation allows for greater post-divorce stability. In contrast to the adversarial nature of the traditional litigation system, your mediator seeks to improve the ability of you and your spouse to communicate with each other. This helps the divorce process move forward and achieve better results.

You may also return to your same mediator if conflicts arise in the future. Your mediator can help moderate disputes and clarify or modify your agreement as time goes by. Your mediator already knows your agreement, is attuned to your family's issues and dynamic, and can be available when you need it.

9. Mediation only involves the spouses. In mediation, you and your spouse discuss and work out your issues with just the mediator present. The mediator does not decide or rule on the issues as a judge does. It is up to the spouses to come to an agreement. Mediation takes place in a quiet, private office or conference room with no outside parties present.

> **Better**
>
> *Be impeccable with your word.*
> *Don't take anything personally.*
> *Don't make assumptions.*
> *Always do your best.*
>   –Don Miguel Ruiz,
>   *The Four Agreements*

In a court hearing, testimony is put into public record. Anyone can come into the courtroom, sit down, and listen to you and your about-to-be ex-spouse fighting over your divorce issues. Then the judge decides.

10. Managing Conflict: "I Assumed." What is the number one source of conflict? Before you read further, pause for a moment and consider your answer. Words like communication, money, religion, and relationship might come to mind. All of these would be accurate and typical responses. And yet, embedded in each of these words is a very simple, two-word phrase that I believe is the root cause of conflict.

"I assumed..."

Think about all of the times you became angry, judgmental, or sad. Was it because you had an expectation or made an assumption about something or someone else?

- *I assumed* we would go to my family's home for the holidays this year because we went to your family's home last year.
- *I assumed* that you would clean the kitchen because that's what you usually do.
- *I assumed* that you would not use the credit cards anymore because we are trying to save money.
- *I assumed* that the children would receive religious education.

Imagine a conversation about parenting plans. Mom suggests one plan, and Dad another. Each assumes that their respective position is obviously the best or preferred choice. And when they are asked to elaborate, their language is often filled with criticism and judgments.

One of the most important aspects of mediating is *bringing clarity to the conversation*. It involves gently probing exactly what each person meant by certain statements or circumstances. A mediator can highlight the what-ifs and several different scenarios to make sure that there is a jointly held understanding. Mediation is alert for the "I assumed."

I have an MOU. Now what?

Some couples take the MOU to their respective attorneys for review. Then one of the attorneys will complete the required forms to file the legal separation or divorce action with the court system.

> **Better**
>
> *Some clients have the MOU reviewed by their own attorney, and then use the neutral scribe attorney to process the agreement. It saves money.*

Other couples decide to have the MOU processed into the legal system by using one neutral or "scribe" attorney. This attorney will file the papers, but neither represents nor gives legal advice regarding the content of the MOU to either person.

> **Better**
>
> *The MOU is a completed agreement. The scribe attorney is simply adding the formatting and legalese required by the court system.*

The MOU can still be reviewed by your attorney prior to this, and edits can be made if needed before using the scribe attorney.

In both cases, the attorney(s) will file the documents on the clients' behalf with the court system. In an uncontested divorce, it is very unlikely that the couple needs to make an appearance in court.

New York State does not require couples to use the services of an attorney to obtain a divorce. However, I alert my clients that it is prudent to have the MOU reviewed by an attorney and to have the final MOU processed by an attorney.

Chapter 2

Moving Off Square One: When You Know Your Marriage is Over

"We must be willing to get rid of the life we planned in order to have the life that is waiting for us."
–Joseph Campbell

Maybe you and your spouse argue all the time, or maybe your home has become a place of tense silence. Perhaps there has been a major change in your life or your spouse's life that has made your relationship unsustainable. Whatever the reason, you know it's time to end your marriage.

But are you and your spouse on the same page? Do you both know that your marriage is over, or will the news come as a surprise?

It's time to make sure you are both ready to move to the next step and begin to end your marriage. Let's look at some ways to do this.

> **Bitter**
>
> *When the air in your home becomes polluted from tension, everyone is gasping for breath. Ending your marriage gives your family the chance to breathe clean air again.*

"This marriage is over for me."

When people call me regarding the first mediation consultation appointment, they often ask: "What if my spouse won't cooperate?"

That's when I ask, "Does your spouse know you want to end your marriage?"

Often the response is, "Well, he (or she) should know, we fight all the time."

When you have concluded that your marriage is over, and you are sure, you need to say to your spouse: "This marriage is over for me." You have to be clear

> **Better**
>
> *"Over" means nothing will influence your decision to end the marriage. For example, if there's substance abuse in a marriage, one party may promise to stop ... again. The person wanting to end the marriage needs to be able to say, "I hope you do that for yourself, but you're not doing it for the marriage, and you're not doing it for me. This marriage is over."*

and gentle. Do not say it's over for him or her, or us—say it's just over for me. You cannot be ambivalent or vague. At that point you need to focus on HOW you are going to process the end of the marriage, not IF.

The "how" comes down to mediation (cooperatively) or attorneys (which sometimes can be contentious and escalating). Those are the typical choices.

After you have told your spouse that your marriage is over, it's not unusual for your spouse to become defensive or sometimes bullying. Remember, change is scary. Once you are sure your marriage is over, following these four rules will help you move the situation forward.

1. **No Defending Yourself**: Your spouse may start blaming you, calling you names, and labeling you all sorts of things. Your response is simply, "OK, that's who I am." You say it gently, kindly, and let it go. You do not defend yourself. Every time you defend yourself, try to correct the record, or otherwise disagree, you are fueling the same old conversation you have been having for months or years.

> **Better**
>
> *You do not need your spouse's permission to end the marriage, although you would like his/her cooperation.*

2. **No Persuading**: You will not persuade your partner by reminding him or her that your marriage has been over for a while, or that neither of you is happy, or that the kids are miserable, or we'd be better off not fighting. Those points just initiate more of the same conversations that you have already had. Do you actually imagine that he or she will stop, listen, and say: "You're right, that makes sense, and we should end our marriage."?

3. **No Negotiating**: Another typical reaction is: "Fine, you want a divorce? You're not going to get anything. No house, no retirement money, no nothing." Your response should be: "You may be right, but we have to figure that out." You don't say, "That's not fair, that's not legal, you can't do that." Your spouse is scared or hurt or angry, or may be looking for your fear and your Achilles' heel, which is a useless conversation. You will have a guide to help you, either a mediator or an attorney. You do not want to negotiate at your kitchen table when you are both scared and angry. Remember, you are not going to sign anything until you have all the information you need.

4. **Next Step**: You then say: "We can choose to do this cooperatively or not. We can meet with a mediator or we can both make appointments with separate attorneys. It's your choice. We just need to get on the mediation train or the attorney train by ‹choose date›." And then stick to it. During this period, your spouse may attempt to draw you into one of the above kinds of conversations. You need

to stay cool and kind and determined; do not engage in the old conversations.

Managing these discussions is like being on a diet. You need to refrain from engaging in those old conversations just as you refrain from eating a cookie when you are on a diet. Some times are harder than others, but if you

> **Better**
>
> *There are two primary choices in life: To accept conditions as they exist, or to accept the responsibility for changing them. Make the choice for change.*

stay determined and firm, the choices for moving forward will emerge. As with a diet, ambivalence will sabotage you. You need to have a plan every day to not engage in the old conversations.

If you want to explore the "why" and "if only" of your marriage ending, then you both still might benefit from counseling. You need a professional to help you navigate the marital issues and their resolution. If you could have mended your marriage at your kitchen table by yourselves, you would have done it already.

Being the initiator of ending a marriage is a difficult position to be in. The guidance I provide here is a path to moving forward for both of you.

One More Try—Counseling

When I meet with clients for the first time, there is always one person more ready to end the marriage than the other. Clients are never on the same page. During our conversation, I may learn that they have either been to counseling or one has begged the other "for years" to go. Now, when reality sets in, one or both may want to reconsider counseling.

> **Better**
>
> *Discernment counseling is a way for couples to look at their options before making a final decision about divorce. This kind of counseling can be very useful even if it ends up being a gentler way to say goodbye, rather than reconnecting and continuing the marriage.*

Couples are often surprised at how supportive I am of counseling. I encourage them to try counseling, but to consider several important guidelines:

1. **A set number of visits.** Commit to go a certain number of times, usually three to five—a finite amount of sessions where both must show up, regardless of how they feel. This frees them to be honest and limits the indecision. When all sessions have been completed, the couple decides whether to commit to another number of sessions or return to mediation. The key is that both will have learned important things about themselves, the other, and their marriage.

2. A softer landing. Another reason counseling is so useful is that the one who wants the marriage to continue will not retain the illusion that everything would have worked out if only they had gone to counseling. If the counseling confirms that the marriage is over, the couple knows they did all they could (at least at the end). They honored the request of the one partner to try—and ultimately the need of the other to move forward with ending the marriage.

3. Help the counselor. Be upfront with the counselor about the number of sessions you expect and that you want to focus on partnership qualities. Often counseling may digress into some of the family issues, kids, money, and so on. The agreed-upon sessions are valuable opportunities for each person to examine what he or she really wants in a partner for a long-term relationship or marriage.

4. Focus on partnership qualities. Write a list of at least 25 desired qualities in a partner. This may seem like a long list and may take a week or two to complete, but you'll be surprised at what comes up. Then define the quality in three or four sentences, so you understand what you are looking for (see "Must Love Dogs" on page 203). Decide which ones are most important. Discuss these with each other with the counselor's guidance. This exercise may clarify your needs and develop a clearer picture of whether your partner can truly meet them. For example, couples often use words like trust and respect, but they are not sure how these are expressed in behaviors. Such lists can also help you and your partner articulate why the marriage is ending, what has changed, and what each is feeling now.

These simple steps can help reduce long-term conflict, build mutual respect, and set the stage for future interactions through the divorce process and afterwards, especially if there are children involved.

When Hopin' Ends, the Healin' Begins

Dusty Springfield sang a song in the early 1960s called "Wishin' and Hopin'." The chorus went like this:

> *Wishin' and hopin' and thinkin' and prayin'*
> *Plannin' and dreamin' each night of his charms—*
> *That won't get you into his arms.*

Those lyrics are wise words. It takes much more than wishin' and hopin' to reverse a marriage that is on the cusp of ending. Clients are rarely on the same page when a marriage ends. Invariably, one person still clings to the hope of reconnecting and recommitting to the partnership. On the other hand, the person who is psychologically out of the marriage is not immune to the sadness and hoping either. This spouse is often at a loss on how to comfort but not encourage the other.

Often the hopin' party becomes addicted to the conversation about "why" and "if only." There is a belief that a magic word or two could change the outcome. The need or request to keep talking is sometimes a way to procrastinate rather than end the relationship, a way for the reluctant partner to maintain the status quo. Sometimes the kindest option is to set a time limit on conversations—or not to engage in these conversations at all.

Redirecting the conversations from "if" we are going to end the marriage to "how" we'll end the marriage (choosing between using mediation and/or attorneys) is a way to move forward. Creating the option for the hopin' spouse to make some decisions may be helpful.

It is not unusual for one party to express confusion and incredulity that the marriage may really end. There is often a lot of pent-up emotion and urgency to communicate. One or two sessions of goodbye counseling may be useful for both of you. It is a time to hear the other's loss and grief in a safe environment.

This is not a shame-and-blame opportunity, but rather a chance to gift each other with being heard and understood. Quite often the hopin' spouse will be much more cooperative and less angry and ready to proceed.

We all know that kids pout when they do not get their way. Sometimes they slam doors and shout. It does not often change the outcome: They still can't go to the party or watch TV, but they want you to know they are angry.

Adults pout, too. When a marriage is ending, the wishin' spouse wants the other spouse to know, without a doubt, that they are hurt and upset and often afraid.

Bitter

Adult pouting looks like the cold shoulder, the silent treatment, sniping, and worst of all, bad-mouthing the other spouse.

What may help the pouting partner is to let him/her know that you sincerely care that he or she is in pain and deep sadness. Empathetic listening means that you can be present with the other's feelings without problem-solving or minimizing. While the hurt does not disappear and the wishin' may continue, it is likely the pouting and acting out anger may be reduced. There is healing for both parties when people feel understood.

It is hard to imagine that the spouse that is ready to end the marriage can influence the hopin' spouse in a positive manner. One of the kindest ways to ease the

Better

An old Yiddish proverb says, "You can't put your tush in two saddles." It may seem counter-intuitive, but healing will only begin when the hopin' ends.

pain of a hopin' spouse is to be consistent and gently firm that nothing will influence your decision.

Do you love your spouse or the marriage?

Very few couples come into my office on the same page emotionally. It's pretty clear there is a "trailing spouse"—in this case, one who followed the other to mediation without really believing the marriage is over. It shows up in body language, tears, and a look in the eyes that pleads, "I do not want to be here." And yet there is also courage and a willingness to at least listen. During that first consultation, sometimes healing begins as the reluctant spouse starts to accept the situation.

There are two parts of letting go. It's useful to distinguish the difference between loving your spouse and loving the marriage. I have described these by using two hands.

On one hand: The Spouse

There is letting go of the spouse: the actual person, the human being. In most cases, letting go of the partner is not that hard. One or both have concluded that the other just does not have the partnership qualities the other needs for a relationship. They have good and fine qualities but not the ones needed for you to sustain an adult, positive relationship. Often both people acknowledge that this is true.

At the very least, a relationship requires being with someone who wants to be with you. (This will likely come up in the list of qualities you've been making, as we discussed earlier.) If you wake up every morning feeling you have to thank your spouse for staying with you, you will realize that you deserve more than that. This realization may come all at once or happen over time.

On the other hand: The Marriage

Letting go of the marriage is hard and complicated. It takes time. The issues to consider include the kids, the money, the family and friends shared for many years, and how to handle holidays. For many people, the perceived stigma of divorce is a difficult issue with concerns about the opinions of others or simply the desire not to be in that "club." The end of a marriage also ends dreams, potential, illusions about the relationship, and the future that is no longer possible.

Mourning, grieving, and healing from the end of the marriage often takes two to three years. It takes time to learn that the healing, attitude, and choices are all in a person's control, even though having the marriage itself no longer is.

Confusing Loving the Other Person with Loving the Marriage

People often confuse loving the other person with loving the marriage. They will declare love for the other, but, in fact, they are clinging to the marriage. When people separate these two issues—partner and marriage—they begin to heal more clearly and more efficiently.

Consider this: Would you want your children to have the same type of marriage you have now? No couple has ever said to me, "Yes, this would be fine for our children." When imagining their children experiencing similar feelings in a future relationship, couples always want more for their children.

You both also deserve to have more. Living separately may be the pathway to having a better life.

The Valley of Indecision: Trial Separation

Sometimes it's hard for a couple to finally admit that the marriage is actually over. They arrive at the consult to inquire how they can sort out financials or parenting plans while they "just spend some time apart to see what happens."

If you come to me to negotiate a trial separation, of course I can help you "sort things out." But it's also a time for you to clarify what your actual intention is. Sometimes I ask, "What additional data are you looking for to make a decision to keep or end your marriage?"

> **Better**
>
> *Time apart is not going to provide magical insights regarding the potential for your marriage.*

What about the children? As hard as limbo is on adults, it's even harder on children. If children believe there is a chance that Mom and Dad may reunite, they get their "magic wand" out and try to intervene. Children calibrate their parents' behavior and end up angry at one or both of them. Why can't Dad stay for dinner? How come Mom isn't coming to the show? They become confused and frustrated.

Initially time apart may feel good and relaxed. There is a break from the ever-present tension and difficult conversations. If you believe that you may be able to reconnect, you need to work with a marriage counselor. The truth is if problems could be solved on your own, you would have solved them. A marriage counselor can guide honest sharing in a manner that lets you hear each other.

What I emphasize is that more than financial and parenting ground rules need to be established. What is essential are emotional and behavior ground rules. Otherwise the dreaded default of "I assumed" will sabotage any chance of reuniting. For example, one might say to the other: "If you thought that ignoring me was going to get us back together, well, think again." And the responder says: "I wasn't ignoring you, I was just giving you space." These are two very different interpretations on how to live separately.

During a period of trial separation, couples have to be clear about many of the following questions:

- Do you want to "date" each other?
- Will you date others?
- Will you be intimate with each other?
- Do you want to only discuss the children?
- Will it be OK to ask about each other's feelings?
- Will you attend family events like weddings and birthdays together?
- What are you telling the children? (see Chapter 13)
- What are you telling your friends and family?

As each person ponders this list, they become aware of how difficult "I assumed" can be. It is clear that if the answers to these sorts of questions are not clarified, then the couple is very likely to end up angrier, sadder, and more disappointed. Sometimes a trial separation is really just postponing the inevitable. It's scary making the decision to end a marriage. People become emotionally paralyzed and think that the valley of indecision is better than a decision. Parents may think that this final research step is gentler for children, but in fact, it is disruptive and promotes anxiety. The emotional roller coaster of indecision is hard on everyone. If at all possible, complete your process, consider marriage counseling, make a decision, and avoid temporary solutions.

If you have explored your relationship through counseling and reached an impasse, or if you both know that your marriage is over, it's time to decide which path you will take: an *uncontested divorce* negotiated with the help of a mediator

Better: A Book on Clarity

I frequently recommend an excellent book by Marshall Rosenberg that emphasizes how essential clarity is and elaborates on ways to incorporate clarity into your daily words and relationships. The book is Nonviolent Communication: A Language of Life: Life-Changing Tools for Healthy Relationships. *The concept is referred to as NVC, and there are workshops and study groups to enhance your knowledge and application of the NVC method. You can find additional information at the Center for Nonviolent Communications' website at* www.cnvc.org.

or an attorney, or a *contested divorce* involving attorneys and perhaps the court. In the next chapter, we'll talk about all the nuts and bolts of proceeding with your divorce.

Domestic Violence: This Changes Everything

Ending a marriage when domestic violence is a factor complicates the process. Whether you work with an attorney or a mediator, the abuser is likely to hear things that may trigger an event. There is a significant debate whether mediation can be used if domestic violence is a factor. Of course, personal safety is the highest priority, and honesty without fear of consequences is essential. However, in my experience, mediation can be successful and may actually minimize angry retaliations that can occur with escalating attorney involvement.

If there are already court orders precluding contact or other restrictions, they can often be removed to allow for mediation appointments. In some cases, however, attorneys may provide clients the necessary insulation and separation from each other.

Before you initiate a conversation with your abuser spouse about ending your marriage, it is essential that you seek professional advice and a strategy for your safety. If you are in a potentially violent situation with your spouse, or if the violence has already started—whether it includes physical assault or verbal abuse or both—your safety is more important than papers and records.

An abuser will use violence, name calling, insults and other verbal abuse to make their partner feel hopeless, weak, and helpless. This kind of controlling behavior can make you believe that there is no way out of the relationship. Intimidation, threats, isolating the victim from family and friends, withholding money, using the children against you, and then minimizing the violence and blaming you for "making" them lash out are all methods of violence and domination. You do not have to live with this.

If this is happening to you, take these steps to protect yourself and your children.

- **Get away from the abuser.** Friends or family are most likely to help you, but if you can't reach them or they are reluctant to get involved, call the domestic violence hotline in your area. (In New York State, this is 800-942-6906.)
- **Take your children to a neutral place.** Your parents or grandparents may be the right environment, or a friend who has children of about the same age as your own may provide a place where your children can be comfortable. A battered spouses' shelter may be able to keep your children's location secret.
- **Don't destroy or throw out anything.** The property in your home is marital property, and it will have to be divided equitably. If you deliberately destroy

or hide something, your spouse may see that as an act of violence on your part.

- **Start working with a mediator or attorney.** Not only may you need a temporary restraining order or Order of Protection to keep yourself and your children safe, but you will want to move on to divorce as soon as possible. If you hope to salvage a cordial relationship with your spouse, look for a mediator with experience in dealing with domestic violence cases.
- **If more violence occurs, call the police.** Your safety is the top priority. Be willing to move ahead with charges against your abusive spouse. Studies show that when the victim of abuse first tries to leave the abuser, this can be the most dangerous time in the relationship. The domestic violence hotline can help you find the protection you need, and law enforcement will have information about shelters and other safety measures.

If you are in danger because of the way your spouse treats you, there is no choice—you must separate from your spouse as quickly as possible. There are many people and organizations who are ready to help you.

PART 2
The Legal Divorce

Chapter 3

Divorce 101: The Basics

"Grant me the serenity to accept the things I cannot change,
Courage to change the things I can,
And the wisdom to know the difference."

−*Reinhold Niebuhr*, The Serenity Prayer

You and your spouse may have agonized for months or even years over whether to end your marriage. These conversations are difficult and include lots of wishing and hoping. Perhaps counseling has been useful, helping to discern whether you are just having a rough spot or it's time to say, "This marriage is over."

What I hear repeatedly is that, once the decision is made, both people want to start the process and then get on with their lives. At this point, the *five stages of divorce* begin.

Many people liken the end of a marriage to a death, and, in many respects, that is accurate. It is the end of a dream and a vision that had sustained you for a long time. The stages of divorce can be compared to the four stages of death described by Elisabeth Kubler-Ross in her book *On Death and Dying*. As a divorce mediator, I have seen thousands of couples go through these stages, just as they would if they were grieving for the loss of a loved one.

Keep in mind it's very unlikely to go through these stages linearly, one after another. It's very common to circle back to a previous stage. You may find yourself letting go of anger, moving towards sadness, and then something will trigger your anger again. Over time, you will find you stay in each stage for shorter and shorter periods, healing more quickly, with less disruption of your life and fewer repetitions of the stages.

Four of the divorce stages are similar to those associated with healing from the death of a loved one. I've added a fifth that is specific to divorce.

1. **Anger:** Furious at your partner, you feel betrayed, rejected, abandoned, and misunderstood. This is a natural reaction as you search for meaning and explanations and deal with fear and loneliness.

2. **Grief:** Grief is gentler and personal. You are mourning the loss of a dream without casting about for someone to blame.

3. Depression/Blahs: You feel deep sadness, despair, and hopelessness. Life as you knew it has ended. Sometimes a sense of paralysis takes over.

4. Acceptance: Your heart and mind begin to come together. You find peace with your circumstances and are able to think about a new future.

5. Prolonging the Relationship: This is the stage that is unique to divorce. It may happen between any of the stages above or even after acceptance. In this stage, you and your partner continue to rehash the "why" and "if only" of your circumstances. This is an ongoing and endless conversation in which you try to get your spouse to agree with your version of why this marriage is ending. Or just as you are beginning to heal, you find yourself in yet another conversation about what went wrong and who is to blame for your marriage coming to an end.

If the "why" questions are still alive for you both and you want to explore them further, it may be the right time to work with a marriage counselor who can guide you through the conversations. But for many couples stuck in this stage, it becomes a way to stay engaged with one another, because it feels so hard to let go. You may be "addicted to the conflict."

There is no specific timeline to experience these stages. Be patient with yourself and trust your inner voice on when you are ready to do certain things. On the other hand, be aware that you might be stuck in a certain stage. For instance, anger or grieving may seem like a useful currency of social conversation and attention. Be alert if you find yourself repeating your story over and over, asking for affirmation, or gathering allies to support your truth.

Remember, the stages are not just checked off and then done. Things like a holiday, a parenting issue, or even a casual remark may make you feel you have slipped down your ladder of courage and resiliency. The key is that the more that time goes on, the faster you are able to rebound from these feelings.

In the beginning, you may have such intense feelings that it seems like you are hemorrhaging. After some time, it will be a slow bleed, then a scab will form, and finally a scar. Sometimes your scar may itch and feel tender, but you know that, inside and out, you have healed.

Better

The secret is that you and your spouse do not have to agree upon the reason your marriage is ending. Each of you can have your own story. The healing happens when you stop trying to influence your spouse to agree with your version.

Denying the good times and your own accountability is denying part of your-self. The important point is to give yourself permission to honor your past and your marriage.

The Many Ways to Process the End of Your Marriage

What's the first image that comes to your mind when you think about getting a divorce? You would not be alone if you conjured up a court battle with a warrior attorney at your side. Let me be clear that your divorce does not have to go that route—most people find it comforting to learn that statistically, only about 5% of divorces actually end up in a court trial. There are many other viable options, depending upon your circumstances.

When you file a complaint for a divorce, you are actually initiating a lawsuit. There is always a *plaintiff*—the person filing for the divorce—and a *defendant*. This is true even if your divorce is uncontested; the court requires one spouse to request a divorce from the other. The lawsuit concludes with a judge's signature that decrees and confirms what the terms of the divorce will be. The vast majority of couples never actually see a judge. The papers are processed through the court system, and couples are notified by telephone or mail when the judge has signed the papers.

Each state has criteria that must be met to initiate a divorce. To file for divorce in New York State, you must meet one of the following criteria:

1. The marriage ceremony was performed in New York State and either spouse is a resident of the state at the time of the commencement of the action for divorce and resided in the state for a continuous period of one year immediately before the action began, OR

2. The couple lived as husband and wife in New York State and either spouse is a resident of the state at the time of the commencement of the action for divorce and resided in this state for a continuous period of one year immediately before the action began, OR

3. The grounds for divorce occurred in New York State and either spouse is a resident of the state at the time of the commencement of the action for divorce and resided in this state for a continuous period of one year immediately before the action began, OR

4. The grounds for divorce occurred in New York State and both spouses are New York residents at the time the action is commenced, OR

5. If you and your spouse were married outside of New York State and you never lived together as husband and wife in this state, and the grounds for

divorce did not occur in this state, either you or your spouse must presently be a resident of New York State and have resided continuously in the state for at least two years prior to bringing this action for divorce.

There are several ways you can process your divorce, and they have different emotional and financial impacts, as well as different levels of complication. The following information is based on upstate New York data, but the processes are similar in any state.

Pro Se Divorce (Uncontested)

Pro se is Latin for "on your own." Couples looking to save the cost of attorneys or a mediator can obtain the required forms at no charge at the Supreme Court or county clerk's office, or download the forms from the court's website and print them at home. *Pro se* divorces usually do not involve an attorney.

In any divorce, there are as many as 26 forms to complete. (If you don't have children, several of these forms will not be necessary.) Some are fairly complicated, especially if you are not used to dealing with legal forms, or if you have unusual circumstances that deviate from the state's divorce guidelines. Most people say completing these forms is very complicated and daunting, as the court reviews each and every document for accuracy and completeness without regard to your

> **Better**
>
> *Of course, you can represent yourself in any judicial proceeding, but, in my opinion, it is worthwhile to have an attorney help process the papers.*

pro se status. In other words, there is no leeway because you are not familiar with the forms. The judge looks for a specific presentation of the information with the appropriate forms and affidavits completed, most of which require notarization. *Pro se* filings are sometimes returned several times by the judge for the couple to correct errors or change the way that information is presented.

Whether you file *pro se* or with an attorney, there will be court fees for every divorce. In New York State, the court fees as of this writing usually run about $400. This includes the purchase of an Index Number for $210 to begin the process, a Request for Judicial Intervention (RJI) for $95, a Note of Issue for $30, and a Certificate of Dissolution for $5—plus the cost of duplicating all the paperwork. In some cases you may have to hire a process server for an additional cost of $45-60.

While there are many ways to complete a divorce filing, *pro se* divorces are often the most problematic, difficult, and ultimately unsuccessful. Couples may not have all the issues sorted out before they fill out the forms, or they may do the paperwork incorrectly. If the court rejects your *pro se* divorce for technical reasons, you may need to hire an attorney. This, in the long run, will most likely cost more money than if you had engaged attorneys or a mediator at the beginning of the process.

Do-It-Yourself (D-I-Y) Divorce (Uncontested)

There are several businesses that will help you complete your divorce yourself. Each of these businesses provides the appropriate forms needed to file for a divorce. Each charges a fee of approximately $500 (the cost varies from one service to the next) to guide you through the process of completing and processing the forms. In addition to the service fee, you will pay the court filing fees of approximately $400, so a D-I-Y divorce costs about $900.

These businesses do not mediate or help you and your spouse negotiate issues. When you start the process with a company like Divorce Yourself, CompleteCase.com, or GetDivorcePapers.com[1], for example, you need to have all of the decisions made and complete the documents yourself. One such service asks on the landing page of its website, "Can you and your spouse agree to the division of property, assets and all child related issues?" If so, you qualify to fill out the required documents on their website. If not—and this is a big *if*, as you may have overlooked a number of issues simply because you didn't know they were relevant—you are not ready to "take the express" with one of these companies.

On the other hand, if you do not have children or a lot of assets, and you and your spouse can make a clean break without a great deal of negotiation, this kind of service can be successful for you.

Divorce Mediation (Uncontested)

Divorce mediation creates a safe and affordable environment where your issues can be discussed and resolved. The mediator provides information that lets you make well-informed decisions regarding the parenting plan, child support, retirement assets, debt, spousal maintenance, equitable distribution, health insurance and taxes (i.e., everything that is listed in this book). Mediation is efficient and affordable and creates an opportunity for couples to hear each other's worries and concerns.

Mediators provide information regarding state guidelines so that their clients can make informed decisions that will be durable, fair, and respectful to each person. Mediators also are highly trained conflict resolution specialists, so they are ready to help you through divorce circumstance, regardless of whether you and your spouse are amicable or in high conflict.

[1] *I am not recommending any of these services; they are just listed here as examples.*

In my experience, and that of my clients, divorce mediation is the process that is more affordable, more efficient, and gentler than other options.

Dr. Robert Emery is Professor of Psychology and Director of the Center for Children, Families, and the Law at the University of Virginia. He concluded in a 2001 study that couples that choose mediation have more durable and lasting agreements and a much better co-parenting relationship. The couples in the study spent an average of five hours in mediation, and all families were followed for twelve years. Here are some of Dr. Emery's findings:

- Less than 20 percent of the couples in mediation appeared before a judge.
- Twenty-eight percent of nonresident parents who mediated saw their children weekly twelve years later, compared to 9 percent who litigated and 11 percent in the national averages.
- Fifty-two percent of nonresident parents who mediated talked with their children weekly twelve years later. This compares with 14 percent of nonresident parents who went to court and 18 percent in the national averages.

The bottom line was that the decisions reached did not matter (both mediation and litigation couples all decided on the same things), but the process of reaching those decisions did matter.

In Chapter 1, I discussed the benefits of mediation and the process that you and your spouse will experience. Here I will just summarize the costs involved, so you have this information as you compare your options.

Mediators generally charge an hourly rate. Mediators often complete the process in a fraction of the time that attorneys need, so there are fewer billable hours and their hourly rate is considerably less than an attorney for each spouse.

At the end of the mediation process, most clients use the services of an attorney, a review or a neutral "scribe," to draw up the documents the court requires. If you use a neutral attorney, he or she will generally charge a flat fee for meeting with the clients, preparing the documents, and taking the papers to the court system. Fees may vary depending upon the specifics of each case. You also will pay court fees for filing the divorce.

Collaborative Law Attorneys (Uncontested)

Collaborative law is a relatively new concept for divorce attorneys, one that came to the public consciousness in the 1990s. These attorneys will work collaboratively with each other and with the clients, minimizing the adversarial relationship that often comes from a contested divorce.

In order to be designated a collaborative attorney, the attorney takes a number of comprehensive professional training courses that emphasize cooperation and mediation, and that focus on needs of both parties and settlement, not litigation. Both attorneys involved in the collaboration should be on the International Academy of Collaborative Professionals' panel (list) of approved collaborative attorneys.

In addition to individual client meetings, the four people (two attorneys and two clients) meet together, usually for two-hour sessions. The clients and attorneys sign an agreement that precludes the attorneys from using the court system, attempting to compel evidence, or initiating a judicial intervention regarding the case.

Attorneys charge an hourly fee—and they require an upfront retainer that usually runs in the thousands of dollars. The retainer often only covers a portion of the process, and additional funds may be needed.

According to several Rochester collaborative attorneys, the process usually takes between six and twelve months. Clients and attorneys usually meet in six or eight sessions, and then the final paper work is drafted for signatures, which adds additional billable hours. In addition to the collaborative meetings, paid specialists on parenting or finance are often included, as well as separate individual client meetings. If the clients cannot reach a settlement, and they want to escalate to litigation and use the court system, they must each retain new attorneys. The collaborative attorneys are precluded from commencing litigation.

Individual Attorneys (Uncontested or Contested)

Before alternative dispute resolution options were available, couples who wanted a divorce usually went directly to separate attorneys. Couples still do that today for many reasons. Some people are not familiar with alternative options like mediation or collaborative law. These spouses will seek individual representation. Clients who go to individual attorneys can still have an uncontested divorce.

Bitter

Unlike mediation that has one professional, using attorneys requires two professionals—one for each spouse.

Litigated divorce cases can require many billable hours. Attorneys will use the court system to compel information to confirm assets and debts, to provide temporary orders, and to referee challenging questions. They often will get on the court calendar to have periodic meetings with the assigned judge in preparation for a trial, if that becomes necessary. The assigned judge may try to influence a settlement before a trial by alerting your attorney as to the likely outcome if the litigation ends up in court.

Attorneys generally bill an hourly rate, and they also require a retainer fee (down payment).

Bitter

About 5 percent of divorces end up in court trials.

Court Trial (Contested)

If you have exhausted all hope of a settlement and continue to argue over issues, the last resort is a court trial where a judge will decide (decree) the terms that are in dispute. There are many matrimonial judges, and while they are guided by statutory law and case law, each judge can draw his or her own conclusions. You will not know in advance of your lawsuit which judge will preside. Your attorney may provide an insight or try to predict an outcome, but there are more surprises than consistency.

A court trial is the worst-case scenario, but only about 5 percent of divorces actually end up in a courtroom with a judge. Trials can last days or weeks, and you will each pay for your respective attorney's preparation time and presence at the trial. Despite what you've seen on television, divorce trials do not usually include a lot of emotional drama. There is little if any opportunity to vent your frustrations, nor will a judge provide you with a forum to do so. If you are hoping to drag your spouse through an ugly court battle with histrionics in the courtroom, you may be disappointed that your investment in your attorney's time did not result in this.

Better

Divorce can be the springboard for renewal and hope. It can transform your relationship from husband and wife to Mom and Dad and be a positive learning opportunity for your family.

Bitter

Or divorce can be a nightmare that escalates and leaves lasting resentment and scars for you and your children alike. It's up to you and your spouse to choose your path.

Economic issues of equitable distribution or spousal maintenance are generally fairly efficient to resolve. Child custody court cases, however, can take a year or more to resolve and are very expensive. Your child(ren) under age 18 will be assigned an Attorney for Child (AFC), an attorney who is not required to consult with the parents. We'll talk much more about this in Chapter 10, but let me say that under these circumstances, it is very hard for children to hear about or witness the behavior of their parents.

In the end, few people are satisfied with the results of a divorce decided by a trial. It often feels like there is a winner and a loser, but it is more likely you both are bruised and wounded, and the possibility of any sort of positive relationship with your former spouse generally vanishes.

According to several Rochester, NY, attorneys, cases that actually go to trial usually take a year or more to resolve and can cost as much as $60,000.

Are You Eligible to Get a Divorce?

If you would like to get a divorce, you are eligible to do so. All states now offer no-fault divorce, so you do not have to prove that your spouse did something wrong; nor does he or she have to point the finger at you. If you feel your marriage is over, you can file for divorce. No-fault divorce filings in New York State today simply say the marriage has been "irretrievably broken for a period of six months or more." In other states, the language may be "irreconcilable differences" or "incompatibility."

The fault grounds in New York still exist, but are hardly used. There is no benefit to using a fault ground in New York State because grounds are not punitive. You will not receive a larger settlement or more alimony because you use a fault ground.

The legally acceptable reasons (grounds) for divorce in New York State are:

- Cruel and inhuman treatment—a pattern of behavior that rises to the standard of cruelty.
- Abandonment (away from the marital residence for more than one year).
- Imprisonment for three or more consecutive years since commencement of the marriage.
- Adultery, which requires evidence provided by a third party, such as a private investigator.
- Living separate or apart pursuant to a separation judgment or decree for more than one year.
- Living separate and apart pursuant to a separation agreement for more than one year.
- The marriage has broken down irretrievably for at least six months.

In 2010, New York State became the fiftieth state in the country to permit no-fault divorce. In the past, to avoid having to use uncomfortable or even nasty fault language, couples opted to file a legal separation, wait a year, and then convert the agreement to a divorce. (This option still exists in New York and many states.)

There are several important differences between a legal separation and a no-fault divorce:

1. During a legal separation, the couple can continue to share health insurance (in most cases, though, there are some exceptions). Divorce ends the sharing of health insurance.
2. During a legal separation, the couple can still file their federal and state taxes as "married, filing jointly." The ability to do this ends once a divorce is final.
3. During a legal separation, retirement and pension assets cannot generally be distributed until there is a Judgment of Divorce.

A legally filed Separation Agreement or commencing a Divorce Action by suing your spouse with a Summons for Divorce are the formal ending dates for marital debt or asset accumulation. This is known as the **Date of Commencement.**

Today using the one-year legal separation is no longer necessary to avoid using fault grounds, so many couples file their agreement as a divorce rather than as a legal separation. This has made the count of divorces increase—but the actual number of couples ending their marriages has not.

Legal separation (a minimum one-year waiting period while living under the terms of the agreement) via a separation agreement is still available as grounds for divorce, and there are benefits for taking this route. Some couples file a legal separation rather than a divorce to extend health care benefits for a spouse. There can also be good reasons to continue to file taxes as "married, filing jointly" to secure a larger refund in a specific circumstance, deal with capital gains on an investment, maximize the number of dependents claimed, or for reasons that are unique to your financial situation.

> **Bitter**
>
> *Fault grounds are generally inflammatory, and there is no legal or financial benefit to using them now.*

For the majority of private companies and virtually all city, county, and state employees, spousal health insurance options end only after the divorce decree is signed. If health insurance is not an issue, then many people choose to file a no-fault divorce and prefer the closure that follows.

There are other practical reasons why divorce may be preferred over legal separation that have to do with retirement distributions and real estate.

Chapter 4

Divorce Process

*We all need to plant seeds to spring to life. Similarly, you can't climb
a mountain starting at the top. It takes preparation, tools, and skills,
and a set path to follow one step at a time.*
– Catherine Pulsifer

Divorce Homework

Whichever method of divorce you decide to use, you will need to gather information to get started. We will go into each topic in depth in Chapter 5, but it's good to start thinking about where all of your important documents reside and getting them together in one place.

First, make a list of all of your assets, owned together or separately, and the balances on these. Assets include things you own and accounts that hold your savings and other money: your house, your bank accounts, cars, and mutual funds, for example. The following is a longer and more thorough list, but most people only have some of these items:

- Your marital home and any other real estate you own
- Liquid cash (bank accounts)
- Bitcoin accounts
- Stocks and other investments
- Ownership of a business with associated financial records
- Automobiles, boats, or other transportation
- Antiques, artwork, and household items
- Contents of the house (furniture, accessories, appliances, electronics, digital assets)
- Retirement plans (defined pensions, 401(k)s, IRAs, SEPs)
- Miscellaneous, including patents, copyrights, royalties, and money others owe to you or to your spouse
- Cash value of whole life insurance policies

Next, make a list of all of your debts, and find the most recent documents for each of these:

- Credit card statements
- Home equity loan, or line of credit statements
- Auto, motorcycle, and boat loan statements
- Mortgage statement showing the remaining balance

- Student loan statements
- Loans borrowed from life insurance policies, IRAs, or 401(k)s
- Debt in your business, if you own one
- Letters or statements of money owed to family members or friends
- Any other debts not listed here

Find all of the important documents that pertain to your assets. It's good to know where these documents are, though they are not always required. These may include the following:

- Deed to your current house
- Purchaser's closing statement
- Receipts for the costs of any capital improvements on your home
- Mortgage documents, including a statement with your current balance
- Your most recent tax assessment of your home, which may show its current value (or a recent appraisal)
- IRS Form 2119 showing any capital gains, if any, from selling a previous home that were rolled over into this home
- Closing statements from any other homes you have owned as a couple
- Statements for each of your bank accounts and investments
- Statements of auto loan balances, or the titles if the cars are paid off
- Life insurance policies and beneficiary information
- Health insurance policies, including information on COBRA options if your insurance comes through one spouse's employer
- Cash on hand, if you keep more than pocket money in the house
- Benefits statements from your employer(s) about your pension and retirement plans
- Current pension, retirement and 401(k) statements
- A document from your employer(s) that details your annual salary or regular pay, and whether you receive additional income from bonuses, tips, or commissions
- Statements for any royalties, copyrights, patents, or other intellectual property payments you receive
- A current paycheck stub for each job
- Statements of gross business receipts and annual expenses, if one or both of you own businesses
- Most recent federal and state tax returns—both personal and for your business, if you own one

Better

You should assume that the language of the separation agreement will be the same as the divorce decree. It is difficult to change any of the language later in the process when you convert the separation agreement to a divorce, unless you and your spouse agree upon the changes.

Processing a Legal Separation

Once you have considered all of the relevant assets and debts, you and your spouse will make decisions regarding equitable distribution. You will also discuss and decide the details of child support, parenting and all the other aspects regarding your circumstances.

When the conversations and decisions conclude, your mediator will summarize all of your decisions into a document called a Memorandum of Understanding (MOU). This is a non-binding summary of your decisions. When your MOU is ready to be processed into the legal system it is scribed by a neutral attorney into a Separation and Property Settlement Agreement (SAPSA). [1]

If you are working with your own attorney, the summarizing document is the SAPSA. It is prudent to have the SAPSA prepared by an attorney because the language is the foundation for your divorce.

If you want just a legal separation rather than a divorce, just the SAPSA is signed and notarized in the presence of your separate or neutral (shared) attorney and you are contractually separated. To be "legally" separated, the signed and notarized SAPSA is recorded or filed with the county clerk's office where you are residing. The SAPSA is a voluntary contract between you and your spouse.

The signed SAPSA is contractually binding and enforceable. If one party is not in compliance with the agreement, it can be enforced by discussing the issue(s) with an attorney who will represent you in the court system as appropriate. (Enforcement is discussed later in this chapter).

In order to change or contest a SAPSA before it is converted to a final divorce decree, a spouse would have to claim fraud or that the information contained in the agreement had not been fully disclosed to him/her, or that there was not an opportunity to confer with an attorney, or that a spouse withheld information. It is considered difficult to prevail in changing the terms of the SAPSA. That is why it is prudent to have your own attorney look over the MOU on your behalf before the (scribe) attorney processes the SAPSA.

[1] The use of the term Separation and Property Settlement Agreement (SAPSA) is only used in this section of the book to describe the legal term of the separation agreement. Throughout the rest of the book, I refer to a Memorandum of Understanding (MOU) or separation agreement as the non-binding document that is created for clients by a mediator.

Processing a Divorce

If you want to be divorced, the SAPSA becomes the foundation document for the proceedings, but there are as many as 26 additional documents that need to be processed to create the total divorce packet.

Better

Initiating a divorce is actually starting a lawsuit. Even in an uncontested divorce, there is a Plaintiff—the one initiating the divorce, and a Defendant—the one accepting the divorce.

If you use a neutral attorney (scribe), you and your spouse will sign your documents together. The scribe prepares all of the paperwork for the court.

The scribe will prepare the documents required to commence the divorce action with the court, which require your signatures. If you use separate attorneys, the same documents will be signed separately and transferred between attorneys. The plaintiff's attorney will file the documents.

Whether you are using a neutral attorney or one of your own, you should be prepared to sign many documents. Please refer to Appendix H for links to New York State forms.

Once you have contacted the scribing attorney or separate attorneys, the mediator forwards the approved MOU to the attorney, who completes the papers. The attorney then submits all of the documents (called a Judgment Roll) to the court, and the wait begins for them to be reviewed by a judge and returned to the attorney. The wait may take as little as three to six weeks, or it may be longer, depending on the time of year the filing is made, the case load of the judge assigned, and the county in which the divorce is filed.

Better

When using a neutral attorney, the "summons" is just one of many papers signed in the scribe's office and is not "served" on the Defendant in an outside setting.

When the attorney (either scribe or separate) receives the Judgment Roll back from the court and confirms that the judge has signed the required documents, the Judgment Roll is filed in the county clerk's office, where the filing of the Summons and Complaint at the commencement of the divorce action was filed. This is a sealed record. No one but the attorney(s) of record and the two spouses can open this record unless they designate (using a signed and notarized document) that a surrogate can open it.

Enforcement of Agreements/Divorce Decrees

It's important to understand that an MOU drafted by a mediator is not a legal document, and the decisions reflected within the MOU are not enforceable in court or binding until put into a SAPSA prepared by a neutral or separate attorney(s).

When clients sign their legal papers, the hope is that everyone will "do what they say." There is always a worry about enforcement and honoring the agreement. Some terms in the agreement are easier to enforce than others. Generally there are two categories within the agreement: **Behavior** issues and **Quantitative** issues.

Behavior issues are things like being on time for parent transitions, being dependable, following agreed upon parenting rules, transportation issues, and the like. Clients make these agreements with good intentions, and yet compliance with behavior issues can be subjective and often become a source of resentment and conflict. Returning to mediation to clarify and modify understandings is useful. Enforcing behaviors in the court system can be problematic. It's hard to substantiate behavior issues and difficult to monitor them.

Quantitative issues of enforcement regarding child support, asset distribution, spousal maintenance, or who can remain in the house are less subjective and easier for the courts to enforce.

Mediation Before Escalation

Most agreements (whether written by attorneys or mediators) have language that encourages clients to attempt to resolve disagreements in mediation prior to escalating and commencing adversarial action against each other. Agreements usually have some aspect of the following understandings:

- Prior to the signing of their Agreement, the parties agree to return to mediation to deal with any changes to their mediated agreements that may be suggested by their respective attorneys, or to deal with any and all other disputes or differences that may arise between them.
- Subsequent to signing the agreement, in the event that one party requests mediation to resolve a dispute, the other party will participate and make a good-faith effort to resolve the disagreement within 30 days of the request.
- The parties generally share equally the fee for the first mediation session, and the fee for the preparation of the summary of the new agreement, unless otherwise mutually agreed.

- A commitment that each party will notify the other of any change in his/her residential address or telephone number within five (5) days of any such change.

When mediation is successful, and both parties agree to the changes, the parties would return to a scribe (or separate) attorney. The attorney would prepare a Modification Agreement which would be filed in the county clerk's office. Only when the Modification Agreement is attached to an Order called "Order Modifying an Agreement" would the Modification Agreement be enforceable. The Order would be presented to a Supreme or Family Court Judge who would sign the Order. If the Modification Agreement is not attached to an Order, the Modification Agreement would not be enforceable in a court of law.

Judicial Intervention

If mediation is not successful, or not attempted, each party can challenge the agreement through attorneys and the court system. Any contract can be challenged; the question is how likely is it that you will prevail. That's when a good common-sense attorney is important. Initiating a frivolous or unsubstantiated lawsuit is expensive.

Generally, the following rules of enforcement are included within your agreement:

- In the event that any provision of an agreement is deemed invalid or unenforceable for any reason, it does not give permission to review or invalidate the entire agreement. In other words, if you are challenging the compliance of the parenting schedule, you do not have the option to review the way retirement funds were shared.
- If one person does not comply with the terms of the agreement, it does not give permission for the other party not to comply. In other words, there is no "tit for tat." If child support is not paid, it does not mean that the other parent can change the parenting plan. These are separate issues and all of the other issues should continue in full force and effect.
- If one person chooses not to insist on the strict compliance of the agreement, it does not mean that he/she has waived rights to the full compliance in the future. For instance, when sharing uninsured medical expenses, perhaps one party does not request reimbursement of expenses per the agreement for months or even years. That does not mean that in the future, the person cannot then require the reimbursements within the Statute of Limitations.

- What happens if one party defaults in the performance of any of the terms or obligations in the agreement? If it becomes necessary for the other party to commence litigation to enforce the agreement, the party found to be in default may be responsible for payment of any and all expenses, including reasonable attorney fees incurred by either of the parties as a result of such proceedings.
- During the mediation or litigation prior to a divorce, or as long as there remains an obligation of either party within the agreement, each party will produce any and all necessary documentation to properly enforce the provisions of their agreement. This includes documentation such as verification of income or health insurance coverage. This may occur when adjusting health insurance coverage expenses or considering modifying child support. So a person can ask for income verification, but that does not mean access to future tax returns, which are often considered private—especially after remarriage.

There are studies that indicate that mediated agreements are more durable and have fewer post divorce litigations. The research reports that divorcing couples feel they have been heard and respected in mediation and can genuinely accept the decisions that have been reached. Most people stretch pretty far to avoid escalating issues, and statistics indicate that the vast majority of divorces do not require judicial intervention.

Better

If you are going to briefly change a monetary arrangement within your agreement, it's prudent to document what the intention is. Perhaps in an economically hard time, a person receiving child support says the payor does not have to pay for three months. Is that non-paid child support intended to be repaid, or is it "forgiven?" This is where the ugly "I assumed" creates conflict.

The Spiritual Divorce

In addition to all the legal considerations, if you are a person of faith, you may want the option to end your marriage according to your religion. These methods have no legal standing, but they may be required if you want to marry again within your religion. New York State is one of the only states that requires a spouse to cooperate with the other spouse if he or she wants to pursue a religious divorce.

The Catholic Church

The Catholic Church sees marriage as a permanent union according to the teachings of Jesus in Matthew 19:6: "Therefore what God has joined together, let no one separate." This means that the church does not recognize a civil divorce, because a court or a state can't undo what God has done.

That being said, the church does not excommunicate people who receive a civil divorce—in fact, it encourages these people to continue to come to church and to receive the holy sacraments (take Communion). The civil divorce only becomes an issue if one of the spouses wishes to marry again in the Catholic Church. To be married again, the spouse either needs to be widowed, or he or she needs to seek an annulment.

It is a myth that an annulment means that in the eyes of the Church, no marriage had actually taken place—nor does it brand your children as illegitimate. If an annulment is granted, it simply means that the marriage was not valid according to Church law. An annulment can be granted decades after a marriage as long as the criteria are met.

A Catholic marriage has six points that must be fulfilled for the marriage to be considered valid:

- Both spouses must be free to marry.
- Both spouses are capable of giving their consent to marry.
- The spouses freely exchange consent to marry.
- The spouses both have the intention of marrying for life, being faithful to one another, and being open to having children.
- Their intentions toward one another are good; in other words, they do not intend to harm one another.
- They both give their consent in the presence of two witnesses, and before an authorized minister of the Catholic Church.

To obtain the annulment, the spouse (the petitioner) submits testimony in writing to a tribunal of Catholic Church officials. The tribunal then examines the testimony to determine if something essential was missing *at the time of the wedding*, based on the points above. Once the petition is submitted, the respondent—the other spouse—will have the opportunity to read it. The petitioner and respondent may each be represented by a Church advocate, and the Church will appoint a "defender of the bond," a representative who will present arguments against granting an annulment.

Some petitions for annulment take place in a local or regional judicial process, while others go all the way to a Roman court. The people within your diocese

Better

You do the right thing because it is the right thing to do. If someone else is not compliant, it does not give you permission to not be compliant.

who handle annulment tribunals will be able to tell you how long the process might take.

Jewish Annulment

The Jewish religion has three main denominations of worship: Orthodox, Conservative and Reform Judaism. The Reform and Conservative denominations have less stringent requirements for receiving a *get* (annulment), a document in which the husband states that the marriage has ended, and will sometimes accept a divorce that has been decreed by the civil court. Orthodox congregations require that the husband give the wife a *get*. Jewish people believe that this procedure comes from the law God gave to Moses in Deuteronomy 24:1: "Suppose a man enters into marriage with a woman, but she does not please him because he finds something objectionable about her, and so he writes her a certificate of divorce, puts it in her hand, and sends her out of his house; she then leaves his house..."

The *get* is a document written by an expert rabbinic scribe in which a husband states his intention to divorce his wife. The document says that the husband is "under no duress" and willingly consents to the divorce, and that the wife can "have authority over yourself and go and marry any man you desire." Jewish custom mandates the wording of the *get*, which is why the scribe who writes it must be an expert. Each *get* is written specifically for the husband and wife involved, so there are no forms that you can fill out to expedite the process.

The procedure for securing a *get* takes place in front of a *beth din*, a rabbinical court with three presiding rabbis. When the scribe completes the document, the husband hands it to the wife in the presence of two qualified witnesses—two Jewish men over the age of bar mitzvah (13), who are not related to the bride or groom or to each other.

It may look as if the wife has no rights or choice in these divorce proceedings, but this is not the case in modern times. Today the wife must consent to the divorce.

Islamic Annulment

In traditional Islamic marriages, the husband can divorce his wife simply by saying to her, "*Talaq*," the word for divorce in Islam (although the wife cannot divorce her husband this way). Saying "*Talaq*" the first time suspends the marriage for three months, during which time the husband is required to continue to support his wife and allow her to live in his house. During this suspension, the husband can decide to take his wife back, though he must declare this before two witnesses.

Two more declarations of *Talaq* actually end the marriage in the context of the religion. Islamic teaching discourages doing this, as some men say it out of momentary anger or disagreement and regret the decision later.

While many other religions officially discourage divorce, they generally accept a civil divorce as valid, and permit divorced people to remarry in a religious ceremony.

Secular/Civil Annulment

Annulment is not restricted to religion. Secular or civil annulment is a court action that declares a marriage null and void. It usually takes place after a very short marriage, because it states that a marriage never existed—that the marriage was not legal due to some defect in the proceedings or the contract. Some of the factors involved include bigamy, duress (a forced marriage), fraud, incest, incompetence, insanity, mental disability, or misunderstanding because of drug or alcohol abuse. The most common civil annulments happen between blood relatives for whom marriage is illegal, or they involve some kind of diminished capacity (drugs or drunkenness), an underage spouse, or a spouse who is already married. In many of these cases, a judge can declare that since the marriage was illegal, it never happened—it is therefore nullified. In others, the marriage contract (the understanding between the two spouses) can be voided because of misrepresentation on one spouse's part, or misunderstanding by either spouse. The result is that a court hands down a judgment of annulment.

> **Better**
>
> *"Out beyond ideas of wrong-doing and right-doing, there is a field. I'll meet you there."*
>
> *– Rumi*

PART 3
The Economic Divorce

Chapter 5

Money and Assets: Getting Started

"New beginnings are often disguised in painful endings."
– Lao-tzu

An elderly Cherokee Native American was teaching his grandchildren about life. He said to them, "A fight is going on inside me. It is a terrible fight, and it is between two wolves. One wolf is evil—he is fearful, angry, jealous and negative. The other is good—he is happy, peaceful, positive and content."

The grandchildren thought about it for a minute, and then one asked, "Which wolf will win, Grandfather?"

The elder smiled and replied, "Whichever wolf I feed."

Ending a marriage is an emotionally difficult time. People often describe their thoughts as a roller coaster of ups and downs. It's as if you have two wolves inside of you vying for your energy and attention.

Many clients come to mediation with their angry, fearful wolf screaming loudly. They are afraid that the New York State guidelines or pension distribution may be unreasonable in their circumstances. There are practical decisions to be made about sharing money in divorce that may get hijacked by emotional reactions.

I often ask clients, "Would you rather be happy or right?" There is rarely just one answer to a challenge, and each party may cling to their "truth" because the alternative feels so scary.

When budgets and the guidelines are looked at together, more positive and gentler solutions tend to emerge. Mediation offers a neutral setting to explore what would be a difficult conversation at your kitchen table. It helps both people find a way to feed the gentler and more positive wolf.

Marital and Separate Property

Divorce involves dividing the family's property. This process can be complicated and contentious, especially if there are significant assets to be considered.

"Property" includes homes, vehicles, boats, furniture, artwork, and jewelry, as well as cash, savings, investments, securities, retirement accounts, and more.

One of the first issues a couple going through divorce deals with is determining whether an asset is *marital property or separate property*.

Marital property. Property acquired from the date of the marriage through the date of legal separation is marital property. Property acquired during the marriage is considered marital even if the title to the item, such as a vehicle, a retirement account, or a pension, is held in one name.

Separate property. Any asset acquired by each spouse before they married each other is considered separate property. You and your spouse may exclude this property from the marital estate via a prenuptial or postnuptial agreement, or by not comingling the funds by keeping them separate at all times. Without such an agreement, there is a presumption that property acquired during the marriage is marital property, while separate property (as defined below) belongs to the designated individual.

Separate property usually includes the following categories, but the manner in which assets or debts were treated during the marriage may influence the outcome of separate vs. marital:

- Property acquired by gift, legacy or descent from someone other than the spouse, either before or during the marriage.
- Property acquired in exchange for property acquired before the marriage, or in exchange for property acquired by gift, legacy, or descent.
- Property acquired by a spouse after a Legal Separation or Date of Commencement.
- Compensation you received for personal injuries during the marriage not related to loss of wages or earning capacity during the marriage.
- The increase in value of separate property, such as stock appreciation, interest, or real estate appreciation.
- Property acquired by either spouse before the marriage.

Throughout the divorce process, you will have opportunities to decide with your spouse how you want to split your property between yourselves. When the divorce court is processing your divorce decree, the judge will usually accept your written separation agreement on how you want to divide your property.

If you cannot reach an agreement with your spouse, the court will have to step in to make decisions for you, includ-

Bitter

If the courts are involved in your divorce, they have no authority over separate property, although they may be involved regarding what is or is not considered separate property. However, separate property such as savings can be taken into consideration by the court if the other spouse requires spousal maintenance.

Better

New York was once a "common law property" state, so property was distributed at divorce based on which spouse held the title to each item. If just one spouse's name was on the deed to the house, for example, the house went to that spouse. Equitable distribution replaced common law in 1980, so both spouses have equal options regarding marital property.

ing what is and isn't marital property and what the *equitable distribution* plan will be.

The most complicated part of identifying separate from marital assets is when separate assets are commingled with marital assets. If you and your spouse are going to court to establish equitable distribution of marital property, what you believe to be separate property can lose its separate property status if it has been combined, or commingled, with marital property. This is where property issues can become very murky and require analysis to resolve. Generally, if you mix or commingle separate property with marital property, the court may consider part or all of that separate property to be marital property when determining the equitable distribution.

The issue of commingling property often arises during divorce. Here are some of the situations that come up:

• **You own a home before you marry, and it becomes your marital residence:** A portion of the property may be considered marital in the future. That is because, in most cases, "marital money" went into paying for the mortgage, taxes, repairs and the like. Determining the separate from marital portion is part of the mediation or litigation process.

• **You own a property prior to marriage that you want to remain separate, such as a cabin in the woods or rental property:** You can maintain the separateness by remaining the sole owner and making sure marital money was not used in the home. If marital money was used for taxes, repairs, or renovations, a portion of that property could turn into a marital asset.

• **You and your spouse purchase a home together after marriage, and he/she contributes a portion or all of a separate property (e.g., an inheritance) towards a down payment:** That contribution to the purchase will normally remain your spouse's separate property. He/she may be able to get that contribution back after the marital house is sold.

• **You inherit stock and deposit it into a jointly owned investment account that both you and your spouse worked to grow:** Generally this dilutes the separate property. The majority, if not all, of the funds may be considered marital property, and it can be divided up as such.

• **You have a bank account started prior to the marriage in your name, and after the marriage you add your spouse's name:** By adding his/her name, there is now a presumption of a gift to your spouse of one-half the value of the account.

In New York State, equitable distribution is the fair division of property between spouses. This doesn't necessarily mean the court will create a 50:50 split of your assets. Instead, the judge will strive for a fair outcome, considering more than a dozen factors in making the decisions. See Appendix F for the list of factors.

> **Better**
>
> *Marital money is any money earned during the marriage, regardless of who earned the money.*

While the court can decide what is separate or marital property, the court can include only marital property when deciding the equitable distribution.

How to Divide Up Marital Property

There are four basic steps in the process to determine who takes what.

1. Identify all assets held by either or both of you.
2. Categorize each asset as marital or non-marital property.
3. Assign a value to each asset.
4. Establish a plan for division of the assets, considering the guidelines in your state.

The Statement of Net Worth and Why You Need It

Nearly every divorcing couple is required to fill out a Statement of Net Worth. This is a standardized document provided by most states. The long, detailed list of income, assets, expenses, and liabilities can seem daunting to anyone, even if you deal with household finances on a regular basis.

The Statement of Net Worth becomes a sworn legal document. It describes your entire financial background—everything you earn, spend, save, own, and owe. Your mediator (or attorney, if you choose this route) will use this document to help you make important decisions about how much money you will need once your divorce is final. That's why it is important to provide all of the information you can as accurately as possible. Making wild guesses about what you spend in a month on groceries, laundry, dry cleaning, or auto expenses like gas and oil changes could leave you with less money than you actually need to cover such expenses.

One way to be sure you are taking all items into consideration is to save all of your receipts for a month or two before you fill out the form. At the end of the month, sort the receipts into categories including groceries, dining out, auto expenses, clothing, laundry, and so on, and add up each pile. You will see what you spend in a typical month—and it may be different from what you imagined.

Better

Creating a realistic budget is the best way to avoid surprises after your agreement is signed. Take your time and be thorough.

The Statement of Net Worth is a sworn legal document, so it can be a crime to fill it out incorrectly—especially if this is done deliberately. Some people think that withholding information in an attempt to hide assets makes them clever or smart, but the fact is that you can face a charge of perjury for doing so. Chances are that your spouse has a clear idea of what should be on the Statement of Net Worth, so he or she will know what is missing and will bring this up in mediation or in negotiations between attorneys.

In mediation, all of the information required for the Statement of Net Worth is collected and discussed. The information is included in the MOU. The actual court-required Statement of Net Worth is completed as part of processing the divorce papers.

Better

It's prudent to request your credit report during the divorce process and to follow up three months after the divorce: first to see what debts you have, and then to ensure that the decisions regarding debt have been implemented.

How Divorce Affects Your Credit

One of the biggest worries many divorcing couples have is how divorce affects their credit and finances. It's a complicated issue that needs to be addressed in your divorce process.

You and your spouse each have your own separate credit history beginning with the first credit card or loan you received—your car loan, student loan, or mortgage, for example. You also have your own credit score based on your individual history. The most commonly used score is the Fair, Isaac and Company (FICO®) score, the one that provides a rating up to 850 points based on your credit history, the amount of credit to which

Bitter

Through the eyes of divorce, all marital debts are a shared responsibility. Through the eyes of creditors, only the name on the account is responsible.

you have access, the amount of debt you carry, and the way you use your credit cards and loans. If you've never used credit, you may not have a credit score or report.

FICO is not the only score, however. Each credit reporting agency calculates its own credit score.

> **Better**
>
> *It is important to have at least one or two credit cards in your own name before you end your marriage. During the marriage, you can use household income to apply, even if the card will be in your name only.*

All of the credit bureaus (the main ones are Experian, TransUnion, and Equifax) use the same criteria to judge your "credit worthiness." While the bureaus often come up with similar scores, those scores can vary because they have different information, and each bureau may analyze the facts slightly differently.

Your marital status, age, gender, race, job status, savings/investments, and income have no impact on your FICO score. The main thing that matters is your credit history—whether you pay your bills on time. The legal status of your marriage or relationship does not matter where your credit scores are concerned. What does matter is whether you opened a joint credit account together (credit card, mortgage, car loan). How you and your spouse manage those joint accounts will continue to affect the credit scores of both of you regardless of whether you marry or divorce.

Note that being *an authorized user* of a card is not the same as being *a joint account owner*. If you are an authorized user, you get a credit card in your own name that you can use to make purchases, but you are not responsible for paying the bill. Your credit score will not be affected by the account owner's payment history under the FICO scoring model.

> **Better**
>
> *As you begin the divorce process, get a credit report for each of you to create an accurate list of accounts and whose name they are in.*

If one spouse agrees to pay some of the debts, be careful. Your agreement is between the two of you and not with your creditors. Creditors can still look to you for repayment of debt even though your spouse agreed to pay the bills.

Unfortunately, your credit scores can be affected by your ex-spouse's financial behavior long after a marriage ends. If you are still registered as a co-owner of a credit card that is also used by your ex-spouse, you are considered responsible for that debt, regardless of the state of your marriage. (In some states, all accounts opened during marriage are considered joint, regardless of whose name is on them.)

Better

Rather than sharing payments on a joint credit card, consider transferring your portion to a new credit card in your own name. If a debt of $5,000 is in both names and Gail agrees to pay $2,500 of this debt, Gail could transfer $2,500 to a new card in her name only. However, unless Tom closes the account (when paid in full), Gail may remain liable to the creditor for future debt.

One of the most common misperceptions during a divorce is that the divorce decree cancels previous credit contracts. In fact, the divorce decree is simply an agreement between you, your ex-spouse, and the court regarding who will take responsibility for paying the existing debts.

In a divorce, the extent of your liability for credit card debt depends on two things:

- Whether or not the debt is for a joint credit card
- Whom the debt is assigned to in the divorce

The divorce decree does not remove or authorize the removal of a joint credit or loan account from your credit report. In cooperation with the creditor, it may be possible for you and your ex-spouse to close a joint account and open new accounts in your own names separately. The joint account may remain on your credit report as "closed," however. If its history is lowering your score, you will need to approach the credit report companies to dispute the information.

Before closing any accounts, however, make sure that all balances have been paid in full and on time. Keep in mind that closing joint accounts can lower your credit scores, especially if you close multiple accounts within a short period of time.

Deleting a mortgage from either of your credit records will probably require refinancing the mortgage, so the old mortgage appears as "paid in full" on future reports. (See Chapter 6 for more details.)

For a mortgage or a credit card, if the provisions in the SAPSA are not followed, the matter usually is sorted out in small claims court.

If at all possible, work cooperatively with your ex-spouse to find a path that does the least damage to your credit scores and helps you both regain solid financial footing.

Could your spouse be hiding assets?

How can you be sure that your spouse is not hiding assets from you? Remarkably, there are a number of signs that make it surprisingly easy to guess that there may be money in places your spouse has not shared with you. Here are some of the things that may give you a clue that your spouse has not been completely honest with you.

- **Sudden secrets.** Your spouse has always shared your family's finances, and now he/she suddenly won't provide any information to you.

- **Income vs. lifestyle.** Your spouse insists that he/she is not making much money, but he/she makes extravagant purchases that do not show up on your credit card statements.

- **Surprise debts or gifts.** Your spouse decides to pay off a big debt—but you had no idea this debt existed. Chances are your spouse says this debt is to a friend or family member, and they're being paid in cash. This may be a "shell game." The friend is going to hold onto this cash and return it to your spouse once your divorce is final.

- **Sudden large withdrawals.** When you get your bank statements, you see large cash withdrawals without any explanation from your spouse.

- **Custodial accounts.** Your spouse creates a trust or bank account with a large sum of money, placing it in the name of one of your children and using the child's Social Security number. He or she names himself/herself as the sole trustee for this account.

- **Failing business.** Your spouse tells you repeatedly that the business he or she owns is having a terrible year, so there is little or no money. You have seen other evidence, however, that the business is doing well.

- **Pressure to sign.** Your spouse comes to you with documents to sign, wanting you to sign right away without reviewing the documents.

- **Bonus delays.** Your spouse reports that his employer is not giving bonuses this year or that he/she is delaying the bonus, when you know the business has done well.

- **Suspicious charges.** You find charges to your spouse's credit card for gifts, hotel room nights, college tuition, rent, or travel, when none of this activity is for you or your family.

If you see this kind of behavior and you suspect that your spouse is not being honest with you, it may be time to enlist the help of a forensic accountant or a private investigator. "Forensic" means "appropriate to present in court." A forensic accountant collects, analyzes and presents information about a financial situation in a way that can be used as evidence.

Prenuptial and Postnuptial Agreements

Many people think that a prenuptial agreement, or "prenup," means the couple is starting married life with distrust and lack of commitment. People say it's an insurance policy that protects against an "inevitable" divorce.

If someone wants a prenup, isn't the marriage doomed? After all, why would someone worry about sharing assets and debts unless they had some doubts about the marriage or the integrity of one of the parties?

> **Better**
>
> *A prenup avoids the dreaded "I assumed" culprit that plagues many marriages.*

I have mediated many prenups. My research and experience indicates that a prenup often reduces the chances of a divorce. It provides a framework and a process to examine sensitive issues like money and children and to create an understanding and a resolution that is agreeable to both.

A prenup can enhance communications and improve the quality of your marriage. Using mediation to create the prenuptial agreement with a skilled guide may actually reduce the possibility of divorce.

A prenuptial agreement is a written contract created by two people before they are married. It typically lists all of the property and debts each person owns and specifies what each person's property rights will be should the marriage end.

In essence, a prenuptial agreement overrides the laws that govern divorce and estate rights (if one spouse passes away) and lets the couple set the rules. Because of the timing of the agreement's creation, those rules are created with good will and love rather than bitterness and anger.

A prenup is intended to be clear about how accumulated assets and debts and future income might be shared, not only in a divorce but also if a spouse passes away. It is especially important if children are involved. Young adults just getting started in life and marriage may not need a prenuptial agreement unless they have trust funds, family businesses, or other major assets they are bringing into the marriage.

For couples who are marrying a second time and have accumulated assets such as retirement funds or a house—or significant debt from student loans or other sources—a prenup can be essential. This is true regardless of whether children are involved.

Each state has its own rules for prenuptial agreements. Couples should understand the requirements for an agreement before signing because premarital contracts can have long-term effects. New York is in the minority of states that haven't adopted the Uniform Prenuptial Agreement Act (UPAA). Instead, New York State law sets forth the rules and requirements for prenuptial agreements.

Elements of a Prenuptial Agreement

Assets: What will be considered separate rather than marital assets if the marriage ends or a partner dies? Designate what was acquired prior to the marriage, such as the house, retirement funds, defined pensions, mutual funds, and business values/ownership. The prenup needs to state whether the growth and appreciation from the separate assets will be considered marital.

Debts: What debt was acquired prior to the marriage and who will be responsible for its repayment? This is important especially because "marital money" (money earned during the marriage) may complicate how payments toward debts may be made if the prenup is not clear.

Full Disclosure: The prenuptial agreement includes a complete itemization of all assets and debts. This is required to be thorough and comprehensive to avoid any misunderstanding in the future.

Spousal Maintenance: This is an important conversation, especially if there is a disparity of income. The conversation generally considers different conclusions depending upon the length of marriage and the intention to help one party reestablish himself/herself if the marriage ends. The topics of temporary and post-divorce spousal maintenance may also be discussed.

Joint Property and Income: How will the parties create shared marital assets to be excluded from the prenup? What if a recreational home is purchased or a new house is purchased together? What about joint bank and investment accounts? What if a new business is created during the marriage?

Estate Rights: The agreement needs to be clear about how each party's estate will be managed regarding the distribution of assets and debts and the children's inheritance options. The prenup sets forth and overrides state estate laws regarding mandatory spousal distributions after one spouse dies.

Voluntary Exceptions: A prenup does not preclude one party or the other from mutually agreeing to change the terms. It also does not prevent one party to gift or in any way provide more than the prenup indicates to the other.

Applicable in All States: Much like a will, the prenup needs to include language such that its terms will be applicable in any state in which the parties may reside during the marriage or in which either may die.

Sunset Clause: Many prenups include language to provide an increasing percentage of what was once premarital assets to the other as the marriage progresses through the years. What was once premarital often changes over time as the marriage prevails.

Timing: It is considered prudent to create and sign a prenup more than 30 days in advance of the wedding, and with even more lead time if possible. The issue of signing a prenup under "duress" is something that may undermine the ability to enforce the agreement in the future.

> **Better**
>
> I recommend a very useful book, Prenups for Lovers: A Romantic Guide to Prenuptial Agreements by Arlene Dubin. It expands on the details of a prenup and emphasizes the value of clarity and good will when discussing these sensitive issues. The book describes how a prenup can take the worry out of marriage.

Signing and Filing the Agreement: Similar to a mediated Memorandum of Understanding (MOU) for a divorce, it is prudent to have the final version of the prenup processed by an attorney because there is required legal language to make it a binding, enforceable agreement. The agreement is then filed in your local county clerk's office to preserve the original document with no misunderstanding regarding what the final terms of the agreement are.

In order for your prenuptial agreement to be valid, it generally has to satisfy several criteria:

- It must be in writing.
- Both spouses must have signed it.
- Both spouses must have entered into the agreement voluntarily. This has its own set of criteria to be sure you met this requirement:
- The spouse must have had independent representation (his/her own attorney) or have signed a separate document waiving representation.
- The spouse must have had at least seven days to review the document before signing it.
- The spouse must have had a clear understanding of what he/she was signing, including the rights to money and property he/she would lose by signing it.
- The spouse was not under duress or in any way forced to sign against his/her will.
- The agreement must not have been "unconscionable" when the spouses entered into it—that is, it did not waive so many of the spouse's rights to money and property that the spouse would be left with little or nothing if the marriage ended.
- The agreement must have full disclosure of the financial information being addressed.

Postnuptial agreements: A postnuptial agreement is a document drawn up after the marriage, but it serves the same function as a prenuptial agreement. Like a prenuptial agreement, the terms of a postnuptial agreement override the New York State equitable distribution guidelines (see Appendix F). To be valid, it has similar criteria as a prenuptial agreement and cannot be unconscionable or signed under duress.

> **Better**
>
> *Neither a prenup nor a postnup can direct child support or parenting decisions. These issues are always subject to the jurisdiction of the courts.*

Couples may want a postnuptial agreement if there is a large investment contemplated, or if a spouse is about to buy into a partnership agreement, or perhaps to safeguard a large inheritance of property and funds to avoid any confusion regarding separate or marital property if the marriage ends. Another use is if there is a large age gap between the spouses, and one party will continue to add funds to a retirement account while the older spouse is actually drawing a distribution for the retirement funds.

> **Bitter**
>
> *It is prudent to have a prenuptial or postnuptial agreement reviewed by separate attorneys. Without attorney review, enforcing the prenup or postnup may be jeopardized.*

A prenup or postnup often brings clarity to the financial process of separating assets and debts. This avoids additional marital stress during an emotional time.

It is always challenging to separate assets. In truth, both parties end up with less than what they had together, and it is hard to feel safe and OK. Adjusting to a new financial and emotional situation takes courage and acceptance and a willingness to let go of the struggle.

Chapter 6

Putting a Price Tag on Emotions:
Your House, Retirement Funds, and Debt

"I am stronger because of my hard times, wiser because of my mistakes,
and happier because of my sad experiences."
—Unknown

L ew and Donna arrive for their first appointment and announce, "We have everything worked out. This will be an easy mediation for you."

What I know is that divorce mediation is never easy. It may be less complicated, but not easy.

In this case, Lew and Donna have no children and have been married for twelve years. At some point there will be an emotional conversation concerning a financial asset. That's when folks put a price tag on emotions. That's when there is an underlying need that translates into a financial request.

The beauty of mediation is that clients get to make choices that are right for their specific situations. The key to a successful mediation process is when everyone is well-informed. Then they make the emotional and financial trade-offs that work for them, and they may have fewer regrets in the future.

Lew and Donna have worked out everything at their kitchen table, so I respect their effort and ask them to be more specific. As they recite their conclusions, I map their information into the mediation process.

For clients without children, this results in a table similar to Table 1 on the next page. The Item and Value columns show the Assets and Debts as they stand now, before splitting anything.

The "Lew After Decisions" and "Donna After Decisions" columns show the redistribution of assets as discussed in the paragraphs below. The last figure in the Value column shows the result of a 50:50 split. As you can see, the actual dollars are not a 50:50 split.

Bitter
A very common client conclusion is to trade a retirement asset for the value of the house. Pre-tax retirement funds like a 401(k) or IRA, however, are not comparable to house equity dollars that are tax-free.

Table 1: Assets and Debts

Assets	Value	Lew After Decisions	Donna After Decisions
Net equity of house (*)	$40,000		$40,000
Mutual funds	$10,000	$5,000	$5,000
Lew's car	$15,000	$15,000	
Donna's car	$5,000		$5,000
Sub-total	**$70,000**	**$20,000**	**$50,000**
401(k)-Lew	$70,000		
403(b)-Donna	$30,000		
Sub-total retirement (#)	**$100,000**	**$78,000 (see discussion)**	**$22,000 (see discussion)**
Teacher pension	TBD	(see discussion)	(see discussion)
Total assets	**$170,000**	**$98,000**	**$72,000**
Debts			
Car loan-Lew	$5,000	$5,000	
Visa-Lew	$3,000	$3,000	
Visa-Donna	$2,000		$2,000
Total debt	**$10,000**	**$8,000**	**$2,000**
Net Assets	**$160,000**	**$90,000**	**$70,000**
Asset adjustments	For cars	-$2,500 (see discussion)	+$2,500 (see discussion)
50:50 Split	**$80,000**	**Actual: $87,500**	**Actual $72,500**

*Net equity = The fair market value of the house minus the mortgage, and minus refinance or selling costs.
These numbers assume Donna will stay in the house and she compensates Lew for the house using her share of the marital retirement savings accounts.

It is important to understand that Lew and Donna can share their assets and their debts in any way that feels fair and equitable to them. New York State is an "equitable" state, not an "equal" or "community property" state. The presumption is that marital assets and debts will be shared equally, but the equitable distribution guidelines (Appendix F) give reasons why this might not be the case.

What Lew and Donna need to understand is that not every dollar is equal when sharing funds.

Donna would like to stay in the house that has a net equity value of $40,000. Using 50:50 as an equitable distribution guide, she would owe Lew $20,000 as his share. Donna suggests Lew keep $20,000 more of the total retirement savings, and then they will be even.

Under this arrangement, Lew would keep his original 50 percent ($50,000) of the total retirement savings ($100,000) plus $20,000 out of Donna's $50,000 of the total amount of retirement savings.

But here is how the math actually works: The retirement savings accounts are pre-tax, meaning income taxes will be due when the money is withdrawn from those accounts. With few exceptions, there are no taxes paid on the net equity of the sale of a house. If Lew receives an extra $20,000 of retirement savings now, and we assume a 30 percent tax rate, he will really net approximately $14,000 when he starts to withdraw the money, even many years later.

In order for Lew to fully benefit from the extra $20,000, he needs to be compensated now for the taxes he'll have to pay later. Donna needs to give him $20,000 divided by .70 (using a 30 percent tax rate), which comes to $28,000 out of her share of the retirement savings.

Therefore, on the chart you can see that Lew will retain $78,000 of the retirement savings, and Donna will retain $22,000.

Another misapplied strategy is sharing assets or debt by subtracting one from the other. Continuing to work with our couple, Lew's car is worth $15,000, and he has $5,000 left on his loan. The net amount is $10,000. Donna's car is worth $5,000 and has no loan.

Many clients would assume that Lew should pay Donna $10,000 minus $5,000 or $5,000 for the difference in the value of the cars. Instead, subtract any debt directly related to each asset, add the value of the two assets together, and then divide by the number of assets (two in this case). This determines what each person could have in marital assets in order to receive the same value.

Here's the math:

- $10,000 (value of Lew's car after subtracting car loan) + $5,000 (value of Donna's car) = $15,000
- Divide by two= $7,500
- If the couple decides each should have $7,500 worth of car, Lew owes Donna $2,500

> **Better**
>
> *No matter what you decided at your kitchen table, if you learn something new in mediation, you both get to make a different decision.*

Couples often discover in mediation that they have made some assumptions and miscalculations at the kitchen table that could have lasting implications for their finances and their post-divorce quality of life.

Sometimes one spouse wishes to be generous to the other, perhaps as an apology for difficulties he or she may believe led to the end of the marriage. The spouse may say, "I don't want anything for the house—let her keep it," or "He earned the retirement fund, so he should keep it all." While you can make any arrangement that you choose, this may mean that one spouse is walking away from assets to which he or she is entitled—money that can make a difference if the spouse ever intends to buy another home or retire comfortably. A mediator helps separate the emotional from the practical details to reach an agreement that is fair to both of you.

Your New Budget

One of the biggest challenges in mediation is making sure that both parties will be all right financially. Often the previously combined marital income supported a comfortable life with plenty of discretionary spending. Eating out, vacations, and

> **Better**
>
> *Clients have just one financial tablecloth going over two tables. If there's a shortfall, it's helpful to consider "comparable suffering" for both spouses.*

lots of activities for the kids were real options. Now, both parties may have to be more frugal as "one tablecloth needs to fit across two tables."

You and your spouse will need to think carefully about your individual expenses now that you will be living separately. You have the same amount of money you had in marriage, but now you need to split it and support two households. Your money needs to stretch so that each of you can sustain your own homes, and your new standard of living may not be the same as it was before.

Start by making a list of all of your expenses. Each spouse will need to make his or her own list, because you may each have different expenses. I encourage you to do this independently, so you are confident in your personal needs. Regardless of whether you use mediation or attorneys to end your marriage, a budget is an essential element of creating your agreement. This is a good way to learn about future expenses, especially if one spouse is less familiar with the day-to-day expenses of running a household.

Be as realistic as possible about what you need to live on your own, including your children's expenses. In Appendix G, you will find a sample budget to help you start to plan. If you are proceeding to a divorce, whether no-fault or otherwise, this budgeting process is required.

You may have other expenses not on the template. Be as comprehensive as possible in creating your budget, so your mediator or attorney can help you prepare for your new financial reality.

Bitter

On average, adding a separate household costs at least $20,000 annually in duplicated expenses.

Many spouses arrive in my office without ever having examined what they spend in a month or a year on their home, transportation, clothing, food, communication, entertainment, and all the other expenses that pile up on a daily basis. Almost invariably, this can lead to a spouse believing that he/she spends much less than a carefully computed budget would reveal. I work with my clients to determine a realistic budget so that there are no surprises in the future.

One of the biggest budget considerations is who keeps the house, and how that spouse will pay the mortgage and related expenses. Couples often believe that the best arrangement for their children is for the custodial parent to keep the house, so the children's living situation will not be disrupted significantly by the divorce. They may overlook the hidden expenses of owning a house. The parent with whom the children live may not be able to afford the mortgage, property taxes, upkeep, and maintenance of keeping the home. It may make more sense for the couple to sell the home and avoid an undue financial burden on either spouse, even though this will create a temporary disruption for the children. There is more on this topic later in this chapter.

It's also important to understand what happens to debts during a divorce. Each spouse may continue to be responsible for shared credit card accounts in the eyes of the credit card companies. The divorce agreement needs to spell out exactly who will pay the credit card debt—or, ideally, if the debts will be paid off using available funds before the divorce is finalized. Otherwise, you may find that a debt still appears on your credit report. If it is not paid per the agreement, your credit score will be impacted.

Your Home

One of the biggest financial (and emotional) decisions to be made during a divorce is what happens to the marital home. Most of the time, the property is titled and mortgaged in the names of both spouses, so there are multiple issues that need to be decided. Regardless of how the home is titled, however, there are many factors that influence who retains the home, such as the children, the school district, and the pets. These are all legitimate issues, and in the midst of sorting out the finances the practical details also need to be addressed.

Option 1: Sell the Marital Home to a Third Party

If neither spouse wants the house (or neither can afford it) then it will be sold to a third party. Each of you moves to a new, separate dwelling. You will need to make some major decisions:

- When will the house be put on the market?
- What needs to be done to make it market ready, and who will do that work?
- Who will be the listing agent?
- What is the asking price?
- How will you handle open houses and visits by prospective buyers?
- How will you agree on a presented offer?
- When will both spouses (and children, if applicable) be out of the house so the new owner can move in?
- How will utilities, mortgage, taxes, homeowners insurance, and upkeep be paid until the house closes?
- How will the proceeds from the sale be allocated to you and/or your spouse?

Option 2: One Spouse Buys the House

If one of you wants to keep the house, then the process can become more complicated. The first step is to agree upon the fair market value of the house. Sometimes clients use the bank's appraisal required for the refinancing of the mortgage. Sometimes clients ask several realtors to provide the market value.

Arrangements have to be made so that the spouse keeping the house becomes the sole owner (title) and has the mortgage placed solely in his or her name.

So if Barbara is to keep the house, she needs to qualify for the mortgage in her own name. Alan will have to work with Barbara to have his name removed from the title and end his obligation for the mortgage. The timing and method of the title transfer (ownership) and the refinancing (getting the mortgage in one name) have to be coordinated to prevent problems for either party down the road.

The bank sometimes will let Alan's name be removed from the mortgage liability without refinancing. This is a very good and affordable option, but it does not happen very often. Usually this is done when the person whose name is being removed from the mortgage was not an income provider—an at-home parent,

> **Better**
>
> *It's up to the clients to agree on the fair market value of the home. No specific document is required, although some form of third party appraisal is useful.*

for example. The legal and bank fees involved in this method are much less than in refinancing.

However, removing Alan's name from the mortgage does not remove his name from the title of the home. Alan will need to produce a written document to legally transfer ownership of the property from himself to Barbara. There are several types of documents that can be used to do this. The most common is a quit claim deed. (Sometimes people call this a "quick claim" deed, but that is inaccurate.)

The quit claim deed is part of the refinancing process. Refinancing a house during divorce is usually done to pay off the current mortgage that's in both names. Then the spouse who is keeping the house obtains a new mortgage. That spouse becomes the only one financially responsible for the mortgage.

> **Bitter**
>
> *Do not take your name off the title (the deed) until your name is also off the mortgage.*
> *In the unlikely event that your spouse dies after you sign a quit claim deed, but before the joint mortgage is refinanced, you may still be responsible for a mortgage on a house you no longer own.*

When you get close to finalizing the refinancing, the bank will need the signed (but not yet filed) quit claim deed. After your name comes off the mortgage, the bank will then file the quit claim deed in the county clerk's office.

Sometimes the quit claim deed is held in escrow by an attorney who is not part of the bank's refinancing. That attorney can send a letter to the mortgage lender bank and alert the bank that he/she has the signed document. When the name is off the mortgage then that attorney will file the new deed.

To refinance the mortgage, the person seeking refinancing must have good credit. The bank will take his or her existing debt into consideration as well.

> **Better**
>
> *It's not unusual for couples to say, "He can keep the house; I'll sign over the deed." Couples do not always understand that the change in title does not take your name off the mortgage. You need to have the spouse's name removed from the mortgage with the approval of the mortgage lender.*

As with the initial mortgage, refinancing also involves a variety of bank fees that are usually added to the amount being financed. To estimate these charges in your situation, myFICO.com provides a refinancing cost calculator (see Appendix H for the link). In addition, attorney fees and filing fees may be involved for the transfer of title on the deed.

> **Better**
>
> *Clients often share the refinance and attorney fees because it is part of the divorce process.*

In a divorce situation, the mortgage lender considers the amount of child support and spousal maintenance in determining whether you are eligible to refinance:

- The amount of child support or spousal maintenance is considered as a debt to the provider of these funds.
- The amount of child support and spousal maintenance is considered as income to the receiver of the funds, generally after 3-6 months.

The mortgage lender usually wants to see a final legal separation document or divorce decree to finalize the transaction.

The bank will do an appraisal of the house to obtain its current fair market value. Then the current mortgage balance and refinance fee are subtracted from the market value to determine the house's net equity. As an example, let's look at Barbara and Alan's house situation:

- Fair Market Value: $150,000
- Subtract the current mortgage balance: $100,000
- Subtract the refinancing fees: $4,000 (or other negotiated refinance or selling fees)
- Current Net Equity in the House: $46,000

If the net equity is divided 50:50 to determine the leaving spouse's share of the house's equity, then the leaving spouse's share usually is added to the staying spouse's new mortgage, so the staying spouse has cash to pay the leaving spouse his or her share of the net equity.

In the above case, Barbara has to increase the mortgage by $4,000 to refinance (unless she makes other arrangements with Alan), and then by $23,000 to pay Alan his share of the net equity. That adds $27,000 to Barbara's mortgage. Thus, Barbara must be able to qualify for a new mortgage of $127,000.

While many people balk at a 30-year mortgage, it will likely keep monthly payments as low as possible, which is very important in your new financial circumstance.

Option 3: The Leaving Spouse Stays on the Mortgage

It is not unusual for the leaving spouse to stay on the mortgage for a specified period of time after the divorce is final, for one or more reasons:

- The staying spouse needs to stay a few months until his/her child support and spousal maintenance can be counted as income. This would allow the staying spouse to qualify for a mortgage.
- The staying spouse may want to stay to allow a child to finish the school year or graduate from high school.
- The staying spouse wants a short period of time to decide to sell or refinance.

> **Bitter**
>
> *Being house-poor affects the quality of life for children. Consider reducing your house expenses by refinancing for a 30-year mortgage, so you are not house-poor, and you can have more discretionary expenses with your child(ren).*

Here's an example: Ellen and Jeff are divorcing, and Ellen needs Jeff to stay on the mortgage until his spousal maintenance payments become part of Ellen's income.

- Their separation agreement/divorce decree specifies a length of time—in this case, 24 months—until Jeff's name will be removed from the mortgage.
- The agreement should provide Jeff with a legal form of an IOU (specifying the defined payment schedule and due dates) for him to be paid the equity that is owed him.
- As long as his name is on the mortgage, Jeff is protected—he may order the house to be sold if the mortgage payments are late (for example, to avoid damage to his credit score).

On occasion, one spouse may die during the process of changing ownership of the house. While this is a rare occurrence, it's good to know what the process is if this takes place. During marriage, the co-title is referred to as *tenancy-by-the-entirety*. When one person dies, the surviving spouse gets the entire value and ownership of the home. Other types of ownership are joint tenancy with right of survivorship, tenants in common, and joint tenancy.

After divorce, if the house is still co-titled, the title automatically changes to *tenancy-in-common*. In this case, each ex-spouse would own an equal share, but neither spouse receives the other party's shares if the other party dies. Each specific share of the home is directed according to his or her will.

This may not be the result the divorcing couple wants. It's important to make sure your wishes can be carried out after your death. Your mediator or attorney

> **Bitter**
> *Staying on the mortgage and title may result in a homeowner liability if something unforeseen happens. Be sure to include language about who will pay if an accident or other issue takes place on the shared-ownership property.*

can explain the options for managing the different situations that can arise under these circumstances, but the most important thing you and your spouse can do to protect yourselves is to update your wills as soon as possible following your divorce. (See the section on wills in Chapter 14.)

Dividing Household Items

Who gets the holiday china, the leather recliner, Christmas ornament collection, and the dining room table? Dividing up the accumulation of items that fill every married couple's house can be emotional, but surprisingly there is usually a high degree of cooperation regarding this issue. Each person may have a sentimental attachment to specific items, and some items have a higher market value than others. When both spouses want to keep the same items, it can be difficult to find a way to satisfy them both, but fortunately, today, photos, CDs, and many sentimental items are easily replicated. (See also the "Special Property Categories" section of Chapter 7.)

Imagine putting every item in your home on the lawn for a one-day garage sale. Consider all the computers, TVs, washer and dryer, and so on. That's the value of your household. Would you guess you'd get $10,000-$12,000 for everything? If one person is keeping the majority of items, then the leaving spouse may get a buy-out allowance or a certain percentage of the total estimated value.

If you and your spouse have already separated, the leaving spouse probably took some household items with him/her. What remains in the house may include some other items the leaving spouse intends to have when a suitable residence is available. Walk through the house together and make lists of things each of you would like to have. This may be enough to divide things equitably, with the understanding that each spouse may have to purchase new items or replace those the other spouse received.

You may find that there are some items on which you can't agree—things both of you want to take

> **Bitter**
> *Household item values are generally set at garage sale prices, not what you paid or the replacement value of the item.*

> **Better**
>
> *Surprisingly, most clients distribute their household items to their mutual satisfaction without the need for attorneys or the mediator's involvement.*

away with you from the marriage. Make a list of all of these things, noting things that should be kept together, like a bedroom set or a stamp collection. Flip a coin to decide which spouse goes first, and take turns picking one item at a time from the list—like choosing sides for basketball teams—until all of the items are taken. You may not get all the items you want, but you will get some of them in the fairest way possible.

If there are items of significant value on this list—heirloom furniture, antiques, sterling silver tableware, works of art, and so on—bring a list of these items to your mediation appointment. These may need to be specifically included in the equitable distribution of your assets. Mediation can help you agree upon a fair value and distribution of these items.

> **Better**
>
> *Taking turns choosing items avoids the personal merits of why one person feels entitled to an item. By alternating choices, you self-define what's most important to you.*

Retirement Accounts and Divorce

Funding retirement is one of the hottest topics in personal finance today. Add a divorce to the mix, and the discussion about retirement accounts between separating spouses becomes even more emotional and confusing.

> **Bitter**
>
> *Avoid focusing on just one "sacred issue" as you begin to negotiate. I call that "cherry-picking." Your mediator can help you see the whole orchard, in order to provide a larger perspective on the issue.*

Let's start by reviewing the three main types of retirement funding:

Defined-benefit pensions: An employer funds this entire pension; you or your spouse do not contribute. The "defined benefit" is the amount the employee will receive per month at retirement. The employee has no say in the amount invested or paid. Most government and union pensions are defined benefit plans.

Defined-contribution plans: These include 401(k), 403(b), and 457 plans. In these plans, the employer does not promise a specific benefit amount at retirement. You or your employer (or both) contribute to the individual account under the plan, sometimes at a set rate (say, 5 percent of your annual earnings). These contributions are invested on the employee's behalf. The employee has control of how the money is invested, but investment options are limited to those available within the fund.

Individual Retirement Accounts (IRAs): These are opened by individuals and are not connected to any employer plan. There are four types: Traditional, Roth, SEP, and SIMPLE. To make things more confusing, the law does allow employers to make contributions to some of these plans.

These funds are generally invested in stocks and mutual funds, so they are subject to the volatility of the financial markets.

It's important to have a list of all retirement-related accounts owned by you and your spouse during the divorce process. The list should indicate the type of account and the current balance. If you are not sure of either, contact your employer or the financial planner who set up your accounts to get this information.

Defined Benefit Pension

Here is how a defined benefit pension is handled as part of the asset distribution during a divorce.

A defined benefit pension plan is a company pension plan in which an employer promises to pay the retiree a specified monthly benefit on retirement for the rest of his or her life. The monthly benefit amount is predetermined by a formula usually based on the employee's earnings history, length of service, and age at the time of retirement.

Today very few companies provide a traditional defined benefit pension to employees. However, virtually all city, county, state, and federal employees are currently eligible for a defined benefit pension.

There is something about a defined benefit pension that is very emotional. Perhaps it is because for the most part, people who receive such pensions have challenging careers, such as firefighters, police, teachers, mail carriers, and military personnel. In many cases, a pension is a symbol of very hard, sometimes dangerous, and stressful work.

When a couple is ending a marriage, financial security is a huge worry, and it is often downright scary. With so many variables regarding the future, a defined benefit pension represents a safety net because it promises a guaranteed income for life. Sharing that safety net with your ex-spouse, often many years in the unpredictable future, can feel scary and unfair.

Let's sort out the facts from the myths around defined benefit pensions and divorce. First, it's a myth that your spouse will automatically receive 50 percent of your pension. Your spouse may be eligible for part of (and typically 50 percent of) the marital portion of your pension. You and your spouse come to agreement on how to divide the marital pension. I explain this below. Your pension is like a savings account that was accumulated on your behalf by your employer during your marriage. So, the marital portion of your pension is just like any other marital asset.

You may feel that you are the one who worked at this job all these years with the crazy hours and dangerous situations, so you should not have to share this benefit with your ex-spouse. During your marriage, however, your spouse partnered with you in order for you to work the stressful and difficult hours. Perhaps he or she managed the home front and did most of the child care. Your spouse certainly spent time being worried about you while on the job and hoping you would come home safe and sound.

The fact is that your pension does not necessarily have to be shared. Your pension, like any other asset, is part of a larger conversation of asset and debt distribution in your divorce. In mediation, clients make informed decisions and may trade off one asset for another. A spouse may say, "No, thank you," to your pension, for lots of reasons. Any decision is fine as long as everyone is well-informed.

What if the pension does not exist in the future? Both parties share the risk of the loss, and neither party will receive anything from the pension.

As mentioned above, a defined benefit pension is shared in a manner quite different from an IRA, 401(k), 403(b), and so on. In New York State, the Majauskas Formula is used as a standard for determining how defined benefit pensions are to be shared after divorce, should the couple decide to do so.

The Majauskas Formula defines the marital portion of a pension as a percentage of the full pension. The percentage is calculated by dividing years of service credit accrued during the marriage by the total years of service at the time of retirement.

The formula ONLY defines the marital portion that is eligible to be split between the spouses. **Then the couple decides whether they want to divide the marital portion between them, and if so, how.** They can split it 50:50 or in any other way they both find agreeable.

Let's return to our example of Lew and Donna. Here are the assumptions:

- They were married for 12 years.
- Donna was a teacher for all of those 12 years.
- The pension rules set by Donna's employer say her pension will be 60 percent of her final average salary.
- Donna decides to retire after 30 years of working as a teacher.

- Donna's final salary at retirement is $80,000.
- Therefore, her annual pension will be $48,000 (60 percent of $80,000).
- Lew and Donna decide to split the *marital* portion of her pension 50:50.

Here is how the marital portion is calculated for Donna and Lew based on the above assumptions and using the Majauskas Formula:

- The marital portion of Donna's pension is the number of years Donna worked as a teacher during the marriage (12) divided by the total years Donna worked (30). So the marital portion percentage is 12/30, or 40 percent.
- Donna's full pension is $48,000. Multiply $48,000 by 40 percent to get the marital portion: $19,200.
- Since they decided on a 50:50 split, Lew is then eligible to receive half of the $19,200, or $9,600, annually for the rest of Donna's life.
- Donna will receive $38,400 annually ($48,000 minus $9,600, Lew's share) for the rest of her life.

If Donna works for only 20 years, the marital portion will be higher: 12/20 = 60 percent. But the dollar value of the marital portion is likely to be smaller because her annual pension will only be for example 40 percent of her final average salary.

So what are the benefits of the Majauskas Formula?

- Because the actual calculation is completed at the time Donna retires, there is no guesswork about the value of the pension. That means actual numbers will be used instead of estimates or guesses.
- Lew will receive his part of the marital portion directly from the pension provider, in this case New York State. A separate court document is prepared after the divorce that instructs the state to do the distribution. That form is called a Domestic Relations Order. For most private plans the court document is called a Qualified Domestic Relations Order and referred to as a QDRO (pronounced "kwa-dro"). (This document is among those prepared for the divorce. See Chapter 4.)
- Lew has the option to reduce his share of the marital portion by a certain amount to ensure that he will receive his share of the marital portion over the course of the rest of his life versus the rest of Donna's life. This is referred to as a survivor benefit within the pension plan.

Sometimes clients will say: "Donna can keep her pension, and I will keep the house." This means at the time of the divorce, Lew would not pay Donna her half of the equity in the marital house. That may seem like a fair trade.

However, to truly understand what is being traded, the expected future dollar value of the pension must be converted to today's dollars. Then that value needs to be figured into the overall picture of the couple's assets and debts to be divided.

Making this trade-off is problematic because you never know what might happen to a pension. There are plenty of cases where promised pensions have been lost due to the death of the participant before retirement, underfunding of pension investments, company bankruptcies, and other situations. It is wise to be cautious about trading off today's assets for a future asset.

How might this trade work in Lew and Donna's example? If Donna retires at 60 and lives to 85 (an insurance actuarial estimate), she will be retired for 25 years. Let's use Donna's annual pension from the earlier example: $48,000. Lew's share of the marital portion of that was calculated to be $9,600.

So if Lew shares her pension, he would receive $9,600 annually for 25 years (Donna's life expectancy). That comes to $9,600 x 25 years or $240,000.

The next step is to figure out how much the estimated future total annuity, $240,000, would be worth in today's money (present value). The question is: What would you have to invest today to have it provide you $9,600 annually for 25 years?

Let's imagine that the final calculation of the present value of $240,000 equals $30,000. Lew now has a $30,000 asset to trade off with Donna, regarding the house and other assets.

Bitter

Most professionals are cautious about using the present value of a pension because it is based on so many variables and must be calculated by an expert.

To resolve this, Lew and Donna should use the help of an appropriate financial professional to work through the math. Important questions to be answered are the interest rate that will be used to calculate growth of an investment, and what Donna's life expectancy is. Those assumptions can make a big difference.

By going through these steps, whatever they decide, Lew and Donna will have confidence that they were well-informed and made a decision that works for them.

Discussing money and finances and security are complicated and hard conversations in the best of times. Throw in emotional upheaval and the heartache of ending a marriage, and it is very challenging.

As a mediator, I guide clients to separate the emotional and the financial worries in order for each of those themes to be heard and valued. I find that when space is created for both conversations, clients are often reassured and sometimes even surprised at the outcome.

Let's look at each of the other types of retirement accounts in more detail.

Defined Contribution Retirement Plan (401(k), 403(b), 457)

- A **401(k)** is a retirement savings plan spon- sored by an employer who usually also makes contributions to your fund. It lets workers save and invest a piece of each paycheck before taxes

> **Better**
>
> *A person feels rich when what they want is what they have.*

are taken out. Taxes aren't paid until the money is withdrawn from the account. You control how your money is invested. Most plans offer a range of mutual funds composed of stocks, bonds, and money market investments. There are complex rules about when you can withdraw your money and costly penalties for pulling funds out before retirement age.

- A **403(b) plan** is a retirement plan for certain public school employees, em- ployees of nonprofit organizations, and ministers. Individual 403(b) accounts are established and maintained by eligible employees. The employer may determine the financial institution(s) at which individual employees may maintain their 403(b) accounts, which in turn determines the type of 403(b) accounts that the employees may establish and fund.

- A **457 plan** is a type of tax-advantaged, deferred-compensation retirement- plan that is available for government and certain non-government employers. The employer provides the plan, and the employee puts part of his or her earnings into it on a pre-tax basis. This may not be a retirement plan; some high-earning employees can choose to defer a portion of their income each year into this plan to avoid paying taxes on it. They may choose to withdraw the money at a set time, such as five or ten years down the road, or they can leave it in the plan until they retire. If you have a spouse with significant income, you will want to find out if he or she has placed money in this kind of "non-qualified" account.

Individual Retirement Account (IRA)

An IRA is an account set up at a financial institution that allows an individual to save for retirement with tax-free growth or on a tax-deferred basis. The three main types of IRAs each have different advantages:

Traditional IRA: You make contributions with money you may be able to de- duct on your tax return. Any earnings can potentially grow tax-deferred until you withdraw them in retirement. Many retirees also find themselves in a lower tax bracket than they were in pre-retirement, so the tax-deferral means the mon- ey may be taxed at a lower rate when it is withdrawn.

Roth IRA: You make contributions with money you've already paid taxes on (after-tax). Your money may potentially grow tax-free, with tax-free withdrawals in retirement, provided that certain conditions are met.

Rollover IRA: This is a traditional IRA intended for money "rolled over" from a qualified retirement plan. Rollovers involve moving eligible assets from an employer-sponsored plan, such as a 401(k) or 403(b), into an IRA.

Both 401(k)s and IRAs have rules and regulations regarding the maximum annual contribution and under what terms you can withdraw funds. Although there are exceptions, there are generally penalties for withdrawing retirement funds prior to age 59 ½.

The method required to share a 401(k) versus an IRA during a divorce has some special (but not complicated) considerations.

> **Better**
>
> *First and foremost, regardless of whether you are over or under age 59 ½, <u>do not withdraw retirement funds directly and give the funds to your spouse.</u> The distribution needs to be part of the divorce decree to avoid unanticipated taxes and penalties.*

For example, let's return to our couple Ellen and Jeff. Ellen has a 401(k) of $30,000 and Jeff has a 401(k) with $70,000. They want to share the total assets of these funds equally between them. The total is $100,000, and 50% is $50,000.

Because Ellen already has $30,000 in her 401(k), she would be owed $20,000 from Jeff's account. She would keep 100% of her own account.

If the distribution is processed through a Qualified Domestic Relations Order (QDRO), the following applies:

- There are no taxes or penalties to Jeff, the owner of the 401(k) from which funds are being removed to give to Ellen.
- Ellen has the option to put her share of Jeff's 401(k) into a tax-deferred account such as an IRA. Then she will pay no taxes or penalties.
- Ellen also has the one-time option to take some or all of her distribution in cash before putting funds in a tax-deferred account. Ellen will pay taxes but no early withdrawal penalties on the amount she takes in cash.

In New York State, the distribution of these funds can only take place after the Judgment of Divorce is signed. The distribution is usually available several months following the divorce decree, as the plan administrator of the 401(k) must approve and process the distribution.

Taking cash without paying penalties is only an option when funds originate in a 401(k)-type investment. This is not an option when funds are taken from an IRA-type investment.

Let's imagine that Ellen and Jeff both have IRAs in the same amounts listed above, and neither has a 401(k) plan. The math to calculate the sharing is the same; Ellen will receive $20,000. Here's how the IRA sharing works:

- The distribution can only take place after a Judgment of Divorce.

> **Better**
>
> *The option to take cash without penalties is a one-time only option and must be done before the funds are placed into another tax-deferred account.*

- In virtually all cases, a QDRO is not needed to initiate the IRA distribution.
- The distribution commences upon the Authority of the Judgment of Divorce, usually within a designated time from the final divorce decree.
- Jeff would provide the divorce decree that indicates the distribution to the IRA plan administrator. The funds would be transferred to Ellen's IRA, or Ellen can start a new IRA.
- If Ellen decides to take the $20,000 in cash instead of moving it into an IRA, she would pay taxes and withdrawal penalties.

If you have a Roth IRA, you do not pay taxes on your withdrawals when you are eligible to use the Roth IRA's funds (over age 59 ½).

> **Bitter**
>
> *Unlike a 401(k) distribution, taking cash from an IRA distribution before you are 59 ½ will trigger an early withdrawal penalty.*

Let's say Ellen's $30,000 is in a Roth IRA, and Jeff's $70,000 is in a pre-tax IRA account. That means Jeff's account was built with money on which he paid no income taxes prior to putting it in the account.

When the amount in a Roth IRA is significant, it is usually most equitable to split the Roth IRA separately from distributing the 401(k) or IRA funds. Sharing the funds in this manner eliminates the need to calculate the taxed versus pre-tax dollars. The Roth IRA does not require a QDRO. If they prefer to share the Roth IRA funds with 401(k) funds, they would want to equalize the taxes between the accounts prior to the distribution.

Distributions from retirement funds can be a good way to free up cash if it is needed to pay off marital debt or to fund a new home, especial-

> **Better**
>
> *If you have several old 401(k) plans from previous employers, do not consolidate them into an IRA until after the divorce. This will preserve the option of taking penalty-free money after the distribution.*

Better

Sharing retirement funds apples-to-apples (Roth to Roth) rather than apples-to-oranges (Roth to 401(k)) provides a more equitable distribution of retirement assets.

ly if the receiver is the lower income party. Your mediator can help you consider the options that may help you reach your financial goals.

Chapter 7

Health Insurance, Taxes, and Other Inevitabilities

"Learning is a gift. Even when pain is your teacher."
–Maya Watson

Deciphering and determining health insurance options for the family is one of the biggest hurdles of divorce. I talked with my colleague, Mark Shannon, a senior marketplace advocate at Bond Financial Network in Pittsford, New York, to get the most up-to-date perspective on your health insurance options.

As of this writing, health insurance is accessible to everyone under the Affordable Care Act, and the possible changes to the current laws have not been enacted. Before that law, health insurance was largely only available through your employer, if the company offered it.

Note: This discussion applies only to residents of New York State. If you live in another state, please check your state's health care website for information.

Better

A divorce is a qualifying life event that allows you to change (enroll or drop) health insurance options any time of the year.

First, be aware that choosing not to obtain health insurance in the tax year 2018 means you may pay a penalty for not being covered when it comes time to file your federal income taxes. The new 2018 tax code eliminates the health insurance penalty for the tax year 2019.

Virtually all health insurers do not allow the continuation of insurance for divorced spouses, so one spouse may lose health insurance if he/she was covered by the other spouse's plan. In New York, the law even requires divorcing spouses to acknowledge they are aware that they will no longer be allowed to receive health care coverage under a former spouse's insurance plan once the divorce is final.

If you know that you will lose your health insurance in your divorce, you have a number of options. One is insurance under the Consolidated Omnibus Budget Reconciliation Act, or COBRA, a federal law that provides you with the right to continue your insurance coverage in a group health plan for three years. COBRA allows a spouse who was formerly covered under his/her spouse's plan to obtain coverage from the same insurance company. However, the premiums can be quite expensive because the spouse's employer does not contribute to the cost. The couple's separation agreement should address the issue of health insurance and state the arrangements to which the couple agreed regarding covering the cost. After three years, you will need to find another method of insurance coverage.

You have other options for enrolling in a health insurance plan that may be less expensive for you and your family:

- Through your employer's benefits program
- Through an individual or family policy with the New York State of Health (NYSOH) Official Health Plan Marketplace at **www.nystateofhealth.ny.gov/**
- Through state programs like Medicaid, if you make less than 138% of the Federal Poverty Level for the size of your taxable household and have less than $2,500 in savings

Children do not lose health insurance at divorce. They remain eligible as the children of both parents and can be enrolled in either parent's health plan. As of this writing, they can remain on your health plan until they are 26 years old unless they have an employer that provides health coverage.

New York State statutes create an obligation for each parent to contribute to the cost of health insurance as part of the child support determination, based on the prorated amount of income for each parent (see Child Support in Chapter 8).

A state program called Child Health Plus, now available through the New York State of Health Marketplace, meets children's health insurance needs. This plan can significantly decrease a family's out-of-pocket costs while increasing the benefits for children. If you have children under the age of 19, Child Health Plus can provide savings that will help you manage health insurance costs.

If you cannot afford private coverage but your family income is too high to qualify for Medicaid, the Children's Health Insurance Program (CHIP) may help. It was established in 1997 to provide new coverage opportunities for children.

Divorces can happen any time throughout the year, so you are able to enroll in health insurance outside of the open enrollment period (November 1 to January 31).

Divorce or legal separation are qualifying events that trigger a Special Enrollment Period (SEP), if your spouse can no longer include you on his or her policy. The window for enrollment is *approximately 30 days from the Judgment of Divorce*, but that window can be any time during the calendar year.

The Marketplace offers the option for individuals and families to purchase health insurance directly from insurance companies. Depending on your taxable household size, adjusted gross income (AGI), and county of residence, you may apply for a program called the Essential Plan. It offers the same essential health benefits as the main plans but is designed to be more affordable if you meet criteria for income relative to household size. For example, a household of one individual who has an annual income of $23,760 or less will pay $20/month (in 2017). This plan provides individuals the benefit of having no deductible and low co-payments for all needed health care services.

If you need assistance in finding a plan, there are resources available to you.

In-Person Assistors (IPAs)/Navigators provide in-person enrollment assistance to individuals, families, small businesses, and their employees who would like help applying for health insurance through the Marketplace. IPAs/Navigators provide culturally competent, linguistically appropriate, and disability accessible enrollment services. They are available at convenient times, including evenings and weekends, at no cost to enrollees. You can find IPAs in your area at **http://info.nystateofhealth.ny.gov/IPANavigatorSiteLocations**.

Authorized brokers can also assist in choosing the right plan for you. There is no fee to you; the broker receives a commission from the insurance carrier. You can find a broker in your area by visiting **https://nystateofhealth.ny.gov/agent/ hx_brokerSearch**.

Social Security Benefits After Divorce

Social Security is one area that may offer some good news to spouses approaching divorce.

The benefits you will receive from Social Security when you retire are based on your own employment records. This includes all information stored by the Social Security Administration since the day they issued you a Social Security card—primarily about your earnings from your work history.

For the most part, the Social Security rules for divorced couples are the same as those for married couples, as long as you are married for ten years or more. Survivor benefits when your ex-spouse is deceased may be different.

Social Security benefit eligibility, amount, and entitlement are all part of federal law, so no negotiation regarding Social Security is needed between the divorcing spouses. What you

> **Better**
> *Couples can voluntarily share Social Security benefits to equalize future income, but that is not part of the Social Security laws.*

will or won't do concerning your benefits is not part of your divorce decree. The law at the time each ex-spouse applies for benefits will determine how much each is eligible for, when you can apply for benefits, and so on. What each ex-spouse chooses to do regarding their Social Security benefits has no effect on the Social Security benefits the other receives.

> **Better**
>
> *To expedite your application for Social Security benefits, keep a record of your ex-spouse's Social Security number.*

In order for either of you to be eligible to receive Social Security benefits based on the other's record, you first need to be married to each other for ten years or more. If you are at least age 62, unmarried, and your ex-spouse is entitled to Social Security retirement or disability benefits, you may be eligible to receive benefits based on his or her Social Security record. You will need to provide a certified copy of your divorce decree to claim benefits. Social Security will not notify your ex-spouse of your claim, and **your claim will not affect your ex's benefits or the benefits his or her next spouse may receive based on your ex's record.** As of this writing, Social Security will pay you either your own benefit or 35 percent of your ex-spouse's benefit at your age 62, or 50 percent if you claim it at your age of 66 years or more. This assumes full Social Security benefits at age 67. The percentages vary based on your specific full retirement age. Social Security will not pay you both amounts.

How do Social Security benefits work? Let's revisit fictional divorced couple, Tom and Gail. Here's their background:

- They were married for more than ten years when they divorced.
- Tom is now 67, and Gail is 66.
- Both are eligible to receive Social Security benefits.
- Both have the relevant information about the other such as Social Security number, etc.

Tom and Gail have the same options for receiving Social Security benefits. Let's say, based on their own Social Security records, Tom's benefit is $2,400 per month and Gail's is $900 per month. Tom receives the $2,400 per month based on his own benefit. He receives this full amount regardless of what Gail's choice is for receiving Social Security benefits.

Assuming Gail meets Social Security eligibility requirements, as Tom's ex-spouse, she is entitled to an amount equal to half of Tom's benefit, or $1,200 per month. The federal government will add $300 to bring her total benefit to $1,200 per month. Gail's "extra" $300 is not taken from or paid for by Tom; it comes from the government. His Social Security benefit remains unaffected.

Gail doesn't need Tom's permission to make this choice. Social Security will not notify Tom that she is drawing Social Security based on his record.

If, however, Gail's own benefit were $1,300, then her only option is to apply for that. That's because $1,300 is greater than the $1,200 she would be entitled as an ex-spouse of Tom. **Social Security will pay only the higher amount of the two benefits—your own or what you qualify for as an ex-spouse.**

> ### Better
> *Any spousal Social Security benefits require that you were married to the spouse for more than ten years. If you are on the cusp of ten years of marriage, it may be prudent to file your papers after your tenth anniversary to preserve your Social Security options.*

Even if your ex-spouse has not applied for Social Security benefits, you may be allowed to collect spousal benefits. For you to qualify, your former spouse must be eligible for Social Security benefits, which means he or she must be at least 62; and the two of you must have been divorced for at least two years.

If your former spouse has died, you may be entitled to Social Security survivor benefits as a former spouse if your marriage lasted at least ten years, you're at least 60 years old (or 50 if you are disabled), you didn't remarry before you turned 60, and your deceased spouse had contributed sufficiently to Social Security before his or her death.

If you remarry before age 60, however, your subsequent marriage makes you ineligible to collect benefits based on your prior ex's record. Should your later marriage end by annulment, divorce, or the death of your later spouse, then you become eligible again to receive benefits based on your first ex's record. If you remarry multiple times, you may be able to choose to take the benefit from the ex-spouse that has the highest benefit if you were married more than ten years to that spouse.

If your ex-spouse remarries, you won't lose your ability to collect Social Security survivor benefits should he or she die. However, if you remarry, your ability to collect Social Security survivor benefits could be impacted, depending on the age at which you remarry.

If you or your ex-spouse should die while you have minor children, the children receive a death benefit from Social Security until they are age 18, depending upon the amount in the parent's Social Security record. This benefit can be useful if the former spouse that died was the one paying child support.

For the most up-to-date information on the topic of Social Security survivor benefits, please check Appendix H.

Adding Insult to Injury: Federal Taxes During Divorce

Tax complexity increases during and after divorce. I asked my colleague Jamie Block, CPA at Mercer Advisors in Rochester, New York, to provide us with as succinct a description as possible of the federal tax requirements involved in divorce.

As most readers know, there are significant changes to the tax code as of 2018. The changes are a result of the Tax Cuts and Jobs Act passed by Congress in December 2017. Therefore, it especially important to review your personal tax situation with a tax professional.

Let's start at the beginning of a tax return and dive into filing status. The Internal Revenue Service (IRS) has a great tool to determine your federal tax filing status at **https://www.irs.gov/uac/what-is-my-filing-status**. In a nutshell, here are your income tax filing status options:

1. Single
   - Not married during the calendar year for which you are doing taxes.
   - Have obtained a divorce, separate maintenance agreement
     (legally separated), or annulment by the last day of the year (12/31).

2. Married Filing Jointly
   - If you are legally separated on the last day of the year (12/31), you can still choose to file a joint tax return.
   - You are legally married on the last day of the year (12/31).

In most cases (but not all), filing a joint federal tax return will save on income taxes. There are some credits and deductions that are not available with the married filing separately filing status (see below) such as American opportunity credit, lifetime learning credit, tuition and fees deduction, student loan interest deduction, and the earned income credit.

The extra deductions come with a trade-off, however: If there is an error on jointly filed returns, both spouses are equally liable for the tax due. There is innocent spouse relief available in certain cases, but that is beyond the scope of this discussion. If you think your spouse is not reporting all of his/her income on the income tax return or is claiming bogus deductions, you may want to consider filing your return as "married filing separately" to prevent any backlash down the road.

3. Married Filing Separately
   - You are legally married on the last day of the year (12/31).

One advantage of married filing separately is that you do not need to communicate as much with your spouse. This is especially helpful if the divorce is charged with emotions. You do need your spouse's name and Social Security number. You also need to determine if your spouse is itemizing deductions. If one spouse itemizes deductions, both must itemize (even if the result is $0).

NOTE: If you provide more than half of the support for a child, you may be able to use the head of household status (see below).

4. Head of Household

- You are single at the end of the year (see "Single" filing status on previous page) or are considered unmarried. You are considered unmarried if:
  - You file a separate return (not a joint return).
  - You paid more than half the cost of keeping up your home for the tax year.
  - Your spouse didn't live in your home during the last 6 months of the year.
  - Your home was the main home of your child, stepchild, or foster child for more than half the year.
  - You must be able to claim an exemption for the child. (There are some exceptions to this rule).
- A qualifying person lived with you in the home for more than half the year. (There are some exceptions to this rule).
- Note that if there are two children, both parents can claim the head of household status as long as the above qualifications are met.

Exemptions

Once you have figured out your filing status, then you need to determine your exemptions. The following information comes from the *IRS Publication 17* for 2017. **For 2018 through 2025, exemptions have been eliminated and replaced with a higher standard deduction.**

Personal Exemptions

- You can claim an exemption for yourself.
- You can claim an exemption for your spouse if you file a joint return (see "Married Filing Jointly" above).
  - If you file a "Married Filing Separately" return, you can claim an exemption for your spouse if the spouse had no gross income, isn't filing a return, and wasn't a dependent of another taxpayer.
  - If you obtain a divorce or separation agreement, then you are not able to claim your spouse's exemption (even if you provided all his/her support).

Dependency Exemptions

There are 2 types of dependents:

- Qualifying child
- Qualifying relative

This discussion focuses on the qualifying child. There are five tests that must be met in order to claim a qualifying child as dependent:

1. **Qualifying Child Relationship Test.** The child must be your son, daughter, stepchild, foster child, brother, sister, half brother, half sister, stepbrother, stepsister, or a descendant of any of these.

2. **Qualifying Child Age Test.** The child must either be under age 19 at the end of the year and younger than you (or your spouse, if filing jointly); or be under age 24 at the end of the year and a student, and younger than you (or your spouse, if filing jointly); or permanently and totally disabled and any age.

3. **Qualifying Child Residency Test.** The child must have lived with you for more than half the year. Temporary absences for school count as living with you. For children of divorced parents, typically the custodial parent will claim the dependency exemption.

However, there is an exception. The child will be treated as the qualifying child of the noncustodial parent if all four of the following statements are true:

1. The parents:
    - Are divorced or legally separated under a decree of divorce or separate maintenance, or
    - Are separated under a written separation agreement, or
    - Lived apart at all times during the last 6 months of the year, whether or not they are or were married.
2. The child received over half of his or her support for the year from the parents.
3. The child is in the custody of one or both parents for more than half of the year.
4. Either of the following statements is true:

    A. The custodial parent signs a written declaration that he or she won't claim the child as a dependent for the year, and the noncustodial parent attaches this written declaration to his or her return, or

    B. There is a pre-1985 decree of divorce or separate maintenance or written separation agreement that applies to 2016 and:
    - The decree states that the noncustodial parent can claim the child as a dependent
    - The decree or agreement wasn't changed after 1984 to say the noncustodial parent cannot claim the child as a dependent

- The noncustodial parent provides at least $600 for the child's support during the year.

If statements 1 through 4 above are all true, the noncustodial parent can claim the child as a dependent and as a qualifying child for the child tax credit.

However, this *does not allow* the noncustodial parent to claim head of household filing status, the credit for child and dependent care expenses, the exclusion for dependent care benefits, the earned income credit, or the health coverage tax credit.

Since no divorce or parenting arrangement is the same or simple, the IRS has developed tiebreaker rules to help determine who gets to claim the dependent:

1. If only one of the persons is the child's parent, the child is treated as the qualifying child of the parent.

2. If the parents file a joint return together and can claim the child as a qualifying child, the child is treated as the qualifying child of the parents.

3. If the parents do not file a joint return together but both parents can claim the child as a qualifying child, the IRS will treat the child as the qualifying child of the parent with whom the child *lived for the longer period of time during the year.*

- If the child lived with each parent for the same amount of time, the IRS will treat the child as the qualifying child of the parent who had the higher adjusted gross income (AGI) for the year.
- If no parent can claim the child as a qualifying child, the child is treated as the qualifying child of the person who had the highest AGI for the year.

4. If a parent can claim the child as a qualifying child but no parent actually claims the child, the child is treated as the qualifying child of the person who had the highest AGI for the year, but only if that person's AGI is higher than the highest AGI of any of the child's parents who can claim the child.

Here are some things to note about the Qualifying Child Residency Test:

- For the child tax credit ($1,000/child under the age of 17 in 2017), you must have a qualifying child (explained above) who is claimed as a dependent on your tax return. You do not have to file as head of household to claim this credit. **In 2018 to 2025, the child tax credit will be $2,000 per child with higher income phase-outs.**
- For the credit for child and dependent care expenses, you must have a qualifying child under the age of 13 who is claimed as a dependent on your return. It makes sense here to use the head of household status for more favorable tax brackets. If you are not considered unmarried and file a married filing separately return, you cannot take this credit.

- For the American Opportunity Tax Credit ($2,500/eligible student in 2016) or the Lifetime Learning Credit ($2,000/return in 2017), you must have a qualifying child who is claimed as a dependent on your return and is a student. Again, using head of household status will give you a more favorable tax bracket for this. You cannot claim this credit if you are married filing separately.
  - The Earned Income Tax Credit is not allowed when married filing separately.
  - Lastly, you cannot deduct student loan interest on your return if you file as married filing separately.

4. Qualifying Child Support Test. The child must not have provided more than half of his or her own support for the year.

5. Qualifying Child Joint Tax Return. The child must not be filing a joint return for the year (unless that return is filed only to get a refund of income tax withheld or estimated tax paid).

As you can see, there are many rules and exceptions to the rules that can make taxes complicated. For more information and guidance, we recommend that you work with a certified public accountant to be sure you're filing your taxes correctly and receiving all the exemptions you deserve.

Life Insurance

With the responsibilities for child support and spousal maintenance added to the other financial considerations of a divorced person's new life, it's also time to think about what will happen to your ex-spouse and children if you should meet an untimely death.

This is not an easy topic, and no one likes to think about it. It is an important part of the divorce process, however, and one that should be addressed sooner rather than later to protect your children, if you have them, and a spouse who may depend on you for support long after your marriage has ended.

When you divorce your spouse, chances are you no longer wish him or her to profit from your demise. To change the beneficiary on your life insurance policy when your marriage ends, you will be required to sign a new beneficiary form to have your spouse's name removed. It is prudent to determine the life insurance obligations within your divorce agreement before you make any beneficiary changes. If you purchased an irrevocable policy, however, you cannot change the beneficiary.

If you own a life insurance policy, it may have a cash value that will count as an asset on your statement of net worth. *Whole life* and *universal life* policies not only pay a death benefit, but they also accumulate a cash value with each payment you make, acting as a savings vehicle that grows over time and accrues interest. If you have one of these policies, you receive a statement of the policy's value on an annual basis. This will need to be counted as you determine the equitable division of your assets in your divorce.

> **Better**
>
> *When there is a spousal obligation for life insurance, the beneficiary may decide to own the policy and the ex-spouse is the insured. This way, you always know the premium is paid and the life insurance benefits will be paid.*

Term life insurance policies do not have a cash value in addition to the death benefit—they simply provide an amount of money to your beneficiary if you die. These policies are usually less expensive than whole life or universal life policies, and they do not have to be considered when determining your net worth.

If you do not have life insurance, however—or if you are the spouse receiving maintenance and child support and you want to protect your own best interests and those of your children—it is time to buy a policy.

The purpose of a life insurance policy after divorce is to protect your child support and alimony income. If you are the spouse with primary custody of the children and you are receiving financial support from your ex-spouse, you need to take steps to make certain that these funds will continue to be available even if your spouse passes away. The most efficient way to do this is to take out a life insurance policy on your ex-spouse.

This does not need to be an expensive policy that will net you millions of dollars. Simple math will tell you how much money you would need if your spouse were no longer able to make child support and spousal maintenance payments.

Let's say, for example, that Lori and Jim have a ten-year-old child, and that Jim is paying Lori $10,000 annually in child support and $12,000 in maintenance. Lori will receive child support until the child is 21, so that's another 11 years—and in that time, Jim would pay Lori $110,000 in child support.

Now let's assume that Lori expects to receive spousal maintenance for five years. That's five years at $12,000 per year, or $60,000.

Child support	=	$ 110,000
Maintenance	=	$ 60,000
Total		$ 170,000

Lori may want life insurance on Jim with a death benefit of $170,000.

Many clients consider that the child support and maintenance obligation should be protected by having an amount of life insurance to cover the obligation. In this case, the amount would be $170,000. Also consider that this would be supplemented by Social Security benefits for the child until age 18.

Clients frequently discuss who will pay for the life insurance premiums. That decision usually depends on the cost of the life insurance and whether both parties have an obligation to maintain a death benefit.

Many agreements stipulate that the amount of life insurance can be reduced annually by the annual amount required. In this case, the annual amount for the first five years of payment is $22,000. So each year the life insurance obligation could be reduced by that amount, and then $10,000 annually for the balance of that obligation.

Often clients discuss who should be the beneficiary of the insurance policy for the child support amount. In most cases, it is the spouse receiving the funds in order for him/her to be able to provide for clothes, education, shelter and the like. Children under age 18 cannot receive life insurance funds directly, so a trustee would be named (most often the other parent), so it simplifies the distribution of funds if the surviving parent is named as beneficiary.

Another important conversation is what happens if the parent receiving the money (Lori, in this case) passes away. Should Lori have life insurance? Because Jim is no longer paying child support (or maintenance) to Lori, there is often no obligation for the "receiving spouse." However, if there are considerable childcare expenses or other extraordinary expenses, it might be wise for the "receiving parent" to have a modest insurance policy and name the other parent the beneficiary.

Many clients have life insurance in excess of the obligation, and those "extra funds" generally are designated to the party's estate by creating a will. (See more on wills in Chapter 14.) Through a will, an executor (usually not the ex-spouse) would be named to manage the estate, including life insurance, house, retirement funds, and the like for the children until they reach a certain age determined by the will.

Your investment professional or insurance agent can help you find an affordable policy that will provide you with the peace of mind you need as a single parent after your divorce.

Bankruptcy

Financial stress may be a factor in the decision to get divorced. Divorce itself may also cause financial stress. Many couples who were able to handle the household debt while living together may find it difficult or even impossible to pay that debt once they have separated. As a result, you may find yourselves considering both divorce and bankruptcy.

I asked my colleague, Deborah Schaal, Esq., a partner at Gordon and Schaal LLP, to share her expertise in bankruptcy law. Here is the information and advice she provided on New York State law.

Individuals can file for one of two chapters of personal bankruptcy: Chapter 7 and Chapter 13.

Chapter 7 is called a *liquidation bankruptcy*. You can obtain a discharge of most of your unsecured debts (such as credit cards, medical bills, car loans, and unsecured personal loans), but you may have to turn over non-exempt property in return. The Bankruptcy Code offers exemptions for many of assets that most people have, including retirement accounts and home equity, so in reality, most people can obtain a discharge in Chapter 7 without losing any assets.

A Chapter 13 bankruptcy involves *repayment of debt over a three-to-five-year period*. Someone may opt for Chapter 13 when they have a debt they want to repay but need extra time to do so, such as mortgage arrears or certain tax debts. Chapter 13 may also be the only bankruptcy option for someone who is over the median income for their family size for their state. In the state of New York, the gross median income for a single person as of February 2017 is $50,768; $65,233 for a family of two; $74,925 for a family of three; and $90,852 for a family of four. If a couple is over the income limit for Chapter 7 while still living together, they may qualify individually for a Chapter 7 once they have physically separated.

Filing bankruptcy is a big decision. A Chapter 7 filing will stay on your credit report for ten years, and it may adversely affect your ability to get future credit. For people who have kept current on all of their debt payments until now, a bankruptcy filing will cause a bigger drop in their credit scores than for people who have already fallen behind on debt payments. If you are delinquent on debt payments, a bankruptcy filing will have a much smaller impact on your credit score.

Bankruptcy is designed to give you a fresh start, free of wage garnishments, bank restraints, collections calls, and many debt payments. That being said, certain debts, including the obligation to pay child support and maintenance, are not discharged in bankruptcy. Most income taxes also do not go away in bankruptcy. Nearly all student loans survive bankruptcy. Whichever Chapter of bankruptcy you choose, it is imperative that you disclose all of your assets in your paperwork.

When someone files bankruptcy, the Bankruptcy Code (Title 11 in the US Code) imposes an "automatic stay," meaning certain actions against the person who has filed bankruptcy cannot continue. Examples of actions that are stopped include collections actions, wage garnishments, collection calls and letters, and foreclosure actions.

If the person who has filed bankruptcy is going through a divorce, the matrimonial court may not order a division of the marital assets until the bankruptcy case is over, or until the bankruptcy court gives permission to continue the division of assets, including the home and retirement accounts. Other aspects of a divorce action, however, may continue even if one of the parties has filed bankruptcy. A matrimonial judge may still decide on issues such as child support, custody and visitation, even if the husband or the wife has filed bankruptcy.

Bankruptcy courts and divorce courts look at debt differently. Bankruptcy courts only look at whose name is on the debt. Matrimonial courts view debt incurred during the marriage as "marital debt" regardless of whose name is on the debt.

For example, let's say a husband has $30,000 in credit card debt in his name, the wife has $10,000 in debt, and they each have similar income. A matrimonial court might even out the debt level by ordering the wife to be responsible for $10,000 worth of debt that is in the husband's name. This means that each spouse ends up with $20,000 in debt, regardless of which of them made the purchases or otherwise created the debt.

If the husband were to file bankruptcy, however, he could likely discharge all $30,000 of the credit cards in his name, leaving only $10,000 in marital debt for the matrimonial court to divide up.

The bankruptcy system ensures that the person who files bankruptcy is paying their domestic support obligations. If the spouse has an obligation to pay child support or spousal maintenance, the spouse will have to fill out a domestic support obligation form giving the contact information for the person to whom they pay the support. The bankruptcy trustee—the person appointed by the bankruptcy court to oversee the bankruptcy case—must inform the domestic support recipient that the person who pays their support has filed bankruptcy, and inform the recipient where the payor works.

In addition, if you file a Chapter 13 bankruptcy (explained below), you cannot get your Chapter 13 plan confirmed or obtain a Chapter 13 discharge unless you can testify under oath that you have kept current on your support obligations since your bankruptcy case was filed.

People often ask whether it is better to file bankruptcy first and then proceed with divorce, or whether they should get divorced first and then file bankruptcy.

In some cases, it is better to do the bankruptcy first. Division of marital debt can be a contentious issue. If either or both parties file bankruptcy, it can eliminate the vast majority of the marital debt, leaving one less issue to resolve in the matrimonial action.

> **Better**
> *Because paying child support or spousal maintenance reduces your income, you may become a candidate for Chapter 7 bankruptcy (discharge of all debt), when you were not a candidate prior to the divorce.*

Also, since a bankruptcy trustee can sometimes undo the division of marital assets (such as the transfer of a house without consideration—i.e., without one spouse owing any money to the other), it may be better to keep the house titled in both names and file bankruptcy. Then when the bankruptcy is done, you can resume division of the martial assets.

However, sometimes it is better to have aspects of the divorce action decided first, such as child support or spousal maintenance. Someone whose income is too high to qualify for Chapter 7 might be able to file Chapter 7 after the amount of support they pay is deducted from their gross income.

If the decision is made to finalize the divorce before the bankruptcy, it is important to make sure that any transfer of assets is supported by adequate consideration in return. For example, let's say the husband and wife jointly own the marital home, it is worth $150,000, and it has a $100,000 mortgage on it—so there is $50,000 equity in the house. The bankruptcy court assumes that each party's equity in the house is $25,000.

> **Better**
> *If you think one or both of you may file bankruptcy, it is important to get legal advice from an attorney knowledgeable in both bankruptcy and matrimonial law before deciding on the best course of action in your divorce.*

Now, let's say the husband transfers his interest in the house to the wife via a quit claim deed, without getting his half of the equity—$25,000—from her in return. If he files bankruptcy within the next 6 years after the divorce, his bankruptcy trustee may undo the transfer of the house into the wife's name and put the house back into joint ownership, to be sure the husband's $25,000 share of the equity is included in the bankruptcy proceeding.

To prevent this, during the divorce, the wife first needs to pay the husband $25,000 to buy out the husband's interest in the property. As discussed earlier in this chapter, this can be accomplished when the wife refinances the mortgage so that the husband is paid $25,000 out of the mortgage proceeds. Alternately, the wife could give up $25,000 of other assets that she would have otherwise received in the divorce.

Bankruptcy laws are complex. If you are considering filing bankruptcy, it is important to consult with an attorney who is experienced in the practice of bankruptcy law in your area.

College Financial Aid: FAFSA

Financial aid can make the difference between an affordable college education and a lifetime of student loan debt. I asked my colleague Brenda Piazza at College Planning Consultant at CAPlus in Honeoye Falls, New York, to explain how financial aid figures into parents' obligation to their child's education in a divorce.

By filling out the Free Application for Federal Student Aid (FAFSA), students will learn if they will qualify for federal and college aid. The FAFSA calculates a number called the Expected Family Contribution (EFC). The EFC is an index number used by the government and college financial aid offices to determine the family need-based aid eligibility. It is essential that this number is correct. Please be sure to have your FAFSA reviewed by an experienced college consultant.

A number of federal aid options may be available to your child:

- **Grants.** The most common are the Federal Pell Grant for undergraduate students and the Federal Supplemental Educational Opportunity Grant (FSEOG) for undergraduate students with exceptional financial need.
- **Work Study.** This program grants students with financial need the opportunity to work in campus-related jobs. Students must interview to gain employment.
- **Student Loans.** These are student loans that do not require a co-signer. They must be repaid (plus interest).
  - **Perkins.** This is a campus-based program and may be offered to students with exceptional need. It will depend upon the availability of funds at the college(s) to which your child applied.
  - **Direct Loans (sometimes called Direct Stafford Loans).** These loans are available to undergraduate and graduate students. There are two types:
    Unsubsidized: These loans are available to all students regardless of need. Interest on these loans will accrue (accumulate) and will be capitalized. The student is responsible for paying the interest. We encourage interest payments be made while the student is in college to reduce the amount of the total principal.

Subsidized: The U.S. Department of Education pays the interest while the student is in school at least half time, or for the first six months after the student has left school (grace period). These loans are available to students who demonstrate financial need.

- **Direct PLUS Loans.** These loans are available to parents of dependent students and to graduate and professional-degree students.

Significant FAFSA changes took effect on October 1, 2016. These may affect your application date and content.

New Launch Date of October 1. You can now file the FAFSA as early as October 1 of the year before your child begins college. This is three months earlier than previous years. This date gives students more time to apply, and for many colleges it aligns with application and financial aid deadlines. Current and first-time college students should be sure to check the college financial aid deadlines in preparation for the FAFSA submission.

Uses PPY (Prior Prior Year) Taxes. The FAFSA will require students and parents to report income from an earlier tax year. For the 2017-2018 FAFSA, for example, you would report your 2015 tax information, and you would not update the FAFSA with your 2016 tax information. I encourage people to use the IRS Data Retrieval Tool (DRT) found in the financial section of the FAFSA to transfer your 2015 tax information. By using the IRS DRT, the college financial aid office is less likely to request additional income information from you (called verification), which streamlines the processing of your application and avoids unnecessary delays.

Note: If you experienced a one-time event during the PPY which overestimated the financial information being reported on the FAFSA, complete and submit the FAFSA as instructed using the financial information for that year, and then call the college financial aid office and explain your situation. Many colleges have a special circumstance form or other process you will complete. The school has the ability to make adjustments to your FAFSA.

If parents of a student are separated, divorced, or living in separate households, the custodial parent's financial information is required by the FAFSA. Even when two parents are not divorced or legally separated but are living in separate households, a custodial parent must be identified. Some parents want to be the custodial parent for emotional reasons. Some believe the custodial parent is determined by divorce or separation legal documents or by the tax return. These documents do not define the FAFSA custodial parent. **The FAFSA defines the custodial parent as the parent with whom the student lived with the most in one year.**

If the custodial parent has remarried at the time of the FAFSA submission, the

FAFSA should include information for both the custodial parent and the stepparent. *There is no exception.* The tax return information must be reported and appropriate asset information provided. So, to the extent that the parents can control the student's living arrangements, the student might be able to qualify for more financial aid if reporting information of the parent with lower income and asset values. However, the living arrangements should be genuine.

> **Better**
>
> *If you have college-age children, consider deferring a pending marriage in order to have financial aid based on your income only, rather than your household income.*

For parents who are recently divorced, legally separated, or living in separate households and have filed a joint tax return at the time of the FAFSA submission, the custodial parent must report on the FAFSA their individual income and taxes paid on the joint return. Parents who are separated but file a joint federal income tax return will not be able to use the IRS Data Retrieval Tool to transfer information from the federal income tax return to the FAFSA. Information must be entered manually. Such a FAFSA is more likely to be selected for verification. Verification is a process by which the college financial aid office will ask the student to supply supporting financial documentation such as income tax returns, W-2 statements, etc., to verify the data reported in the FAFSA.

Valuing a Business in a Divorce

Putting a price tag on a business is a complex task that gets even more complicated when divorce is involved. I asked my colleague Kristen Jenks, CFA, of Lumina Partners, LLC, to provide her expertise in the importance of business valuation in the divorce process.

States view ownership of business interests in a number of different ways, including what share belongs to the non-owner spouse and how to value the personal talents of the business owner.

According to one dictionary, a business is either: (1) the activity of making, buying or selling goods or services in exchange for money, or (2) work that is part of a job. In the first instance, there is likely to be something of value that could theoretically be transferred to a separate party in exchange for cash or other assets. The second case is more akin to collecting a paycheck for work performed, whether the worker is self-employed or is on the payroll of an employer.

One of the challenges for divorcing couples is to identify in which category the business fits and, if appropriate, to determine the value of the business for equitable distribution to each spouse. It can be very helpful to get an independent professional valuation of the business to understand its actual value in the divorce.

In New York and many other states, there are two situations in which a business is considered to be a marital asset subject to equitable distribution in a divorce:

- A business was established during the marriage.
- A business was established before the marriage, and its value appreciated during the marriage.

An independent professional valuation objectively quantifies the value of the business interest. This gives the parties a means to offset the value of the business against other assets or, at a minimum, to make an informed decision about how to address the right to the value of the business. It may also defuse some of the emotional and subjective aspects of business ownership that frequently pop up; e.g., "Trust me, the business is hardly worth anything," or "It's her business; I don't want [or haven't earned] any of it."

It can also provide a road map for settlement of other issues like child support and maintenance, particularly if the business

> **Better**
>
> *What is the value of a business? A simple way to look at this question is this: If you sold the business tomorrow, what would you retain after the sale?*

owner's compensation is above or below what an employee would be paid for similar responsibilities, or if a non-owner spouse has provided services to the business that may or may not continue after the divorce.

The business valuator is trained to identify and quantify all business assets. Sometimes a couple is unsure whether a self-employed spouse is truly a "business owner." While many people operate as sole proprietors, it is very rare for an entrepreneur to have nothing of value associated with his or her efforts other than a paycheck. In some cases, there are tangible items that have value (computers, trucks, etc.). In other cases, there is valuable intangible property such as customer lists, proprietary processes, or trademarks. In most instances, there is goodwill associated with the entrepreneur's name based on performance.

The cost of a valuation varies depending on the size and complexity of the business. For very small businesses, the ultimate value may not justify the financial outlay. It's best to consult with a valuation professional to determine whether it makes sense to proceed with an independent valuation, or whether there may be other approaches that would be sufficient for mediation and divorce purposes.

The task for the valuator is to estimate the future earnings of the business based on the information provided, and then to determine what the value of those earnings is in today's dollars. The process begins with identifying the true earnings of the business. This includes adjusting for discretionary items that frequently exist in family-owned businesses, such as family cell phone charges, family travel associated with business meetings, and the like. In some cases, there may be personal credit card or other debt that is not on the business's books but must be treated as business debt in the valuation.

> ### Better
> *Determining a monetary value for the business is needed to determine how the non-owner spouse may be compensated for the asset.*

Once the earnings capacity of the business is established, the business valuator applies his or her knowledge of the business's characteristics, general economic indicators, and the appropriate financial returns expected by owners of similar businesses to determine the value of the business as a whole today. If the business has any outstanding liabilities, those are subtracted from the total to arrive at the value of the ownership position held by the spouse(s).

In business valuations, it is important to account for owner compensation at a rate that is competitive in the market for the responsibilities the owner carries out, regardless of the actual amount of compensation the owner is receiving. In some cases, a family business owner may enjoy a level of compensation that is substantially higher than he or she would receive to perform the same functions for a separate employer. In other cases, business owners may choose to pay themselves only as much as they need to cover personal expenses and keep the remaining profits in the business.

In order to determine the value of the business if it were sold to a hypothetical third party, it is therefore necessary to establish what the buyer would have to pay in compensation if they hired a person to assume the owner's responsibilities.

It is critical for the divorce professional and the business valuator to work hand-in-hand to be sure that they are consistent in their treatment of income for the business valuation and for other income-based divorce agreements, such as child support and maintenance. This avoids the possibility of "double-dipping," in which the business owner's above-market earnings are counted twice: once in the calculation of the value of the business, and again for the purpose of determining support. The same is true for credit card debt or family-related expenses that are assigned to the business. Care must be taken to account fully for those items, but only once.

The more information that is made available to the valuator, the more accurate the estimate of value will be. A valuation professional will ask for both quantitative and qualitative data about the business, generally including some or all of the following:

- **A detailed description of the business,** its products and services, customers, competitors, business trends, and expectations for the future. This is frequently accomplished through conferences with the business owner(s).

- **Documents describing what type of legal entity the business is** (e.g., S corporation, C corporation, LLC, partnership, sole proprietorship, et al.), including certificates of incorporation, by-laws, shareholder agreements, and other official papers, as well as documents identifying all owners and their respective shares of the business.

- **Tax returns** (for the organization and/or the owner's personal tax returns) reflecting the earnings of the business, generally for the most recent five years.

- **Financial statements** for the most recent five years from the organization's internal records as well as from outside accountants, if available:

   Income statements: Reflect the business' sales, expenses, and resulting net income.

   Balance sheets: Provide details of the business's assets (what it owns, like cash, amounts due from customers, inventory, equipment, and the like); liabilities (what it owes, such as bank loans, payments to its vendors, and taxes it collects and remits to government entities); and net worth (the residual value of the assets after accounting for all the liabilities).

   Cash flow statements: Show how much money came in during the year and how much money went out.

   Statements from bank accounts, investment accounts, retirement accounts, et al.

   Any other supporting details such as marketing materials, web sites, industry or trade association publications, that contribute to the valuator's understanding of the business.

Once the value of the business is known, what happens next depends on a number of factors:

- Whether there are other marital assets to distribute in addition to the value of the business.
- How your state treats business ownership in divorce cases.
- Whether or not the business was started before or during the marriage.
- How active the non-owner spouse was in the business.

- Whether any marital assets were used in the operation of the business, and
- Whether the non-owner spouse will continue to play a role in the business after the divorce

Like many other items you will be addressing in divorce mediation, you may choose to mirror the judicial practices in your state, or you may opt for a distribution of the value of the business interest that accomplishes your joint mediation objectives.

Special Property Categories

Couples who divorce in the 21st century need to consider other kinds of property that may be less obvious or tangible than their home and household goods. In this section, I offer information about determining who gets what, and how.

Digital Assets

Almost every couple owns assets in digital format, including their iTunes music library; Kindle/other ebook libraries; and digital TV shows, movies, and games. I asked my colleague Mary Anne Shew, business and technology consultant with Business Vitality, about the kinds of things you and your spouse should take into consideration.

Little in current law provides rules or guidelines to follow regarding digital and virtual assets. However, there is no indication that a digital or virtual asset would be characterized differently from a tangible asset.

Unlike a set of dishes, a digital book or movie cannot be split in half and still remain useful. Some services such as Amazon Family allow sharing of content. In Amazon's case, it's allowed only between adults in the same household. It also gives access to each other's credit cards.

Furthermore, the user agreements of most sites selling these assets do not address this issue. Of those that do, they may not allow for transfer of an asset. A judge's ruling may not be able to override that agreement. References for related terms of service agreements are in Appendix H.

For couples who have merged all their technology, the situation can be a challenge. Details on how to divide digital goods like a shared photo site or an extensive movie streaming library will be addressed increasingly in divorce agreements and separation plans.

In the case of assets that the couple created themselves such as digital photos and family videos, who gets what is entirely within their control. Those items are often stored in a shared cloud-based account such as iCloud, Dropbox, or similar services. One of the spouses can open his or her own separate account and transfer copies to it.

> ### Better
> "Digital assets are intangibles that only exist in a digital form (i.e., data in the form of binary digits). Such assets may include: e-mail and social network accounts; websites; domain names; digital media, such as pictures, music, e-books, movies, and video; blogs; reward points; digital storefronts; artwork; and data storage accounts. These assets, although intangible, are marital property and are subject to characterization, valuation and division, during divorce."
> —Michelle O'Neil, Dallas, TX divorce attorney

Other digital assets came into the family as part of purchases: airline miles, membership points, and reward points. These often can be transferred. Check with the associated airlines and credit card companies.

Virtual assets are intangibles used in virtual worlds or massively multiplayer online (MMO) role-playing games. Popular online communities such as Second Life draw millions of users worldwide. They spend billions of dollars each year within these virtual realms. Many people also have virtual businesses in these worlds that generate sales that can be translated into "real-world" money. This income may also need to be considered a marital asset.

Sometimes one spouse started a blog before or during the marriage. He or she may have monetized it. That income could be considered as a shareable asset. If the other spouse contributed to the blog by posting to it, editing it, or advancing it in any way, the associated value may become a business asset that needs to be considered.

The best place to start is by having each spouse make a list of all such assets he or she has created or purchased and from where. Each list should include a brief description of what assets the associated website holds, and how many of that asset (e.g., the number of audiobooks or songs). Also write down the web site address to log into it, the username, and the password. Share the lists with each other and discuss how best to distribute and manage them going forward. Your divorce mediator can also help you with this discussion. This will give you a good plan that lets each spouse continue to use the digital assets he or she enjoys most.

You and your spouse also may need to continue to share access to certain online accounts, even after your divorce. Potential accounts include:

- **Checking, savings, and credit card accounts.** Electronic access to statements and transactions; automatic bill payment services.
- **Digital currency accounts** such as Bitcoin.
- **Investment accounts.** Regular and IRA accounts; pension accounts.

- Life, home, auto insurance.
- Medical insurance.
- **Medical and pharmacy records.** Your own, your children's records, perhaps even your pet's veterinary records.
- **Government sites.** Department of motor vehicles, property tax, etc.
- **Your children's school system.** Access to class information, grades, sports schedules, communication with teachers and coaches.
- **Your local library system.** Tracking what's been checked out, by whom, and when it needs to be returned.
- **Netflix/Hulu/Redbox** movie entertainment.
- **Family email accounts,** if you and your spouse share an email account.
- **Billing and payment sites** for all kinds of products and services, including mortgage, utilities, cell phone, cable, Internet, grocery store, retail stores, etc.
- **A shared Google calendar** to coordinate the kids' activities, appointments, and family commitments.
- **Online ("cloud") photo storage and document sites.** Family photos, important documents and other files.
- **Miscellaneous sites** supporting the household: Angie's List, Amazon Pantry, TurboTax, pet food ordering, etc.

As with many technology issues, the law has yet to catch up with sharing or transferring online accounts in divorce. In particular, there are no specific guidelines for sharing accounts or establishing consequences should your former spouse deliberately change a password to lock you out of a shared account.

As you proceed through the divorce process, you and your spouse will work together to decide which accounts you both will need to access, especially those connected with taking care of your children. Depending on the account, you may need to:

- Share a single login.
- Set up separate logins to access the same account.
- Create a new, separate account in one spouse's name and transfer assets to it (as allowed by the account and by law).

One of the most useful software tools available today can help manage the overwhelming number of account logins and passwords we all struggle to track. If you are not using a password management tool now, I recommend you and your spouse pick one (some of these are Dashlane, LastPass, Sticky Password, Keeper Password Manager, Digital Vault, LogMeOnce, Password Boss, and eWallet) and begin to set up your respective password databases. Whether you are sharing online accounts or not, managing your own personal digital footprint is important.

Each of you will have your own private password database (encrypted for security) in your own copy of the app. You each can store info about your shared accounts in your own database.

Another option is to create a third, shared password database, assuming the tool you choose supports this. This database would contain just the logins and passwords that you need to share during and/or after the divorce. You each would have a copy of this database in your password tool. Then, if either of you needs to change the password on a shared account, you update this database, make a backup of it, and then email it to the other person. Your individual password databases remain private. To make this work, it's essential that both of you use the same password management tool on all of your computers, smartphones, and/or tablets.

It's a good idea to list in your separation or divorce agreement the account names and associated web site names (URLs) that the two of you agree will be shared, why, and for how long.

Divorce is difficult enough without having problems getting access to the information and resources you need. Taking the time now to select and use a password tool to organize your online accounts will help smooth the way.

Your Pets: Sharing Fido

Who gets pet custody in a divorce? It might surprise you that the law has not caught up with how people feel about their pets today. Most pet owners consider their dogs and cats to be family while the law considers them to be property like cars, furniture, and other belongings.

A few judges have begun recognizing that pets have a unique and cherished place in the family when deciding a custody dispute. Some state legislators are floating the idea of changing the law to require consideration of the pets' best interests when determining custody.

On the other hand, dogs, cats, and other pets are not children. Already burdened divorce courts are reluctant to devote the time, expense, and resources to conduct proceedings that mirror the complexity of a child custody case.

A 2014 survey from the American Academy of Matrimonial Lawyers (AAML) found a 27 percent increase in the number of couples who have fought over custody of a pet during the past five years. Conflicts over a pet can be just as important to divorcing spouses as any issue when both spouses have developed a special connection to a companion pet and wish to maintain it.

As with most issues in divorce, it's best that you and your spouse work out custody of your pets between yourselves and document your decisions in your separation agreement. If the issue goes to litigation, the judge may focus on existing law rather than what's best for the pets. The judge may base his/her decision on proof of purchase or adoption of the animal.

> **Better**
>
> *Clarity regarding the care of your furry companion is important for your children's well-being and your own peace of mind.*

Note, however, that the courts cannot enforce pet custody agreements because there is no applicable law yet. There is a possibility of using small claims court to obtain funds promised for veterinarian bills or other needs. As of this writing, it appears that the court would not address other issues that fall under the concept of custody. It's best to contact the appropriate small claims court office for information before proceeding.

Small claims courts in New York State impose several restrictions that may limit their usefulness to you in a pet custody case, including:

- You must bring the action in the county where the defendant resides, is employed, or where he/she is doing business at the time you commence the action. You also have the option to sue in the Town or Village Court where the defendant resides, is employed, or is doing business.
- There is an upper limit on the amount of money you can sue for in small claims court.

You and your spouse can decide whether to pursue a sole or shared animal custody arrangement by considering the following points:

- Who usually took on most of the responsibility for meeting the pet's needs (i.e., feeding, walking, grooming, vet visits) when the parties lived together?
- Who spent more time on a regular basis with the pet?
- What arrangement is in the best interest of the pet in question?
- Who wants custody now, and how close will the parties live to one another to share custody?
- Are children involved, and what is their attachment to the pet? Would it be in the best interest of the children to keep the animal in their lives? How can this be accomplished fairly?

Custody issues worked out in a parenting plan for children provide a good template for coming to agreement about your pets:

- Where will the pets live? If in both homes, when and how will the transition occur? How long will the pet stay with each person?
- How will you handle veterinarian-related visits, pet medical expenses, and comfort care?

- Who is responsible for food, toys, bedding, carrying cases, and "day care" or pet-sitting services while the pet is in each home?
- Many separation agreements include the option of right of first refusal. If the primary pet owner is no longer able to care for the pet, custody will be given to the other party.
- Separation agreements also consider a formal visitation schedule and a commitment by the secondary owner to care for the pet (rather than put it in a kennel) if the primary pet owner goes out of town.

As the social status of animals changes from property to family member, the likelihood increases that divorce laws will expand to include guidelines. The more courts start to view pets as something beyond property, the more amenable they will be to allowing couples to create and enforce custody plans.

The Gray Divorce: Baby Boomers at 50 and Beyond

As with so many of life's assumptions, baby boomers are busting through many of the myths regarding aging. Now entering their 50s and 60s, baby boomers consider this period the "youth of our old age." The notion of "until death do us part" has eroded; people over 50 want their golden years to be romantic and energized.

The flip side of this vision is an increase in divorce. Baby boomers expect so much more of marriage than previous generations did. When a marriage doesn't live up to those expectations, divorce is now a much more acceptable option than it used to be.

Fifty years ago, only 2.8 percent of Americans older than 50 divorced. Today more than 17 percent of people over 50 are either divorced or separated. Like many trends, this particular one has been labeled as Gray Divorce. Some reasons are:

- Many people over age 50 are in their second or third marriage, making them statistically more prone to divorce.
- The emphasis on a healthy and active lifestyle.
- Increased life expectancy.
- Increased work experience and greater independence.
- The empty nest.
- Medicines that promote intimacy for men and women.

Regardless of age or the length of the marriage, when a marriage ends, the couple has to consider the *legal, financial, and emotional elements of the divorce.* The elements of gray divorces often require different strategies in those areas than divorces occurring earlier in life.

In most cases, the couple either has grown children or had no children as a couple, so little conversation regarding children and parenting is needed. The emphasis is usually on the economics of the marriage such as marital property, Social Security, spousal maintenance, and health benefits.

At this stage, it is not unusual for a marital residence to have only a small mortgage or no mortgage at all. The equity in the home can be significant. In a divorce, this equity is considered the same way as a savings account. The couple can either sell the property and divide the proceeds in an equitable manner, or one person can buy the other out. In Chapter 6, I described trading house equity for retirement dollars and the considerations both spouses should make if you choose this route.

If either spouse takes over the home, this can be a financial burden on the new owner in a collapsing real estate market. Also, he/she will have to be eligible to secure a mortgage at a time when he/she may have a fixed income. Alternately, if the spouse sells the property, each has the option to purchase something else or to rent a townhome or apartment. Either way, each will have a new monthly expense they may not have had for some time if they paid off their mortgage during the marriage.

If there are retirement funds such as 401(k)s or IRAs, they are intended to supplement Social Security or reduced incomes from full-time or part-time jobs. Withdrawals from these funds may have already started. As part of the divorce, it is likely that these funds will be shared. As a result, each person potentially will have less money to rely on going forward.

For those over age 60, even though you may be able to withdraw funds from these accounts without penalties, you still need to have a Qualified Domestic Relations Order (QDRO) prepared to distribute the funds from one to the other to avoid unexpected tax consequences. The QDRO is prepared by an attorney and is an additional document to the other divorce papers. See more on this in Chapter 6.

Many clients over age 60 who have retired are already receiving a monthly pension check from a previous employer such as a school district, fire department, police department, or corporation. This monthly income is also considered an asset and can be shared between the divorcing spouses. Sharing the monthly annuity also requires a QDRO prepared at the time of the divorce. After the QDRO is processed, each party receives his or her portion directly from the pension fund. (See Chapter 6 for more information about working through the pension fund distribution.)

Social Security (SS) benefits *are governed by federal law*, not state or matrimonial law, so the way they are distributed in a divorce is regulated by the Social Security Administration. For a person to be eligible for the Social Security benefits of an ex-spouse, the couple had to be married for more than ten years before the divorce proceeding begins. (See Chapter 7 for more information on Social Security in divorce.)

The idea of "equalizing" the Social Security benefit so that each person receives the same amount is something that is "negotiated" and not mandated by law. For example, if Mary and Joe wanted to share $800 + $2,400 = $3,200 per month equally, each person would receive $1,600. In this case, Mary would receive her $1,200 from the government, and Joe would have to pay Mary the additional $400 every month. If you would like more information about how Social Security benefits are handled in a divorce, you can review the official Social Security website's divorce section as shown in Appendix H.

> **Bitter**
>
> *Unlike a pension or retirement distribution, if you want to equalize Social Security benefits, one spouse has to pay the other spouse the money directly.*

How will each person live self-sufficiently after the divorce? The guidelines for spousal maintenance (SM) (see Chapter 9) include numerous factors that are to be considered, including the length of the marriage, each person's health, the employability of each person, and the income disparity or income potential between the spouses. If one or both persons are still working, then the issues become how to share income between the two, and how long someone is "expected" to work. The same calculations for spousal maintenance detailed earlier in this chapter will apply to people who are divorcing in their later years.

Just as with younger divorcing couples, any health insurance benefit one spouse receives through the other spouse ends upon divorce, including couples receiving health insurance through a retirement plan. It is important to consider how to bridge health insurance until Medicare eligibility occurs at age 65 for the person who will no longer be insured. One way this is accomplished is by processing the end of your marriage as a legal separation rather than going right to a no-fault divorce.

It's also important to consider long term care insurance. As you move forward as a single person, you no longer have your spouse to advocate for you should you require in-home care or a move to assisted living or a nursing home. You also have a smaller pool of assets on which to draw if your health changes and you need daily medical or custodial care. If you are paying spousal maintenance and/or child support, long term care insurance can help you preserve your nest egg and continue making the payments. If you are the recipient of spousal maintenance, you need to make these payments and your other resources last as long as possible as your health changes.

Long term care insurance can be a great help to your adult children, who will be the most likely to step into the role of caregiver, health care advocate, and attorney-in-fact for your financial health. Knowing that you have provided insurance for your own care in advance will give them peace of mind as well as the resources they will need to ensure that you receive the highest quality care available.

There are many payment options for long term care insurance, including ways to pay off the plan in ten years instead of making payments on it for the foreseeable future. Your divorce professional can help you build these payments into your agreement to make it as affordable and equitable as possible for both of you.

Better

According to Stephanie Coontz, author of Marriage, A History, *"The extension of an active, healthy life span is a big part of the rising divorce rate. If you are a healthy 65, you can expect another pretty healthy twenty years. So with kids gone, it seems more burdensome to stay in a bad relationship, or even one that has grown stale. We expect to find equality, intimacy, friendship, fun and even passion right into what people used to see as the 'twilight years.'"*

ALERT: The rules and laws regarding health insurance, taxes and other issues within this chapter may change frequently.

Please refer to my website **bjmediationservices.com** for up-to-date information regarding the implications of these issues on your divorce circumstances.

Chapter 8

Sharing Money: Child Support

"My mission in life is not merely to survive but to thrive, and to do so with some passion, some compassion, some humor, and some style."
–Maya Angelou

Virtually every client with children emphasizes that the kids are their priority. Both parents assert they want what's best for the kids and the smoothest possible transition. In most cases, the parents are picturing the children's emotional well-being. The flip side of children's emotional well-being is their practical well-being. Children need to have a comfortable place to live, and to the extent possible, a comparable opportunity to enjoy discretionary spending—like vacations or gifts or going to an amusement park—from both parents.

In practical terms, children are a "cost center." The New York State guideline percentages (of adjusted gross income—see below) of 17 percent for one child and 25 percent for two and so on, are intended to express what portion of a budget item (the mortgage, for instance) is allocated as a child(ren) expense. This child support amount, as an example, $20,000 annually, goes well beyond the direct related expenses of a child(ren) and therefore includes every aspect of your household expenses, from your mortgage and utilities to auto repairs and gas.

Who pays child support? *Both parents do.* Who actually pays how much to whom is a function of the parenting plan to which the couple agrees. The New York State Child Support Guidelines provide that the parent who is with the child more (generally based on overnights, but not always) is the primary residential parent (PRP) for the purposes of child support.

In terms of actual money changing hands, let's say Todd is the non-PRP and Jane is the PRP of two children. Todd pays his agreed-upon share of the total child support amount to the PRP (by direct bank deposit or whatever payment mechanism the couple chooses). At the same time, Jane is expected, from her own income, to devote her share of the total child support amount to the appropriate household and child expenses.

Child support law is designed to create comparable environments for the children to feel comfortable in each parent's home after the divorce. It is intended to help fund household expenses such as the mortgage, utilities, food, gas, home insurance, and the like. It is also intended to cover the ordinary expenses of the child such as clothes, school lunches, school supplies, and haircuts.

Regarding the effect of child support on the parents' income taxes:

- It is *not taxable income* for the receiver. It does not increase the income taxes of the person who receives it.
- It is *not tax deductible* by the payor. It does not reduce the taxable income of the person who pays it.

In New York State, child support has two official parts, each intended for specific needs of the children. (See your state's guidelines at the National Conference of State Legislatures' website by referring to Appendix H.)

Part 1: The percentage based on the parents' total income. The portion of the combined adjusted parental income to be devoted to child support is one of the following percentages determined by the total number of children you have:

- One child: 17 percent
- Two children: 25 percent
- Three children: 29 percent
- Four children: 31 percent
- Five or more children: 35 percent

The child support percentages listed above were designated in 1988 and have not been adjusted since that time. However, because incomes have risen, theoretically, child support has also increased.

Part 2: The proration portion is based on the ratio of each parent's income to the total income of both parents. This is intended to be used only for other specific expenses for the children and is paid in addition to the child support determined by the percentage calculation above. The other expenses are:

- The cost for health insurance coverage for the children.
- The actual uninsured medical expenses for the children.
- Child care, if applicable.
- Pre-college education, if applicable.

Let's use our hypothetical example of Todd and Jane (the PRP), who both work and have two children together.

Effect of the Income Cap On Child Support Calculations

As of this writing, the current combined adjusted parental income cap is $143,000. It is adjusted every two years; it was last changed March 1, 2016. So if Todd and Jane have a combined FICA adjusted parental income of $135,000,

Child Support Percentage	Todd	Jane	Total
Gross Annual Income [1]	$75,000	$35,000	$110,000
FICA @ 7.65% [2]	($5,738)	($2,678)	($8,416)
Other Deductions [3]	$0	$0	$0
Net Amount [4]	$69,262	$32,322	$101,584
% for 2 Children 25% [5]	$17,315	$5,495	$22,810

(1) This includes overtime, sales commissions, bonuses, and all sources of income with a few exceptions. (2) FICA tax is collected by the US government for Social Security and Medicare. It is the only tax that is deducted because it is the only tax that is the same for everyone. (3) There are other eligible deductions from gross income that are applied, if relevant, such as child support paid for a child with a different former spouse or spousal maintenance. See Appendix I for details. (4) These are the income amounts to which the guideline percentage is applied. This is referred to as child support income. (5) For 2 children, the guideline amount of annual child support is 25%. Todd pays his 25% to Jane, the PRP.

the cap would not apply and total child support for their two children (25%) is $33,750 ($135,000 x 25%).

If the combined parental income amount income exceeds $143,000, the guidelines permit, but do not require, the use of the child support percentages in calculating the child support obligation on the income above $143,000.

Let's say Todd and Jane have a combined FICA adjusted parental income of $171,000. If there were no income cap, their percentage-based child support obligation would be $42,750 ($171,000 x 25%).

Because of the income cap, the percentage-based child support would be calculated at $35,750 ($143,000 x 25%). The guidelines permit, but do not require, the difference of $7,000 ($42,750-$35,750) to also be considered for this couple's child support obligation.

This is how the guidelines work when both parents are people of means. What if a parent's New York State income is below the US poverty level?

The New York State Child Support Guidelines state that if a parent's income is less than

> **Better**
>
> *Most clients consider income only up to the cap when calculating child support.*

135 percent of the US poverty guidelines for individuals, that parent's annual child support obligation is $25 per month, or $300 annually.

For example, the 2016 US poverty level for a one-person household in the contiguous 48 states is $11,880. $11,880 x 135% equals $16,038.

Therefore, a parent with an annual 2016 income of $16,038 or less has a child support obligation of $300 per year.

> **Better**
>
> *The only states that designate child support through age 21 are New York and Mississippi as well as Washington, DC. The other states designate age 18 or 19 years for emancipation. The emancipation language is different in some states.*

Here are some other things to consider when planning for child support:

- It is useful to *consider having a life insurance policy* on one or both parents, naming the other as beneficiary. (See Chapter 7 for more on this.)
- If a parent dies, Social Security benefits would be provided (if eligible) for children up to age 18.
- Child support may be extended by mutual agreement to continue until a child completes college (usually within 4 years of high school graduation).
- In New York State, child support ends at 21 or prior to 21 upon the child's emancipation (refer to the guidelines in Appendix C). That typically happens if a child enters the military, marries, or does not go on to higher education after high school and is independent.
- Life insurance may also be prudent for the PRP, especially if child care and other costs are relevant.

As previously mentioned, there are other expenses that are also part of the child support guidelines and are calculated using the prorated ratio of the parents rather than the percentages described in Part 1 above. These expenses are paid in addition to the calculated child support amount. The prorated child support is intended for the following other specific expenses for the children and is paid by each parent as shown in the example below.

- The cost of the children's health insurance coverage
- Children's medical expenses that are not covered by their health insurance
- Child care, if applicable
- Pre-college education expenses, if applicable

Let's see how this works out using our example of Todd and Jane. They both work and have two children together. The table below shows their income.

Proration of Children's Expenses	Todd	Jane	Total
Gross Annual Income (FICA adjusted)	$75,000	$35,000	$110,000

Next, let's calculate the percentage of the income each parent has compared to the total income.

Proration of Children's Expenses	Todd	Jane	Total
Gross Annual Income	$75,000	$35,000	$110,000
% of Total Income	68.2%	31.8%	100%

Now, let's add the (hypothetical) amounts spent on eligible expenses for Todd and Jane's two children:

Proration of Children's Expenses	Todd	Jane	Total
Gross Annual Income	$75,000	$35,000	$110,000
% of Total Income	68.2%	31.8%	100%
Children's Health Insurance	$818	$382	$1200
Uninsured Medical Expenses	$546	$254	$800
Child Care	$2,728	$1,272	$4,000
Total Prorated Expenses	$4,092	$1,908	$6,000

Todd and Jane are each responsible for covering the amounts in his or her column for these expenses.

Here is the total picture of what Todd and Jane's child support obligations are for their two children:

Child Support	Todd	Jane	Total
Percentage-Based	$17,315	$5,495	$22,810
Prorated Expenses	$ 4,092	$1,908	$6,000
Total Child Support	$21,407	$7,403	$28,810

What if you and your spouse want to do something different for child support or the prorated share of expenses? Plenty of parents deviate from the guidelines for many good reasons, and the New York State Child Support Guidelines (see Appendix B) set forth reasons why deviations from the guidelines might be warranted.

One of the most common reasons that parents deviate from the guidelines is that their children spend equal time with each parent (which is referred to as a 50:50 parenting plan). When this parenting plan works, parents often look at their respective budgets to make sure that each of them has about the same amount of funds available to provide for household expenses and discretionary income.

If there is a 50:50 parenting plan, keep the following in mind:

- The high-income parent is generally designated as the non-residential parent for the purposes of child support. This makes sense in many cases, so each parent has enough funds to meet expenses.
- If both parents make comparable incomes, they may choose not to exchange child support.
- If no child support is exchanged, it's important to discuss how parents will share direct, related child expenses like clothes, haircuts, and school supplies in an equitable manner.
- The specific child support amount may be guided by budgets as a good context to discuss sharing money.

Depending on the age of your children and their activities, there are other expenses that are important to clarify. There are two main categories of expenses that are not part of the guidelines, so parents generally set forth their intentions within their agreement to avoid misunderstandings and assumptions.

- **Extracurricular Activities:** These are generally expenses for camp and summer programs, sports, music, art, dance, for the children including equipment, registration, and uniforms.
- **Milestone Events and Senior High School-Related Expenses:** These are expenses for large birthday parties, life-cycle events such as religious or graduation events, and larger expenses such as cars, car insurance, college application and preparatory tests, and senior high school expenses such as

Better

When parents share the direct related expenses, a good idea to avoid "chasing receipts" is to calendarize the expenses to keep from questioning what each other spent. For example, one year Mom buys school supplies, and the next year Dad does. Or Mom buys birthday party gifts for other kids for the first six months of the year and Dad the last six months. Even haircuts and clothes can be shared in this way, and things generally even out over the year.

yearbook photos or senior trips. These can also include college expenses for dorm set-ups, technology, or transportation.

> **Better**
>
> *Having an understanding about how to pay these additional expenses is especially important when child support is not being paid at the full guideline amount.*

While child support is intended for the ordinary expenses like haircuts, school lunches, clothes, and school supplies, it does not have to be used for these larger expenses. Without an understanding of how you might share these expenses, your child may have limited options for activities or events. For example, travel hockey or cheerleading are reputed to cost many thousands of dollars a year. It's unrealistic to think these would be funded by just one parent. One caveat is that the agreement usually indicates that these expenses need to be mutually planned and budgeted, so that one parent can not make unilateral decisions and expect the other parent to pay.

When You Deviate from the Child Support Guidelines

New York State child support law allows parents to deviate from the Child Support Standards Act (CSSA) guidelines, provided that they have indicated what their child support obligations would be had they followed the guidelines, have affirmed their CSSA obligations to be presumptively correct, and have justified the proposed deviation to the satisfaction of the court.

When agreeing to a deviation, the parties must show that the CSSA guidelines would result in an "inappropriate or unjust" award, based on one or more of the following factors:

Factor 1: The financial resources of the parents and those of the child

Factor 2: The physical and emotional health of the child and his/her special needs or aptitudes

Factor 3: The standard of living the child would have enjoyed had the marriage or household not been dissolved

Factor 4: The tax consequences to the parties

Factor 5: The non-monetary contributions that the parents will make toward the care and well-being of the child

Factor 6: The educational needs of either parent

Factor 7: A determination that the gross income of one parent is substantially less than the other parent's gross income

Factor 8: The needs of other children of the non-custodial parent

Factor 9: Provided that the child is not on public assistance, extraordinary expenses incurred by the non-custodial parent in extended visitation, provided that the custodial parent's expenses are substantially reduced as a result

Factor 10: Any other factors the court determines are relevant in each case

> ### Better
> *When the child support as agreed upon deviates from the guidelines, the deviation factors have to be included in the papers filed with the court to justify the reasons to deviate. Your divorce professional will work with you on the phrasing of your deviation factors.*

Modifications to Child Support

No one can predict the future. When clients are making a financial obligation to one another, it's natural to worry how obligations will be met if circumstances change. Especially with young children, there are many child support paying years and lots of things can change. Job changes, promotions, disability, and the like are real concerns.

Clients are reassured to know that your child support agreement can be modified if your situation changes. The state guidelines provide eligibility to discuss changes. Child support can be reevaluated based on the following:

- A substantial change in circumstances.
- If three years have elapsed from the commencement, modification or adjustment of child support, on or later then October 12, 2010.
- If there has been a change in either party's gross income by 15 percent since the order was entered, last modified, or adjusted.
- If the deviation factors that might have been used in the original order no longer apply.

Many clients create their own formula for changing child support. They can designate their own percentage of income, agree to look at incomes annually, or designate their own timing to require a recalculation. Some parents build in a cost of living adjustment but do not look at future incomes.

> ### Bitter
> *The modification guidelines provide eligibility to re-evaluate child support, but do not guarantee an adjustment.*

How Is Child Support Collected and Received?

Child support is typically paid by payroll deduction directly into the receiver's bank account. Let's imagine that Frank is paying Helen child support. Frank would set up a payroll deduction directly from his paycheck (similar to a direct car or mortgage payment). Helen needs to provide her bank's routing number. The annual child support is then paid weekly, biweekly, or monthly, coincident to Frank's pay periods. Sometimes clients set up a direct payment from their own bank's online system, rather than going through the employer.

These direct payment options are certainly the most cooperative way to share money. If for some reason Frank is not compliant or child support is not being paid, however, then Helen can initiate payments through the Child Support Enforcement Agency (CSEA—in New York State, this is also known as Child Support Online) and have payments made through automatic wage deduction managed by the state.

If your spouse stops making child support payments, you can apply for state intervention by filling out the application that can be found through Appendix H. Bring this to your local child support office, and CSEA will go to work to collect the delinquent child support payments for you. CSEA takes on the responsibility of locating the parent, establishing support orders, and collecting and distributing child support payments. CSEA then pays you on a regular basis, and your spouse's wages are garnished under the authority of the divorce decree, which is a court order.

Here are some aspects of the CSEA:

- If child support is not paid, CSEA will initiate delinquent consequences. Some couples place enforcement rules in their agreement to make it clear what consequences the payor will suffer if he or she does not keep up with payments. For example, perhaps the parent who gets the tax dependency allowance deduction for paying child support loses this deduction if he/she stops making payments.
- If the custodial parent does not know where the noncustodial parent lives, CSEA will attempt to locate him/her by checking the last known address and place of employment and through other local efforts. CSEA will use federal, state, and local resources to help locate the noncustodial parent.
- The CSEA will initiate steps to collect overdue support. Even if the noncustodial parent has moved and left no forwarding address, the CSEA can intercept the parent's federal and/or state income tax refund, seize bank accounts and other financial assets, suspend the parent's driver's license, file

liens against real estate or personal injury claims, and submit the delinquent parent's name to major consumer credit reporting agencies, so the parent will have trouble getting a new credit card or obtaining a loan. In addition, the CSEA can garnish unemployment checks, send the name of the delinquent parent to the state to initiate tax collection remedies, and intercept lottery winnings to collect child support payments.

- When the CSEA is used, child support is adjusted by 10 percent when the consumer price index (CPI) has a cumulative 10 percent change from the time your child support payments are started. Currently it takes several years for the CPI to aggregate to more than 10 percent, because inflation is low. However, if there is an adjustment, it may not mirror changes to your own wages.

- Most agreements specify that if child support is not paid in full, then Frank cannot claim a dependency allowance for taxes if that's what was in the agreement.

When payments are collected, the state will deposit these into the bank account you specify. You will not have to make further contact with your spouse; the state will pursue the payments on your behalf.

As you can see, New York State does not look kindly on parents who do not make child support payments. Many other states have similar child support collection operations; you can find the one in your state by using your web browser to search on "Child Support Collection Unit" and the name of your state.

> **Better**
>
> *Whether you use a direct payment or the CSEA, you cannot unilaterally stop paying child support regardless of the circumstances. If you lose your job or have other issues, you MUST file a modification request within the court system.*

Temporary Child Support: Living Separately Before Your Divorce

Sometimes parents choose to live (or find themselves suddenly living) separately for months or even years before negotiating an agreement using either mediation or attorneys. Figuring out how to share money and other financial worries generally escalate. It's important to know that the parent who is with the children (most of the time) can apply for an Order of Child Support from Family Court.

Let's say Tanya and Leroy are married and living separately, and Tanya wants to receive child support. She can apply for an Order of Child Support through

> **Bitter**
>
> *If you do not file a modification request and then appear at a hearing for a modification, you may be charged interest and penalties from the time that you unilaterally ended child support payments until the modification, if any, is granted.*

Family Court by completing an application for child support and a petition for custody. At that point, the judge can order a Temporary Order of Child Support (TCS). A hearing date will be set and Leroy will be notified to appear (with Tanya) before a child support magistrate. Each party will provide proof of income and other documents as needed. The hearing officer (magistrate) has the authority to set the child support amount that will be paid and child support usually begins within a few days.

Here are some things to keep in mind about applying for and receiving TCS:

- There is no fee to use the service.
- There is no requirement to have an attorney present, although you have that option.
- Child support will be retroactive to the date of your application for child support—not to the date you started living separately.
- When Tanya and Leroy decide to actually get a divorce, the child support order can be incorporated into their agreement, or it can be modified based on the future decisions they make regarding sharing money or the parenting plan.

What About College?

How to fund college (or higher education) is a very important conversation for parents. Whatever you decide to do, your intentions should be included in your agreement.

Generally, there are two funding concepts regarding college expenses:

1. Making no obligation: The parents do not make an obligation and conclude that each will pay what they choose to pay with no specific obligation.

2. The parents decide to make an obligation to fund college.

1. Making no obligation

When there are relatively young children in the family, most parents have not yet focused on how to fund college. It's not unusual for the agreement to indicate that parents will "figure it out" when the kids get older. Here are some things to consider and to include in the agreement if you choose to defer a college obligation:

Make a commitment to determine what your intentions are by the time the child(ren) enters high school. This way you can guide your child regarding his or her expectations.

- When the decision regarding funding is deferred, it sometimes causes conflict when funding is finally discussed, because circumstances have changed significantly. There may be other children, marriages, or spending patterns that limit what a parent is now willing or able to pay.
- Sometimes parents make no obligation because one or both parents think college funding should be the child's responsibility.

2. Making an obligation

If parents are going to put an obligation into the agreement, the most common method is to use a surrogate or equivalent benchmark. Because most people think that a state school has more "economic value" than a private school, parents often agree to set their contribution at a portion of **tuition only** at a named state school. Here's how that works.

- When parents decide to share up to the equivalent of tuition only (not room and board, books, or other expenses) of a state school, they use the tuition amount when the child is ready to go to school. Let's say it is $12,000.
- The parents then determine what portion they will each pay—perhaps 50 percent each, for example.
  - Fifty percent each equals $6,000 from each parent for each year of college.
  - For four years from high school graduation, $6,000 x 4 = $24,000
  - For two children (for example) $24,000 x 2 = $48,000.
- It's prudent to limit this college obligation for the child(ren) to four or five years from high school graduation. This precludes being obligated to fund college when your kids are much older, or to fund graduate education should your child(ren) pursue this.
- The amount of money "obligated" can be used at any school. The state school concept is a benchmark or a "value" amount and not intended to direct where a child attends school. If a child goes to a private university where tuition is much higher, the funding obligation is still the same.
- Even at a state school, tuition is a considerable amount of money, and that's why room and board are often not included in the obligation. Expenses above the tuition obligation are generally voluntary and may be funded by student loans, financial aid from the college, or other options.

- It's important to let each parent fund his/her obligation in the manner he or she chooses. Some parents start new 529 or college savings plans, some parents put money aside every week, and some parents intend to sign parent loans for their portion. It is generally not useful to require a certain savings program. Each parent is autonomous and will figure out how he/she will meet his/her obligation.
- A positive outcome of this plan is that parents are making every effort to ensure that the child(ren) can actually receive a somewhat debt-free college education, even if the children have to live at home and commute to a community college or a state school.
- Most agreements do not include a financial obligation for education beyond an undergraduate degree.
- Sometimes parents specify that payments will be made only if the child is enrolled full-time and achieves a certain grade point average.

Another way of making an obligation is to determine a set amount annually. Parents can conclude that they will each pay $3,000 per year, for example, for each year the children are attending college within four to five years of high school graduation. This is a more modest and controllable obligation. Parents may want to guide their children to apply to reasonably priced schools to avoid large student debt upon graduation.

Some parents calculate tuition at a community college for two years, and then tuition at a state school for two years.

529 Plans or Other College Savings Plans

A 529 plan is a savings vehicle designed to provide tax advantages when saving and paying for a college education. It is offered by your state of residence or by an educational institution to help you save for college. The plan can be used to pay for college nationwide, not just in the state where the plan is based.

Sometimes parents have already accumulated savings for college. There are important considerations regarding these savings.

- Most people "freeze" the 529 plan at the point of divorce, so it is very clear what has been accumulated "maritally." Let's say there is $20,000.
- If a parent wants to continue using a 529 plan, he/she should start a new plan that clearly reflects what that parent has saved outside of the marital 529 or savings plan.
- Clarify whether the savings that have accumulated ($20,000) are to be used to pay expenses *above* the tuition, like room and board, or *reduce* the parental obligation. The agreement should be clear about this.

- Usually only one parent is on the marital 529 plan. It is important to make sure the other parent is named as beneficiary, and that a Power of Attorney (see Chapter 14) be created in case the named parent cannot make decisions.
- Documentation of the balance should be made available upon request.
- These funds should only be used for the children of the marriage.
- If other people (like grandparents) create savings or leave an inheritance for the children, decide in advance if those funds can be used to reduce the related parent's obligation.

What about child support and college expenses? The New York State guidelines state that child support continues until the child reaches age 21, unless a child is emancipated (see Appendix C)—that is, that the child no longer lives with the parents and is either married, in the military, working full-time year-round, is financially independent, or has ended his or her relationship with the parents. Therefore child support is paid while a child is in college.

Many parents continue child support until the child completes college within four years of high school graduation, regardless of the child's age. If a child turns 21 in November of his fourth year of college, for example, child support would continue until graduation in May. The concept behind continuing child support is that the child's home still needs to be maintained while the child is at school, and certain child support-related expenses still need to be paid, like clothing, allowance, car insurance, cell phone, and the like.

If a parent is obligated by the agreement or voluntarily pays for room and board (in addition to tuition), there is often a conversation regarding reducing child support to avoid "double dipping" or paying for two residences. Parents can create their own agreement regarding how to pay for the non-tuition college expenses. Sometimes the parents create a new child support plan when the oldest child goes to college, but there is often another child still at home, so some child support remains a necessity.

If parents want to consider an adjustment of child support when the oldest goes to college, it's important to remember that the child support calculation for two children, for example, is 25 percent, and for one child the calculation is 17 percent. If an adjustment is made, it would only change the amount of child support by 8 percent (the difference between 25% and 17%).

The amount of child support paid, or what an adjustment to child support might look like because of college, is an important mediated conversation. Clients often consider reductions to child support based on the amount of time the student is home from college and also how room and board expenses are being paid.

Child support in New York State is payable until age 21, unless the child is emancipated, and yet many clients in mediation make adjustments for children in college.

Bitter

Keep in mind that the incremental savings on the household expenses when a child goes to college are generally minimal, such as water and food expenses, compared to the fixed expenses of a mortgage and utilities.

ALERT: Please note that the New York State cap on child support is scheduled to be adjusted every two years with the next adjustment scheduled in 2018. In this chapter, the examples used are based on the current cap of $143,000. The concept will be the same regardless of the specific cap amount.

Please refer to my website: **bjmediationservices.com** for up-to-date information on changes to the cap on child support.

Chapter 9

Sharing Money: Alimony

"Sometimes when things are falling apart,
they may actually be falling into place."
—Unknown

How much money do you need to feel financially safe? This is a provocative conversation during divorce and well-suited for mediation. Most clients consider assets like the house and retirement funds as a safety net and not intended for daily living expenses. Cash flow is a more problematic conversation, because it is how we pay our bills and whether we have discretionary funds. In divorce, cash flow typically has three potential sources (excluding investment income): your personal income, child support, and spousal maintenance (SM).

For clarity, the words alimony and spousal maintenance are often used interchangeably. The federal government refers to the concept as "alimony" and many states (including NY) use the term spousal maintenance.

Spousal maintenance has been around a long time, but the associated laws (in New York State) have changed significantly over the years. Because money is involved, spousal maintenance is often an emotional issue as well.

Many parents accept the notion of child support because it is intended to help the children live comfortably, but the notion of SM often triggers a more emotional reaction. The idea of SM is to provide a safety net for the lower income party to reestablish a more solid financial footing. It is usually time-limited and helps the low-income party find self-sufficient employment or a cushion for training that would lead to a better income. While there are many factors that are considered when determining if someone is a candidate for SM, the main factor is the disparity of income between the parties because that is what is used in the SM calculator as the first test of eligibility.

The purpose of spousal support is to limit any unfair economic effects of a divorce by providing a continuing income to a non-wage-earning or lower-wage-earning spouse. Part of the justification is that one spouse may have chosen to forego a career to support the family and needs time to develop job skills to support him or herself. Another purpose may be to help a spouse approximate the standard of living he/she had during marriage.

In New York State, there are two types of spousal payments: **Temporary Spousal Maintenance (TSM)** and **Spousal Maintenance (SM)**.

Let's look at TSM first. There has always been the option for a judge to direct a party to pay TSM to a person prior to the divorce terms and agreement being finalized. The judicial intervention was and is intended to protect a low-income spouse from floundering economically if he or she had no access to funds while a divorce was being litigated. Imagine a person having no funds during a lengthy, perhaps multi-year litigation. The SM is considered temporary because the final Judgment of Divorce— which may or may not include SM—will supersede it.

In September 2015, the **New York State Domestic Relations Law 236-B** was revised to include a calculator to determine the amount of TSM that might be appropriate. Prior to the calculator, there were no guidelines, and lawyers litigated the "right amount of support." The calculation relies on the income of both parties and was the first step toward providing an income calculation for post-divorce spousal maintenance.

It's important to understand that the law provides *guidelines*, not rules, for spousal maintenance. Nothing in this law prohibits divorcing spouses from deviating from the state's maintenance guidelines. In addition, unlike child support, the final agreement does not have to include justifications for why the parties are deviating from the guidelines.

In January 2016, the TSM was revised and expanded to include a calculation for spousal maintenance. For the first time in New York State, post-divorce SM was now subject to an income calculation formula, rather than the previous, unguided practice of determining SM. The **income cap** for the payor in the TSM formula was lowered in 2016 from $543,000 to the current level of $178,000. If the payor's annual income exceeds $178,000, the court considers additional, specific factors (see the TSM guidelines in Appendix D) in determining any additional award of temporary maintenance based on the income above $178,000. This cap is adjusted every two years based on inflation.

Better

Imagine if child support did not have a calculation defined by law. The amount of support would vary based on emotional data. That's why it is quite significant that TSM and SM now also have a calculator to determine eligibility and provide consistency.

The new SM and the revisions to TSM laws are the product of many attorneys, judges, community groups, and other participants in the New York State legal system who gathered "to address the concerns of lower income communities, domestic violence communities, families with middle class economics, and families with exceptional wealth," according to the language in the bill.

When determining TSM, the New York State court will consider and allocate, where appropriate, the parties' respective responsibilities for the family's expenses (such as mortgage) while the divorce action is pending. The court

Better

Both New York State TSM and SM have a current income cap of $178,000, similar to the child support cap ($143,000). This will be adjusted every two years. The next adjustment is scheduled for 2018.

still retains the ability to adjust the guideline amount of maintenance where it finds that amount to be unjust or inappropriate after consideration of one or more factors (which will be documented in the decision record).

Some of the highlights of TSM guidelines are:

- TSM can only be awarded by a judge after a divorce action has been initiated; however, many clients in mediation use the guidelines voluntarily to share money prior to the final settlement agreement.
- There are 15 factors that can be considered in assigning TSM. These are listed in Appendix D.
- TSM is intended to provide immediate or urgent financial resources. The person who has the higher income (after adjustments are made, as applicable, by the formula) is called the "payor," and the other spouse is called the "payee."
- The calculator is used to determine the "presumptive amount," or the amount that would be due based on the guidelines. The calculator uses two mathematical formulas; the presumptive amount is the lower of the two calculations.
- Income that is used to calculate temporary spousal maintenance is defined in the same way as income under child support guidelines.
- TSM ends when the judge presiding over the divorce issues the Judgment of Divorce. That document will include the amount and duration of the post-divorce spousal maintenance payments, if any.
- You can access the NYS TSM Guidelines Calculator here: http://www.nycourts.gov/divorce/calculator.pdf.

The TSM Guidelines Calculator does not include any deductions for child support payments in the calculation of the temporary maintenance amount. The guideline states that the maintenance amount (temporary or post-divorce) be calculated prior to the child support amount. This is because the amount of tempo-rary maintenance or spousal maintenance reduces the child support calculation.

The duration of TSM remains unchanged in the 2016 guidelines. It terminates upon the death of either party or the issuance of a judgment of divorce. Also, the temporary maintenance award does not prejudice the rights of either par-ty regarding a post-divorce SM award. In mediation, couples may create agree-ments that differ from these guidelines. The courts retain the option of awarding "non-durational" support, meaning no end to spousal maintenance, if appropriate.

Post-Divorce Spousal Maintenance

The notion of SM is intended for post-divorce income sharing. The concept of SM is gender-neutral, but because men still earn more than women on average, and men generally remain in the workforce after children are born, it seems that SM is awarded mostly to women. A higher-earning wife, however, may expect to pay SM to her husband.

Similar to TSM, there is now a formula used to calculate the guideline amount of SM. There is one main difference: The SM formula considers whether the payor (the person paying) is also paying child support. The decision of whether child support will be paid must be made first, as it affects which formula is used to calculate the post-divorce amount. Unlike the child support income guidelines, which take into consideration "combined parental income," the new spousal maintenance guidelines apply only to the payor's income up to the income cap (currently $178,000).

The income definition and the cap on income is the same for both TSM and SM. The main test for whether a person is a candidate for SM is the result of the income calculation. There are also additional concepts that influence the amount and the eligibility of a person who potentially may receive SM.

When determining SM, three main concepts are considered:

- The first and most compelling is the **disparity of income** between the parties.
- **A spouse is fully or partially unable to find self-sufficient employment,** whether due to lack of training, the requirement to care for children or a family member, or a similar factor.
- **SM is provided without regard to marital misconduct.** This is a concept that is often misunderstood. Eligibility for SM is determined by the economics and self-sufficiency of each spouse.

Like TSM, there are approximately 20 factors that are considered when award-ing SM. Many of the factors are similar to what the court considers when decid-ing on TSM. The full list is found in Appendices D and E.

How long do you have to pay?

If SM is applicable, the most common question is: "How long will it be paid, and what conditions might end or modify the payments?"

In most cases, SM is **durational**—it is set for a specific length of time. Another part of the change to SM in 2016 was a formula for determining the actual duration of SM. In mediation, couples may create agreements that differ from these guidelines. The courts retain the option of awarding "non-durational" support, meaning no end to spousal maintenance, if appropriate.

The following table sets forth the guidelines.

Duration of marriage	Duration of maintenance of the length of marriage
0 to 15 years	15% to 30% of length of marriage
15 to 20 years	30% to 40% length of marriage
More than 20 years	35% to 50% length of marriage

There is still an element of discussion required, as the length of the marriage does not correspond precisely to the percentage that applies. For example, if Jane and Jim are married 18 years, the percentage used as a multiplier is between 30% and 40%. Let's imagine the parties agree upon 35%. Eighteen years of marriage times 35% = 6.3 years of alimony.

In some very unusual cases, SM may be for the lifetime of the receiver. This is called **nondurational** maintenance, and it may be appropriate when one spouse is older and unlikely to find employment, or if one spouse has an illness.

The state does stipulate two specific guidelines regarding the termination of spousal maintenance:

- **The remarriage of the spouse receiving SM.** Today remarriage is often extended to include the idea of cohabitation, where the receiving spouse lives full-time with another person and presents him or herself economically and socially as married. The notion of cohabitation is often challenged and is subject to interpretation. It is useful to have specific language in an agreement to avoid conflict in the future.
- **The death of either party.** Because death would end the payor's obligation to make payments, it is often prudent to make provisions for a life insurance policy naming the recipient as the beneficiary to fund the balance of the obligation, especially if the recipient is very dependent upon the funds. (Life insurance options are discussed in Chapter 7.)

There are some other factors that may influence the amount or duration of spousal maintenance, but they are not part of the guidelines. Mediation is a useful place to discuss the following:

- **Social Security Eligibility:** In most cases, the paying spouse is not "obligated" to earn at his or her current level beyond full Social Security age. For instance, if Paul is earning $100,000 and is age 60, his income would be expected to stay about the same (for purposes of SM) until age 67 (or the age at which he achieves his full SS payment level).
- **Change in Employment:** Many couples include language regarding circumstances that would involuntarily affect earnings such as a layoff or disability.
- **Recipient's Income:** The earning potential of the receiving spouse is often considered. Provisions may be included for when/if that party earns over a certain agreed-upon threshold. For instance, if Karen earns over $30,000 annually, perhaps the SM she receives would be reduced by 25 or 50 cents for every dollar earned over that threshold. This provides motivation for Karen to work and also provides for her to still have a safety net of funds.

Taxes and Spousal Maintenance

We all know taxes are already a complicated subject. While I summarize some key points here, I urge you to download and refer to IRS Publication 504: Divorce or Separated Individuals **(http://www.irs.gov/pub/irs-pdf/p504.pdf)** for information applicable to your own situation.

Currently, spousal maintenance is taxable to the receiver and tax-deductible to the paying party. It is often thought of as paying a wage to the receiver ("payee") and as a business expense to the provider ("payor"). To avoid an IRS audit, it is essential that the payor and the payee report precisely the same amount of SM or TSM on their respective tax filings. (See Alert on page 140.)

IRS regulations that govern the manner in which SM can be paid are referred to as recapture. In summary, SM cannot be reduced by more than $15,000 between the second and third years or become significantly different from the first year. For instance, if the first year SM was $35,000 annually and the second year it dropped to $10,000 annually, the IRS may disallow the tax-deductible treatment, or recapture the taxes owed due to the SM. The intent is to avoid having a property distribution (such as a buy-out of a home) be labeled as SM, and thereby be treated as a tax-deductible benefit.

Often, when child support (which is not tax deductible to the payor) is calculated, if there is a gap in income that precludes a comparable standard of living

> ## Bitter
> *You may think that paying spousal maintenance instead of child support is a good way to get a tax deduction, but the IRS is alert to parents paying SM in lieu of child support. Chances are good that this attempt will backfire and result in a higher tax bill.*

for both parties, the gap may be made up in SM. One issue that is also scrutinized is if SM is paid and then stops coincident to when child support might also have ended.

In order for the payor to claim the SM deduction (and for it to be declared as income by the payee), each spouse must file his/her respective income taxes separately, even if you are legally separated and may still be eligible to file as married filing jointly.

If your SM is above a certain threshold (check with your accountant, but often around $8,000 or more annually), it is prudent to file quarterly estimated taxes on the SM, just as you would if you had your own business. This way you will avoid a large and unexpected tax liability, and you can avoid potential penalties if quarterly taxes should have been paid.

The Spousal Maintenance Calculator

The court considers the same factors or guidelines listed earlier for Temporary Spousal Maintenance (see Appendix D) when determining who may be eligible for SM or whether the calculated amount might be adjusted from the guideline amount—with two additions:

- The age and health of the parties.
- The reduced or lost lifetime earning capacity of the payee as a result of having foregone or delayed education, training, employment, or career opportunities during the marriage.

There are two different formulae for determining the guideline amount of spousal maintenance:

- **Spousal Maintenance Formula 1** below is used when child support is being paid or will be paid, and the child support payor is the non-custodial parent.
- **Spousal Maintenance Formula 2** below is used for TSM and SM when no child support will be paid, or the primary residential parent is the high-income parent.

Keep in mind that the decision of whether child support will be paid *must be made first*, as it affects which formula is used to calculate the guideline amount for post-divorce spousal maintenance. Then the SM maintenance amount (temporary or post-divorce) is calculated prior to the child support amount. This is because the amount of SM is deducted in the child support income calculation.

"Income" is gross income (from all sources with some exceptions) adjusted for Social Security and Medicare taxes. It is the same income definition that is used to calculate child support income. (See Chapter 8.) The "payor" is the spouse with the higher income.

When child support is being paid by the maintenance payor, this formula is used to calculate SM to a spouse where there are child support-eligible children:

- Twenty percent of payor's income up to $178,000, MINUS 25 percent of payee's income.
- Payor's income up to $178,000 PLUS payee's income x 40 percent, MINUS payee's income.
- The lower of the two amounts above is the guidelines figure.

When no child support is being paid by the maintenance payor to the recipient spouse, this formula is used when there are no child support-eligible children, or the maintenance payor is also the custodial parent for child support purposes:

- Thirty percent of payor's income up to $178,000, MINUS 20 percent of payee's income.
- Payor's income up to $178,000 PLUS payee's income x 40 percent, MINUS payee's income.
- The lower of the two amounts above is the guidelines figure.

When considering post-divorce spousal maintenance, New York State courts consider items a, b, and c below as well as the 15 factors listed in Appendix D.

a) The spouse lacks sufficient property, including marital property apportioned to him/her, to provide for his/her reasonable needs.

b) The spouse is fully or partially unable to support himself/herself through appropriate employment or is the custodian of a child whose condition or circumstances make it appropriate that the custodian not be required to seek employment outside the home.

c) Maintenance will be in such amounts and for such periods of time as is just, without regard to marital misconduct and after considering all relevant factors.

Let's say Arthur and Carol have been married for 15 years. Arthur earns $125,000 per year, and Carol earns $42,000. They have no children. Based on the calculation, Carol would be a candidate for $1,909 per month, the lower of the two calculations.

Spousal Support Calculator When Child Support is NOT Paid.
Also Used When Income Party (Payor) Is Primary Residential Parent (also used for TSM)

	Rates	Arthur	Carol	Combined
Non-self-employed income		$125,000	$42,000	$167,000
Self-employed income			$ -	$ -
Total Gross Income		$125,000	$42,000	$167,000
Medicare Rate	1.45%			
FICA Cap	$127,200			
FICA Rate	7.65%	$9,563	$3,213	$12,776
Self Employed FICA Rate	15.30%	$ -	$ -	$ -
Over $200,000 adjustment	0.90%	$9,563	$3,213	$12,776
Total FICA		**$9,563**	**$3,213**	**$12,776**
Income for support purposes	$115,438	$38,787	$154,225	
Income Cap	$178,000			
Net Income with cap		$115,438	$38,787	$154,225
Income in excess of cap		$ -	$ -	$ -
Calculation 1				
Payor's Income	30%	$34,631		$34,631
Payee's Income	20%		$7,757.40	-$7,757
Per Year				**$26,874**
Per Month				$2,239
Calculation 2				
Sum of Combined Income				$154,225
Percent of Combined Income	40%			$61,690
Payee's Net Income			$38,787	-$38,787
Per Year				**$22,903**
Per Month				$1,909
Use the lower of the two figures.		**$2,239 per year, or**		
If calculation 2 is less than or equal to zero, then no maintenance.		**$1,909 per month is the presumptively correct ammount**		

Now, let's look at a couple with children. Anita makes $225,000 per year, while Jim makes $110,000. Jim is the custodial parent, and Anita pays child support to him. Based on the calculation, Jim would be a candidate for $854 per month.

Spousal Support Calculator When Child Support is Paid

	Rates	Anita	Jim	Combined
Non-self-employed income		$225,000	$110,000	$335,000
Self-employed income				$ -
Maintenance		$ -	$ -	
Total Gross Income		**$225,000**	**$110,000**	**$335,000**
Medicare Rate	1.45%			
FICA Cap	$127,200			
FICA Rate	7.65%	$11,149	$8,415	$19,564
Self Employed FICA Rate	15.30%	$ -	$ -	$ -
Over $200,000 adjustment	0.90%	$11,374	$8,415	$19,789
Total FICA		**$11,374**	**$8,415**	**$19,789**
Income for support purposes		$213,626	$101,585	$315,211
Income Cap	$178,000			
Net Income with cap		$178,000	$101,585	$279,585
Income in excess of cap		$47,000	$ -	$47,000
Calculation 1				
Payor's Income	20%	$35,600		$35,600
Payee's Income	25%		$25,396.25	-$25,396
Per Year				**$10,204**
Per Month				$850
Calculation 2				
Sum of Combined Income				$279,585
Percent of Combined Income	40%			$111,834
Payee's Income			$101,585	-$101,585
Per Year				**$10,249**
Per Month				$854

Use the lower of the two figures.	**$10,204 per year, or**
If calculation 2 is less than or equal to zero, then no maintenance.	**$854 per month is the presumptively correct ammount**

Changing SM: Motion for Modification

If your circumstances change significantly—you or your spouse lose a job or develop a major illness, for example—it may be possible to modify your spousal maintenance agreement.

In New York, there are only a few scenarios in which alimony can be modified:

- The payor spouse has had a negative change in his/her circumstances due to a problem with the economy (rising prices or taxes) or an illness, and he/she can establish that continuing to pay the SM poses a financial hardship.
- The payor spouse can prove that the payee spouse is cohabitating full-time with his/her significant other—actually living together and functioning as husband and wife. (If this is the case, the obligation to pay spousal maintenance terminates.)

> **Better**
> *Be alert to audit flags! Both parties have to put the same amount of spousal maintenance on their tax returns. If you don't, it's a red flag for the IRS, which can lead to an audit.*

Mediation is a useful first step to discuss modifications to SM. Many concerns can be resolved in mediation.

If you and your spouse agree on the modification, you (or your attorney) can file a motion, get a scheduled court date, and present the motion as an agreement for the judge's approval. It's wise to formalize your agreement with your spouse, even if you have maintained a friendly relationship and you don't expect any future conflict. None of us can predict what may happen down the road, so be sure that a court can enforce the orders if necessary.

Either spouse can bring a Motion for Modification to the court. The motion details the original orders, the changes in circumstances that have taken place since the original orders, and your request for modification of the orders.

> **Better**
> *As with child support, you cannot adjust SM unilaterally. You need to request a modification to the divorce decree.*

If you or your spouse intend(s) to contest the modification, your day in court will become a hearing at which the judge will hear evidence on both sides of the dispute. If you have determined in advance that your orders are modifiable, you (or your attorney) will present the facts that have led you to seek a motion for modification. Your spouse

> **Bitter**
> *If you lose your court challenge, you may have to pay your ex-spouse's attorney's fees.*

will present evidence to prove that the original orders should not be modified, and the judge will make a decision.

Finally, if you are attempting to change orders that are not modifiable, the probability is

> **Better**
>
> *Be mindful of whether your SM agreement can be modified. Most agreements can be modified unless they specifically state that they cannot.*

very high that the judge will not choose to modify them. Before you invest time, anxiety, and money on a futile effort, make certain that you have a chance of achieving your goal and modifying the SM order.

Domestic Abuse and Spousal Maintenance

One of the factors when spousal maintenance is considered details "acts by one party against another that have inhibited or continue to inhibit a party's earning capacity or ability to obtain meaningful employment." These acts generally come under the heading of domestic violence, a living condition that gets special attention during a divorce proceeding.

One method abusers use to assert their power is to force the victim spouse to be financially dependent on them. The batterer may prevent the victim from working, make a rule that the victim must ask for money and keep none of his/her own, give the victim an allowance, and hide information about the family income, debts, and bank and credit accounts. Without money, the victim may be unable to leave the relationship.

If you have been unable to earn a living because of a controlling or physically abusive spouse, the court will take this into consideration when determining the amount of spousal maintenance you should receive. New York State has processes in place to collect this maintenance from the abuser; you will not need to be in contact with your spouse to receive financial support.

ALERT: As a result of the revised tax laws that were passed in December 2017, there will be changes to the tax treatment for Spousal Maintenance/Alimony starting with divorce or separation agreements executed after January 1, 2019. Currently and continuing through 2018, alimony and separate maintenance payments are deductible by the payor spouse and included as income by the recipient spouse.

The new law states that for any divorce or separation agreement executed on or after January 1, 2019, alimony and separate maintenance payments are not deductible by the payor spouse and are not included as income of the receiving spouse. Rather, income used for alimony is taxed at the rates applicable to the payor spouse.

This tax change will make both child support and Alimony taxable to the payor and "tax-free" to the receiver.

The current spousal maintenance cap of $178,000 is scheduled to change in 2018.

Please refer to my website: **bjmediationservices.com** for up-to-date information on the status, implications of this new tax treatment.

PART 4

The Children's Divorce

Chapter 10

Child Custody and Divorce

"You are the bows from which your children
as living arrows are sent forth."
—*Khalil Gibran*

Few issues are more packed with emotion than the question of child custody in a divorce. In mediation, I work to help parents come to the best possible agreement in the best interests of the child or children, with the goal of making the transition as seamless as possible for everyone concerned.

Creating two homes for children is certainly stressful and filled with anxiety. However, it does not need to be a wrenching experience, especially if the parents can come to an agreement that provides for their needs as well as for the needs of the children. Often, parents work out the arrangements cooperatively, rather than building conflict into their ongoing relationship. It is only when parents cannot agree that the matter requires the active participation of the court system.

Child custody guidelines include numerous terms regarding parenting and decision-making. Many clients find the terms intimidating, but the guidelines define different levels of custody based on with whom the child lives.

- **Physical custody** outlines the details of where the children will reside. It specifies the primary residential parent and the parenting plan.
- **Legal custody** is about decision-making. In most cases, and virtually all mediated cases, parents have joint legal custody. This means that they have equal input regarding major decisions about education, religion, healthcare and extracurricular activities. Regardless of the physical custody arrangement, most parents have joint decision-making for their children.

Let's look at these in more detail:

Physical Custody (which I like to refer to as the "Parenting Plan") provides the details of how the children will spend time with each parent. It indicates which parent the child will live with most of the time. That parent is considered the *custodial parent or primary residential parent* (PRP). If the child spends half of his/her time living with one parent and half with the other, the parents have **joint (or shared) physical custody.** For the purposes of determining who pays child support to whom, however, one parent is designated the PRP, while the other is the non-PRP.

Joint physical custody (often referred to as a 50:50 shared parenting plan) requires a high degree of collaboration in the child's life. Daily details and logistics need to be coordinated. There is a high level of commitment and communication skill involved. This plan does not work well with high-conflict parents when the children are exposed to a lot of stressful conversations.

Sole physical custody is reserved for unusual circumstances—usually for purposes of physical protection from an unstable or abusive parent. This means that the child lives full-time with one parent and sees the other on a very limited basis, or not at all.

Legal custody determines how parents will make decisions about the child's education, health care, religion, extracurricular activities, and other issues. In some cases, only one parent has legal custody. When both parents want to remain involved in the child's upbringing, they have **joint legal custody**. Choosing joint legal custody (which most parents do) is not a function of the parenting plan or primary residency of the child. Legal custody is based on what is best for the specific family, and both parents share in making decisions about the child's upbringing, health, and activities.

Split legal custody is when each parent may be the primary residential parent (PRP) for one or more children. This is a parenting plan that works under certain circumstances, such as when the educational or emotional needs of a child require it. Parents still see the "other" children on a regular basis, and often all the siblings are together for weekends or holidays. In some cases, parents choose **split custody**, an arrangement in which one or more siblings live with one parent while the other(s) live with the other parent.

In unusual circumstances, a parent may be designated (usually by the courts) with **sole legal custody**. This usually comes up when there are issues of one parent's fitness to make decisions for the child: in cases of mental illness, substance abuse, or other questionable conditions. Generally, sole custody would not be awarded to one parent based on factors such as: different parenting styles, organizational skills, or annoying behaviors.

Parallel custody is generally the result of a judicial decision that designates one parent in charge of sports, for instance, and the other parent in charge of education or medical decisions. It is usually the result of very-high-conflict parenting situation, and the inability of the parents to make decisions together.

In mediation, parents decide what is best for their children. This is one of the most useful parts of mediation, because parents are able to express their worries and concerns without escalating to legal venues. There are many ways to craft a parenting plan that works best for the parents and the children. If attorneys or the courts are needed to determine the parenting plan, the professionals will use a standard referred to as *the best interest of the children.* You will hear this phrase over and over throughout your custody litigation. The standards for "best interest" vary depending on the state you live in, but here are the factors that tend to be consistent across the country:

- The child's wishes, if he/she is old enough to make that decision, but it is not determinative.
- The parents' mental and physical health.
- The parents' religion as it relates to the child—for example, if the child has been raised as a Methodist, but only one parent will continue that tradition.
- The stability of each parent's home environment.
- The opportunity for the child to continue relationships with extended family, such as grandparents.
- Relationships with other members of the household.
- The school and community in which the child will live.
- The child's age and gender.
- Any sign of emotional abuse or excessive discipline by one parent.
- Evidence of drug, alcohol, or sexual abuse by one parent.
- Which parent has been the "primary caretaker" of the child. This takes into consideration such daily activities as bathing, grooming, dressing, meal preparation, laundry, buying clothing, making health care arrangements, participating in school and after-school activities, and teaching the child to read and write. Many courts no longer assume that the mother is the primary caregiver—and with more same-sex marriages in the court system, the primary caregiver can be of either gender.

If Your Custody Battle Goes to Court

If the parents are so conflicted that they can't come up with acceptable terms for child custody on their own, they may need to take their case to court. This is not the optimal way to resolve your custody issues because the parents lose the powers of choice and control and turn the parenting decision over to a judge. Whatever ruling the judge makes, the parents have no option but to abide by the court's decision.

In Upstate New York, a custody battle in court begins with the judge appointing an attorney for the child (AFC), a lawyer or advocate who will represent the child in court. His or her job is to advocate for what the client (child) wants. This is different from the best interests of the child; under the current system, the AFC advocates for what the child wants, while the judge decides if this is in the child's best interest. However, the AFC can substitute his/her best judgment if what the child wants will put him or her in harm's way. The AFC must tell the judge what the child wants, but the AFC also will share his/her own judgment to keep the child safe.

For example, the child may tell the AFC that he/she loves the mother and wants to live with her, but the court hearing will reveal that the mother is addicted to drugs. The AFC advocates for the child to live with the mother, even though this may not be a healthy environment for the child, because this is what the child wants. The judge will hear all the testimony, however, and decide what's in the child's best interest.

Better

The best security blanket a child can have is parents who respect each other.

The child's age is also a factor in a court battle for custody. Judges know that an older child will have a stronger and more credible opinion of where and with whom he/she wants to live. If the child doesn't want to live with one parent, forcing him/her to do so can create a perpetual problem that may place the child and custodial parent in constant conflict. The child also may tell the AFC that he/she never wants to see one of the parents, and he/she may have valid reasons for this that the AFC will share with the judge, only if the child allows the AFC to share that information with the court.

If the child is not old enough to articulate an opinion, or if the circumstances demand it—in other words, if there is a substantial risk of imminent harm to the child—the AFC will talk to both parents and propose a schedule to the court based on the AFC's professional opinion. This can result in a *substitute judgment*: If a child says he wants to live with a parent against whom there are allegations of abuse or other danger, the AFC can substitute his/her judgment for what the child wants. However, the AFC must still tell the court what the child wants if the child is of a reasonable age.

When the case comes to trial, the judge hears testimony from both sides and issues a decision. A judge may determine, for example, that one parent should get sole legal custody because the parents couldn't resolve the basic issue of the child's residency. To a judge, this conflict indicates the kind of life the child(ren) will have if the parents haggle over every decision as a factor of their contentious relationship. Alternately, the judge may opt to split decision-making responsibility into *spheres of influence*: For example, one parent may be in charge of education issues, while the other may make the health care decisions.

When custody requires judicial intervention, the process can be quite lengthy, even though judges do their best to move the matter along as quickly as possible. Specialists may be required, and parents may have to undergo psychological evaluations. The time and money required increases tensions, and the children and parents are stressed and emotionally wounded.

The parents have the right to appeal the decision to a higher court. The appellate court judges will read the transcripts of the trial and determine if there are appealable issues, but it is unlikely that the appellate court will overturn a custody decision unless the trial court made a significant legal mistake.

In terms of counseling clients about this, I ask them, "Do you want to keep the control of what happens in your family, or do you want a person in a black robe to do it for you?" Most parents want to do what is best for their children, so they will find a way to keep the peace and determine a custody arrangement without a court battle.

Unmarried Parents: The Stipulated Agreement

Unmarried couples don't need to go through the divorce process to end their relationship, but when they have children, they need to formalize their arrangements for custody and child support. You can make decisions together about child support, custody, and visitation and submit these in writing to the court, usually with the help of a mediator or a family law attorney. This document is often called a stipulated agreement, and it requires specific information so the court is satisfied that you are acting in the best interests of your children. An unmarried couple is not required to file a stipulated agreement and make it into a court order, though it is better if they do so, as it formalizes the arrangements they have agreed to and allows for enforcement of the agreement if needed.

Bitter

Unless there is a court order, neither parent has legal custody of the child, and child support may not be enforced.

Issues of child custody between unmarried parents are addressed and resolved in Family Court, instead of in the Supreme Court, where divorcing parties appear.

In New York, if you are the parent filing for custody, you will get a Petition for Custody form from the family court clerk's office. When the petition has been filled out completely, it is returned to the family court clerk's office. In New York, filing the petition is free; check with the family court in the state in which the child lives to find out if there are fees for filing. The parent filing the petition then needs to serve the other parent with a copy, either by process server, sheriff, or registered mail, depending on the state's requirement. You will need proof that the other parent was served to provide to the court. Once the

> **Better**
>
> *The guidelines regarding child support, custody, holidays, vacations, and all other issues regarding the children are the same, whether you are married or not.*

clerk has the petition, you will be notified of your appearance date by US mail, and it is at that time that proof of service is provided.

If both parents have agreed on a custody arrangement and a parenting plan, your appearance before a judge may be a necessary formality, so you can advise the judge of the plan. After the appearance, the stipulated agreement is incorporated into an Order of Custody and signed by the judge. It is now an enforceable understanding between the parents.

Child support—temporary or otherwise—is not automatically included in the Order of Custody. Here in New York, a separate subsection of the Family Court deals with child support matters. The parent with custody files a Petition for Child Support, and then obtains an Order of Child Support by agreement between the two parents, or following a trial and a decision by a support magistrate. (A support magistrate is appointed by the courts to hear and determine child support proceedings.) As noted earlier, this Family Court form is generally for individuals who are not married or who were previously divorced and are back to modify custody or child support; the Supreme Court handles divorcing couples.

Just as in a child custody proceeding for a divorcing couple, however, if the issue cannot be resolved and it looks like the unmarried parents will contest the custody case, the dispute may go to trial.

The court is more likely to accept an agreement in which the biological or legally adopted parent(s) of the child becomes the custodial parent. This means that if one of you is the child's biological parent, however, and the other is not, chances are the court will expect (or require) that the child's primary residence be with the biological parent. If the other parent has gone through the legal adoption process, or if the parents are of the same sex and both have raised the child together, he or she also has a right to share custody.

If one person is neither the biological nor the adopted parent, but this person participated equally in raising the child and wants to stay involved in the child's life, he or she needs to work with the legal parent to determine the most practical arrangement for doing so. If the legal parent is not open to such an agreement, the only recourse is to take the matter to court. Please consult with a family law attorney in your area before taking on such a challenge, to understand the financial and emotional risks involved and the impact this court proceeding may have on your relationship with the child.

Chapter 11

Co-Parenting: Still Being Mom and Dad

"Most folks are as happy as they make up their minds to be."
–Abraham Lincoln

Joint Legal Custody: Clarifications

One of the biggest gifts you can give your children is co-parenting. Even though you are not husband and wife anymore, you will always be Mom and Dad. How you co-parent is a learning opportunity for your children. They are learning how to behave in challenging times. You can teach them cooperation and respect, or you can teach them to carry a grudge and hold resentments.

One of the best ways to be positive co-parents is to be clear about how to manage decisions for your children. There are many nuances and issues beyond the major decisions defined by "joint legal custody." When you create the terms of your divorce, consider adding language about some or all of the following. Once again, being clear avoids "I assumed," which is the root of all conflict.

Minor or day-to-day decisions. Generally parents leave the day-to-day decisions like meals, social activities, school preparation, and clothes to the parent of residence at the time. Of course, it's useful if parents agree in advance regarding overall rules and behaviors. During an emergency in which the other parent cannot be contacted right away, the available parent would make appropriate decisions and contact the other parent as soon as possible.

Handling conflict between the parents. Parents put in the agreement their intention to cooperate to ensure that the children are not knowingly exposed to any conflicts that might arise between them in the future. The parents agree not to use the child to carry messages back and forth between them. Further, they agree not to knowingly do anything to discourage the child from loving, being with, or making contact with the other parent.

Communication between parents. Parents agree to inform each other of all medical conditions and appointments of the child. This is especially important when a child stays home from school. This gives the other parent the chance to express caring and comfort to the child. One suggestion is that the parents have a weekly call (e.g., on Sunday evenings) to confirm the schedule and logistics for the coming week. When both parents are aware of all school activities and conferences, sports, and the like, it avoids difficult scheduling and logistics snafus that are hard for children to hear.

Fortunately, most schools are willing to send all communications to both parents. Make sure the teachers and coaches have both parents' emails. Access and study the school calendar to be well informed about school events. A calendar is on every school website.

Both parents are able to consult with and be informed of any information from any teacher, school authority, doctor, dentist, psychologist, or other specialist attending the child for any reason. Add events to your own calendar. You might even set up a jointly shared Google calendar on which all events, meetings, appointments, trips, and other time-based information affecting the children are located.

Counseling. Counseling is an issue that often requires extra communication skills. If either parent believes that the child is having difficulty adjusting to the family transition, the parents will work together to jointly select an appropriate professional. Then both parents agree to follow the guidance of the professional. Parents generally agree not to initiate or terminate counseling or therapy for the child without the prior consent of the other.

Communication. Parents agree to promote daily contact with the child by telephone, e-mail, and/or text messaging and the like, whenever the child is with the other parent. Electronic video tools such as Skype and FaceTime are an increasingly useful way to stay in touch with your children.

Documents and traveling. In your divorce terms, include language regarding equal access to the child's official documents, including but not limited to report cards, birth certificate, passport, and the like.

Birth certificate. It is very useful to secure an original birth certificate of each child for both parents to have. Requesting an original birth certificate can be done online by accessing the website of the county in which the child was born. (In my home county, for example, the website is **monroecounty.gov**, and there is a link to "order a birth or death certificate.")

Passport. Check the United States Customs and Border Protection website at **www.cpb.gov** to find out what documents are required before you travel out of the country with your children. Parents should agree to cooperate on securing children's passports. Much less paperwork is required to secure a child's passport while you are married than after your divorce.

Travel information. In your divorce terms, include language that states that each parent will cooperatively provide a written note to the other parent when requested regarding a child's travel outside the United States. While it is not the law, many parents report being asked for a note from the other parents and being questioned when entering Canada to confirm that the other parent is aware of the child's travel plans. In your agreement, state that each parent agrees to advise the other of how the child may be reached if they are traveling with the child for more than a certain number of hours (usually 2-3 hours) or the child is staying overnight away from his/her scheduled residence.

> ### Better
> *Traveling anywhere in the United States is the same as traveling within New York State. Every state and most other countries honor the parenting plan in the divorce decree. The issue is not where you go, but rather that the child is returned to the other parent according to the parenting or holiday or vacation schedule.*

Social Security card. Generally the child's Social Security card can remain with one parent, as it is not usually required until the child is older and starts to work. However, both parents need to know what each child's number is, often for medical records and such.

Death of parent. The agreement usually has reassuring language that in the event of the death of one parent, sole legal custody of the child will transfer to the surviving parent. If for some reason this is not the parental preference, legal advice is prudent to understand the difference between another party's guardianship rights and how that affects the surviving parent's parental rights.

Parents often are concerned about who will be made guardian if both parents die. This is less relevant in divorce because, if one parent predeceases the other, then the surviving parent's instructions will prevail. It is less likely that both parents will die simultaneously after divorce than when married.

Grandparents' and extended family's access rights. Another area of concern that is usually outlined in an agreement is the commitment that each parent makes regarding staying connected with the relatives of a deceased parent. The surviving party agrees to make sure that a connection remains to the grandparents and other extended family cousins, aunts, uncles, and other significant adults, even the new husband or wife of the deceased parent.

Religious faith and training. Parents often emphasize in the agreement that neither parent will change the child's current religious affiliation, impose any religious practice upon the child, or initiate or terminate religious education for him or her, except upon the prior consent of the other. Often parents mention the agreed-upon faith for clarity.

> ### Bitter
> *You can both agree and designate in the agreement persons with whom you do not want your children to be left alone without parental supervision.*

The parents acknowledge a respect for each other's religious beliefs and practices, and that each respectively can attend the place of worship of his/her choice. The children can be participants and attend holiday and worship traditions of either parent, with the understanding that the agreed-upon faith of the children is respected.

Surname and parental designation. An important understanding is that the parents agree that the children will maintain his/her surname as decided at birth. Another is that only the parents of the child will have the designation of Mother or Father or the family terms used for that designation.

> **Better**
>
> *A parent who changed his/her surname because of marriage always has the right and option to return to a birth name or any other name that is legally acceptable. Language to ensure this option is written into the divorce decree. While anybody can change his/her name at anytime, it is easier to accomplish when you are actually divorced and provide the divorce decree as evidence.*

When marriages end, couples often disagree about lots of things. They are concerned and filled with emotions and worries. The one thing that couples do agree upon is doing what is best for the children.

The challenge surfaces when parents do not agree upon what the "best" looks like for their children during or after divorce.

I often remind clients that even when they lived together, they did not always agree about parenting strategies. One parent is too strict, another too lenient; one is always there for the child, while the other works more and participates less. The list goes on and on.

Experts are very clear that how well you handle the divorce transition and your own anger will affect your children far more than the divorce itself. Your children love you both; they don't want to hear hurtful shame and blame words. Parental conflict wounds children deeply.

Parenting Plans: Clarifications

In every parenting plan, respect, cooperation, and common sense are key. The more willing the parents are to be respectful and cooperative after the divorce, the easier the arrangements and agreements will be to manage. More importantly, that will contribute significantly to ensuring your children have the happiest lives possible.

The main part of the parenting plan describes where the children will be every day and night and who will be "on duty." There are a lot of other issues, however, that are essential to clarify to avoid conflict as you co-parent. It is useful to consider the following enhancements to the basic parenting plan, so that you and your ex-spouse can have as seamless a relationship with your children as possible.

> **Better**
>
> *Parenting styles do vary, and children learn lifelong lessons regarding interpreting and understanding all sorts of people. It is a way they hone their coping and negotiating skills.*

Right of First Refusal

What happens when a parent cannot be with the children during his/her scheduled time because of a work or social commitment? Each parent wants as much time with the children as possible, so most parents want to have the option of being the first one called. The right of first refusal is usually for chunks of time, like a four-hour time slot or more—not for errands or when a neighbor watches the children for an hour or so. If the other parent is not available, then the parenting parent will find suitable supervision.

Tips about right of first refusal (ROFR)

- When asking the other parent for ROFR, keep in mind that the parent does not have to say yes.
- If you are offered right of first refusal, do not ask the requesting parent, "Why? What are you doing?" The merits of the request are not germane.
- If a parent says, "Sorry, I am not available," do not ask why.
- Provide an answer to the other parent within a very short (30 minutes-ish) time frame, as the requesting parent needs to make arrangements.
- The regular schedule can resume when you are done with your activity. For example, if you have a 5-6 hour daytime (weekend) event that interrupts your time with your children, the regular schedule resumes when your event is over.
- The ROFR is not intended to preclude grandparents being with the children for several hours a day or an occasional overnight. They are an important part of your children's lives and well-being.

Illness/school closings

"Mommy/Daddy, I don't feel well." It's hard to start the morning with an urgent change in schedule. Who's responsible? Generally the agreement states that the parent who wakes up with the child(ren) is the parent who is accountable for figuring out supervision and medical care. In addition, agreements clarify that if the child's day (at school or child care) is interrupted for illness or school closings, the parent who has the child that night is the one accountable to manage the unscheduled circumstance.

Tips for unscheduled events

- Each parent expects to be alerted when a child is ill and stays home from school or has a temperature, or if the doctor has been called.
- Many parents call the other during these unexpected circumstances and negotiate a schedule that works for both parties.
- If multiple days are needed because of illness, parents generally alternate.
- Unless children are extremely ill, the regular parenting schedule can generally continue.

Transportation

It's important to be clear about how children are transported from one parent's home to the other. When children are picked up from daycare or activities, the parent scheduled to be with the child provides the transportation. When transitions occur from one parent's house, it seems to work best that the parent with the children takes the children to the other parent's home. It may seem counter-intuitive, but it avoids one parent waiting (impatiently) while the kids get ready. This can avoid conflict and tension.

Tips for transportation

- Avoid discussing logistics and schedules during transitions. Instead, say something flattering or delightful about the children to the other parent.
- If the distance between homes is longer than "usual," work out a mid-point meeting place.

Extra-curricular activities

Most agreements are clear that the child(ren) may participate in extra-curricular activities—and that when they do, each parent will support the transportation needs of the child. Most importantly, the agreement should be clear that both parents may attend all third-party functions such as sports, school activities and the like, regardless of the parenting schedule.

Tips for extra-curricular activities

- If it is possible that both parents can sit together at events, you can eliminate the child's discomfort in choosing which parent to go to first after the event. Your child will be proud to see you together and getting along.
- If you are bringing a "guest," such as a date or significant other, do not surprise the other parent or your child.

"Use it or lose it."

Parents are often well-intentioned and assert that they will be flexible and switch weekends or days to accommodate the other's schedule. This is a seemingly generous offer, and yet it really messes up the schedule. If you have an every-other-weekend schedule (A-B-A-B) and you switch, then the other parent will have B-A-A-B. In some schedules, there may be a three-weekend gap in seeing the children. With only very few exceptions, it's more predictable for the children to keep the embedded schedule.

Tips for "Use it or lose it"

- When a parent has business travel or needs personal time, consider sharing a couple of hours during your weekend instead of swapping a whole weekend.
- If a parent wants a weekend or days to accommodate an activity with the children, that's when "vacation days with the children" come in handy. See more on vacation in Chapter 12.

Babysitters

It's very useful to have an understanding regarding who will care for the children when neither parent is available. While each parent is the decision-maker during his/her parenting, this is an area where "no surprises" really avoids conflict. Depending upon the age of the child(ren), parents feel reassured when they work together to compile a mutually approved list of sitters. If none of the approved sitters are available, the parent who hires a sitter should make a courtesy call to the other regarding a new sitter.

- As children age, it's important to be clear when the children are able to be by themselves for a period of time, and when an older sibling is able to care for younger siblings.

Cell Phones and Landlines

When parents go from one home to two homes, cost savings are a critical issue. As part of cutting costs, parents "get rid of the landline and rely on the cell phone only." STOP before you make that choice. Depending upon the age of your children, this can be a safety issue. Now that you are the only adult in the home, the children need to know where the phone is at all times and how to call 911. If the cell phone is in your car or under the couch, there will be no phone for them to use. If a babysitter comes and does not have a cell phone, how will you stay in touch? Generally parents agree that a landline is a safety expense until the youngest child reaches an appropriate age of about 8 or 9.

Health and Safety

Nothing feels better to a child who is ill then a hug and a snuggle from "the other parent." It also reassures the other parent about the child. Typically, the agreement will be clear that when a child is ill, each parent will be able to visit the child in the home of either parent, for a reasonable visit (usually an hour or two) regardless of the parenting schedule, at mutually agreed upon times. And in the heart-wrenching moments that a child is hospitalized, both parties can be at the hospital at any time, regardless of the established parenting schedule. In an emergency, the parent available will make appropriate decisions and contact the other parent as soon as possible.

Relocation: A Big Worry for Parents

Among all of the parenting issues, there are two things that almost always have the most discussion, worry and anxiety. Parents care about how they will stay connected to their children on a *physical* level—how far away will the parents live from each other? And how will they introduce a new relationship into their family life? (See more on relationships in Chapter 13.)

Most every agreement has a section on relocation, providing clarity about the distance that parents can live from one another in order to maintain the established parenting plan. For

> **Better**
> *When discussing how far apart you live, consider miles away from each other, not county designations.*

instance, if there is a 50:50 parenting plan that has two nights per week with each parent and then every other weekend, it would be very problematic if the parents lived 30 or 40 miles from each other. It's just too far to maintain that parenting schedule.

How far apart can you live from each other or the school district to sustain the parenting plan that you have created? It seems intuitive that parenting plans that are more robust—50:50 or close to it—would want a shorter distance between the parties or from the school district. This allows parents to maintain spontaneity, to remain in a shared community of interest, and to avoid long car trips for the children.

Sometimes parents will assume that naming the county they live in will suffice, but that can be many miles apart—and, of course, people can live two miles apart and be in different counties. Most parents are more reassured with a designation in miles, rather than simply stating the county.

The agreements generally say something like this: "In order to maintain their established parenting schedule, the parties agree that until the termination of the children's high school education, neither party will relocate his/her residence more than XX miles from the school district the child attends."

What happens if one parent needs to relocate beyond the stated distance? There are two answers: One if a parent wants to relocate as an individual, and one if a parent wants to relocate with the children.

The first one is much simpler. An individual can move anyplace he/she wants. Generally the party who desires to move outside of the boundary would provide an indicated amount of notice (often 90 days) of his/her intention to move. Then the parties would have that time to make decisions regarding new parenting plans as needed, the children's primary residence if it needs to change, child support adjustments, and transportation issues. The established parenting schedule would continue until these details are arranged. Most parents like to keep the new schedule as close to the original as possible to sustain equivalent time with the children.

Relocating with the children is understandably more complicated. If it is within a reasonably proximity, but will require a change in school, a child's education is a joint decision. Especially if the "not-moving" parent resides in the school district, the merits of changing schools is as important as discussing a new parenting plan.

If the relocation is far away enough to make daily or weekend parenting options problematic then it is a much more complicated discussion. The same issues usually apply, but there is usually a large reluctance for one parent to be a far-away parent. Being 100 miles away changes the way parents interact with their children.

If parents are cooperative and willing, new arrangements often can be worked out. Parents create new parenting plans based on school breaks, holidays, long weekends, and summer vacations. Child support is usually adjusted significantly depending on who remains the primary residential parent. Daily FaceTime or Skype calls are often built into the agreement. Technology is a wonderful means for supporting a long-distance parenting relationship.

What happens when a parent is not willing to support a relocation that takes the children (too) far away?

When one parent is not supportive, parents often resort to escalating legally and hiring attorneys—and potentially using the court system. Generally, when both parents are actively involved in parenting and the children's activities, there is not much that would outweigh the not-moving parent's desire to stay actively involved and close to the children. Issues like job opportunities or advancement, family support, or a new spouse that lives elsewhere or needs to relocate for a job may not be compelling enough to have a court support the move. Parenting rights are sacred. However, a court would take these issues into consideration on a case-by-case basis.

On the other hand, if the not-moving spouse is uninvolved, not financially or emotionally reliable, or has other challenging issues, then relocation may be granted to the moving parent by "the courts." The guidelines used to make custody decisions are referred to as the Best Interest of the Child standards (as we discussed in Chapter 10).

As we discussed previously, here are some of the issues the courts will consider in terms of the best interests of the child:

- Which parent has been the main caregiver/nurturer of the child.
- The parenting skills of each parent, his or her strengths, weaknesses, and ability to provide for the child's special needs, if any.
- The mental and physical health of the parents.
- Whether there has been domestic violence in the family.
- Work schedules and child care plans of each parent.
- The child's relationships with brothers, sisters, and members of the rest of the family.
- What the child wants, depending on the age of the child.
- Each parent's ability to cooperate with the other parent and to encourage a relationship with the other parent.

As a mediator, I have helped many parents resolve the issue of relocation and avoid escalating to the courts, which is an expensive, time-consuming and often contentious circumstance. I have successfully worked with parents who live as far away as Hawaii, Florida, and California. Most parents recognize that staying in proximity of each other (until the children complete high school) and being active co-parents is in the best interests of their children, and outweighs the short term goals of work or a new relationship.

In the next chapter, we will look closely at the issues that will come up as your children cope with your divorce, and strategies for working through these difficult times as a family.

Chapter 12

Creating a Parenting Plan

"The curious paradox is that when I accept myself
just as I am, then I can change."
–Carl Rogers

There are no conversations more poignant or heartfelt than those in which you both discuss how you will take care of your children during and after the divorce.

When your children were born, you imagined parenting with your spouse every day and night. Now your time with them is scheduled in advance and limited, with less spontaneity. The quiet of your home and reduced contact in-between visits is hard to get used to.

I have summarized here what I have learned and read over the last 16 years while helping parents decide how they will stay connected to their children when the family no longer lives together. Though I am not

> **Better**
> *I use the term "Parenting Plan"*
> *rather than the legal term called*
> *the "Custody Agreement."*

a therapist, I have gathered information from professional resources, read books, and attended many workshops on parenting—and I have raised my own children. The best outcomes that I have been part of happened when parents started to build their plan by considering the factors listed below.

A parenting plan is part of the memorandum of understanding (MOU) that states when the children will be with each parent (called "parenting time") and how major decisions will be made (legal custody). It includes many details about the logistics and other aspects that are designed with the children's comfort, happiness, and well being in mind.

I am frequently asked to describe the "best" parenting plan. I always say the same thing. The best plan is the one that eliminates conflict and with which you both are most comfortable.

> **Better**
> *The parenting plan that emerges from your discussions will work for the kids if*
> *it works for both of you. A well-written plan provides children and parents with*
> *predictability and consistency.*

Things to Consider When Creating a Divorce Parenting Plan

- Ages of the children.
- How mature each child is.
- The strength of each child's attachment to a parent or routine.
- How far apart the parents live from each other.
- Child care location.
- Flexibility of each parent.
- How transportation will work.
- How well the parents communicate.
- Where the children's friends and community are located.
- How sustainable the schedule will be.
- Whether the children's sleeping patterns are maintained.
- Whether travel time (by car or other transportation) is reasonable.

Parental behaviors that benefit the children

- Encourage and invite the children to have regular contact with the other parent.
- Keep predictable schedules.
- Transfer the children between residences without arguing or discussing logistics.
- Let the children bring items important to them from one home to the other.
- Follow similar routines for meals, snacks, wakeup time, bedtime, homework, and discipline in each home.
- Encourage and support contact with extended family members.
- Allow the children to participate in family celebrations on both sides.
- Provide advance notice about schedule changes.
- Readily provide travel plans and details.
- Support all of the activities of the children.
- Have regular (at least weekly) communication to discuss and confirm logistics.
- Be kind, gentle, and friendly with the other parent when transitioning from one home to the other. Yes, it may be the last thing you feel like doing, but it matters to the kids.
- During the transition, tell the other parent something wonderful about the kids. "Adam's teacher said he was a real big help today." "Lizzy's coach said she was really doing well." The kids have a good feeling, they see you both loving them, and, of course, all parents like to hear positive stuff about their kids.

Parental behaviors that make life difficult for children during and after divorce

- Questioning the children about the other parent's activities.
- Making promises you don't keep or that are inconsistent with the agreed-upon schedule.
- Discussing logistics when bringing the children to the other parent's residence (called "transitioning"). If it becomes an argument, then the kids hear you fighting (again) and using their names during the disagreement, which they may interpret as anger toward them.
- Discussing money or other child support issues with the children
- Using money as a parenting leverage.
- Asking the children to carry messages, to spy on, or to keep secrets from the other parent.
- Undermining the relationship by putting down or criticizing the other parent with the children or in their hearing.
- Making one parent a "porch parent" who is not allowed in the other parent's home. This behavior is a constant signal to your kids that there is conflict, dislike, and lack of respect for the porch parent.

> **Bitter**
>
> *I have dubbed parents who are not able to go inside the other parent's home "porch parents." It's very hard for children to experience this unfriendly behavior.*

A good parenting plan provides benefits with lasting effects

Preserving the children's healthy and ongoing relationships with both parents has enormous positive impact on everyone involved. It is worth your time and effort to build and maintain a good plan so that your children continue to thrive during and after your divorce.

> **Better**
>
> *Positive transitions leave the children with a strong feeling of being loved, supported, and cared for by both parents. And oddly enough, each parent is also more likely to feel respected. It's a win-win.*

Now that you and your spouse are living in separate places, remaining involved in your children's lives can be more complicated. But it can still be accomplished. These are the top parenting issues in divorce that come up in my mediation sessions with clients.

1. **Parents need a plan:** A parenting plan is not just good for the children, but is also essential for parents. You need to know how to plan your week, taking into account where the kids are. Having no plan causes more conflict and extra calls to the other parent asking what the plan is. (See Chapter 11 for helpful checklists.)

2. **"We'll let the kids decide":** The children don't want to decide the parenting plan, no matter what they say. When asked to choose, they will feel conflicted and worry that they are hurting Mom or Dad. There are good ways to secure their input, but it's the parents' responsibility to create the parenting plan.

> **Better**
> *Ending a marriage changes you from being husband and wife, but you will always be Mom and Dad.*

3. **Parents do flourish:** In most homes, there is an organizer and list-maker for all the things the children need. Trusting the other parent with the daily responsibilities that you have done is hard. How will the kids get dressed, hair combed, homework done, and be well fed? What I have seen in my practice is that parents flourish. They quickly pick up new skills to provide a positive environment for the kids. Often the disciplinarian lightens up; the "play parent" develops more organization and routine. As a result, the kids thrive.

4. **No surprises:** The best co-parenting plan is one without surprises. If the children are the messengers of one parent's new adult relationship or even a big planned trip, the shocked look on Mom or Dad's face will make the children think they have done something wrong or shared a secret. Give the other parent information directly, especially if you think it will be an issue. This is not about privacy, but about the kids feeling safe to share information and knowing that Mom and Dad are still communicating.

5. **Transitions between parents' homes:** A lot of research suggests that younger children can tolerate more transitions between homes and benefit from seeing each parent more frequently. As they get older (starting school), children can tolerate and even prefer longer stretches with each parent.

6. **Parents' proximity to each other:** Nothing causes more conflict and makes kids crankier than long rides between parents, especially in the winter (here in the Northeastern US). Keep a reasonable distance between residences to ease conflict and make spontaneity with your children a possibility.

> **Better**
> *"Touch time" is a scheduled opportunity to see the children when there is a long stretch of time away from one parent.*

7. **Not more than three nights:** The parenting plan lays out how much time and when each child

spends time with each parent. Regardless of those details, most parents want to arrange a meal or quality time of two or three hours with their children after spending three nights apart from them. Building in regular "touch time" is very beneficial.

8. I don't want to go to Mom's/Dad's: It is heartbreaking when kids cling to a parent. It happens with childcare, kindergarten, camp, and school buses. Kids do not like change any more than their parents do. When it comes to maintaining the parenting schedule, this is where parents need a united front. Just like going to school, parents have to set forth an expectation that this is the way it is. With few extreme exceptions, it's best for kids to stick with the schedule. Otherwise the parenting schedule will be based on their protests.

9. Use it or lose it: Parents often imagine that trading weekends or days will be easily accomplished.

> ### Better
> *It's wise to create a schedule and give it at least three months so things can settle into a routine. Offline—not while a child is protesting—Mom and Dad can discuss options and consider alternatives if needed.*

> ### Bitter
> *Yelling or blaming the kids for forgetting things all the time often happens when your own resentment and frustration with the circumstances of your life bubble over. This is an area where kids often report a lot of frustration as well.*

For instance, if you have a social commitment for the Saturday of your parenting weekend, you might ask the other parent to cover the day or weekend. Are you expecting that the other parent will give up their next parenting weekend to you, which can cause considerable disruptions in their plans? Or does it mean they get the kids three weekends in a row? Work it out together in advance to keep expectations clear.

Also, most parents want the "right of first refusal." They want to have the first option to be with the kids before third parties are asked. Providing coverage is different from trading a weekend or day; it's important for both parents to be clear on the agreement surrounding the request.

10. The kids keep forgetting stuff: Here's where parents need an extra dose of patience, and, hopefully, access to the other parent's home. It really is hard to keep track of everything (even in one home). This is also where parents can make a difference in the ease and adjustment of their children going from home to home. It is up to the parents to create a routine that minimizes "forgetting."

11. **The agreement is not your authority:** Too often I hear parents report that they told the kids they (the parent) had to do something "because it's in the agreement." Children need to understand that their parents—not a piece of paper—are the authorities in their lives. Children need to trust that both parents know what's best for them. The best parenting plans work because the plans work well for both parents.

> **Bitter**
>
> *The research is very clear that the number one issue that causes harm to children is conflict between the two people they love the most, their Mom and Dad.*

> **Better**
>
> *Your children need to feel safe sharing with each parent their worries and concerns, and that they can love both their parents without conditions.*

12. **Don't believe everything you hear:** When you hear something from the kids or well-intentioned "friends" that sounds alarming (or even unacceptable), go into Neutral rather than Drive. Make a pact with your ex-spouse that you will both report the concern (without accusation) and ask the other for clarification. Neutral sounds like this: "Johnny reported that he was left alone for two hours yesterday, and I thought I would follow up." This is different from blaming and jumping to conclusions: "Why did you leave Johnny alone for two hours yesterday? What kind of parenting is that?"

More and more, separated and divorced parents are opting to spend as much time with their children as possible. Managing this requires a parenting plan that spells out a clear, specific schedule for children as well as guidelines for each parent's co-parenting responsibilities and role in decision-making.

Parenting Plan Options

In my divorce mediation practice, I've seen several parenting plan outlines that have been very useful to the families involved. A solid, workable plan is worth its weight in gold because it brings peace of mind and reduces stress. You'll find examples of these plans below. These are meant to be potential starting points; you will need to customize your parenting plan to meet your family's unique personality and needs.

A parenting plan states when the children will be with each parent (parenting time). A successful parenting plan includes the details about the logistics and other aspects that are designed with the children's comfort, happiness, and well-being in mind.

That said, the best parenting plan is the one that is workable for Mom and Dad.

Research has shown it's important to remember a few key points when thinking about parenting plans:

- Children at different ages have varying needs and abilities to cope with variations in changing families.
- Equal time with the children may not always be the best solution.
- Consider building in a rotation of one-on-one time with a child and not always have all the children at one time.
- Children's development depends less on whether or not children sleep in two homes than on the quality of the parenting and emotional safety of each home.
- From time to time, the family needs to review the arrangement and adjust as needed.

In each plan below, M=Mom and D=Dad, which indicates in whose home the children will sleep each night.

> **Better**
>
> *It's important to clarify when transitions occur. If everyone is off from work and school, who gets the "day"? Most of the time, it's the parent who wakes up with the kids, and then the schedule transitions at 5 p.m. or in the evening.*

Fifty:Fifty Parenting Plans

The 50:50 parenting plan usually has equal overnights with each parent within a designated time. There are several ways to configure the 50:50 plan. The three listed below are the most frequently used. Fifty:fifty shared parenting works best when parents live within close proximity, up to within about ten miles of each other, and have easy access to the school and bus transportation. Transition time is usually after work, or at 5:00 p.m. Attending extracurricular activities is another way for parents to see their kids.

2:2:3 Parenting Plan

	Mon	Tue	Wed	Thu	Fri	Sat	Sun
Week 1	M	M	D	D	M	M	M
Week 2	D	D	M	M	D	D	D

The 2:2:3 plan works well with younger children (perhaps under age 8). Except for the weekend, neither parent goes more than two nights without seeing the kids. Parents often build in a quality time or meal for the weekend they are not with the kids. I call this "touch time." Agree to set the touch time for the oth-

er parent every Thursday night. While flipping Monday and Tuesday may seem complicated, it generally becomes routine for the kids. Sometimes parents provide a symbol for the children, like a soft alphabet letter "M" or "D" each day, so the kids are clear where they will be.

5:5:2:2 Parenting Plan

	Mon	Tue	Wed	Thu	Fri	Sat	Sun
Week 1	M	M	D	D	M	M	M
Week 2	M	M	D	D	D	D	D

The 5:5:2:2 parenting plan works well with older kids (perhaps nine and older). Each parent has five nights in a row, and parents usually build in at least two quality touch times with the children, arranged in advance of each parent's long stretch of time. Because this plan has consistent weeknights, it allows parents to depend on a specific night to do their own activity.

Alternating Weeks Parenting Plan

	Mon	Tue	Wed	Thu	Fri	Sat	Sun
Week 1	M	M	M	M	M	M	M
Week 2	D	D	D	D	D	D	D

The Alternating Weeks plan works well for older children (teens). Teens like the stability of being in one place, and it minimizes forgetting things and working around hectic teen schedules. Parents still work in some touch time with the kids, usually a weeknight or weekend meal. For others, it's a brief shopping trip to the mall. Sometimes parents spend time with just one of the children, having some one-on-one time for each touch time. Consider having the transition day on Friday night, because it allows for a long weekend to settle the children and avoids transitions from a parent's home. As in all the 50:50 plans, the transition time is around 5:00 p.m.

Non-50:50 Parenting Plans

There are lots of good reasons why 50:50 parenting plans might not work. Sometimes it's best for children to consistently be in one place on school nights. Sometimes parents travel for work or live too far from each other for more frequent transitions. Here are some thoughts about other types of parenting plans.

Every Other Weekend (EOW) Parenting Plan

If children can only be with a parent on the weekends, consider extending the weekend through Sunday night. Even though Sunday night is a school night, it is generally a more relaxed day and school work is complete, and it gives the EOW parent some more quality time.

> **Better**
>
> *It's useful to confirm flexible time with the children on the Sunday before so everyone knows the plan.*

It's also useful to schedule a couple of weeknight dinners if possible. Decide on Sunday night when these will be, so everyone knows the plan.

Split Every Weekend Plan

When children are very young or need to be with one parent during the week, because of breastfeeding or other good reasons, it might be useful to split every weekend Friday night to Saturday night and Saturday night to Sunday night. This way the "other" parent is not waiting two weeks to spend overnights with the children.

- Alternate the Friday and Saturday nights (if you want).
- Agree that if a parent wants to go out of town for the weekend (with or without the kids) that they can have the option of Friday through Sunday.
- On Sundays designate time to see the children during the week for a meal.

Flexible Scheduling Parenting Plan (When one parent's schedule varies a lot)

When one parent travels a lot for business or has alternating day and evening shifts or lots of variations in schedule, there are still ways to create a plan.

For example, if you are following a six-week nursing rotation, you generally know your schedule two to three months in advance. Parents can agree to create the parenting plan every three months, or whatever time period is warranted. If the expectation is to maintain a 50:50 plan, or another schedule, it is clarified on a set cycle. Whatever is scheduled is set and honored (with the usual parenting flexibility as needed). This plan and expectation are documented in the agreement.

A Parenting Plan for Older Children (13-Plus)

For kids this age, parents may say "We'll let the kids choose the plan." What parents do not realize is that **the kids DO NOT want to choose.** The inner conflict they feel calibrating whether they are hurting Mom or Dad by their choice(s) is a heavy burden.

> **Better**
>
> *The literature suggests that for young children (under age three), it's important for each parent to see the children at least every two days. This age is when children bond with parents, and quality time (not necessarily overnights) with both parents is essential.*

One way to have the children's input is what I refer to as a "container." You and your spouse decide together how often the kids will be with each of you in a two-week period. Perhaps you decide that five overnights are with Dad, and at least two of those are weekend nights; the other nine nights would then be with Mom. Now you have created a "container," and within this structure, the older children can choose their own nights. They do not have to be the same nights, but there is often an overlap.

Together, the parents and children determine days that will work for everyone. Within each two-week period, everyone knows the schedule, and no one is wondering or "chasing" a child.

When the schedule is set, it is set. The kids value having input, and the parents value knowing what's happening every night.

> **Bitter**
>
> *When the wishes of grandparents and extended families are also a factor, the holidays can be a challenging time.*

Holidays

Discussing holidays with parents is almost always heart wrenching. Parents recall their own experiences (good and bad), and both parents want to create an oasis of joy for their children. It is a special time for connection and each parent wants to maintain traditions and create a family experience. Of course, even without the overlay of divorce, many people have such high expectations regarding holidays that the result is often stressful and disappointing.

One of the best ways to avoid conflict is to have clarity. When it comes to a holiday, this means creating a schedule so everyone knows the expectations. A schedule not only helps the children, but it also helps you. If you know you are not going to be with the children Christmas morning this year, then you have time to create an alternative option that will take care of yourself.

Scheduled Holidays

Most parents are inclined to make a holiday schedule for at least the major holidays such as Christmas, New Year's Eve, Easter, Thanksgiving, Memorial Day, Labor Day, Fourth of July, and Halloween. There are many other holidays during the year, of course, and parents can be as inclusive as they want. Here are some tips when scheduling holidays:

- Designate when the holiday begins and ends.
- Consider starting all holidays the night before. So, for instance, Memorial Day would start on Sunday night at 5:00 p.m. and end on Tuesday morning, when the regular schedule would resume.

- Starting the night before lets everyone have a leisurely wake-up and avoids another parent transition. This works well on Mother's and Father's Day, too, so if you start the holiday Saturday night, you can wake up with your children on that day.
- Consider if you are going to alternate annually where the children wake up on Christmas and Easter morning, which are priority times for holidays.
- Parents also want to alternate annually the prime times of holidays. For instance, Christmas morning and Thanksgiving afternoon are priorities, so they make sure they alternate the prime time, not just the holiday.
- The general hierarchy of parenting plans is: holidays, vacations, parenting plan. So holidays are sacred, vacations next, and then the parenting plan.
- Remember that holidays trump vacation and the parenting schedule, so if it is not designated as a holiday (Columbus Day, for example), then a parent can take the weekend and Columbus Day as vacation time.
- Interfaith parents need to be specific about important dates on each other's holiday calendar.
- For holidays that are not specifically mentioned in the plan, the regular schedule prevails.

> **Better**
>
> *The holiday calendar and selected vacation days trump the parenting plan.*

Not scheduling holidays

Some parents are not concerned about most holidays and may just clarify two or three of the "big ones." For the rest of the holidays, they are willing to determine the schedule two to three weeks in advance and are confident that they can work out the details. This usually works well when the children are older, and when there is a very cooperative parenting pattern.

Birthdays

Most agreements indicate that the regular schedule prevails regarding where the child wakes up on his/her birthday, but that both parents can see the child for a period of time. This works out more flexibly if the birthday is on a weekend, and can be complicated if it is on a school day. It is a terrific tradition (and gift to your child) if you are able (willing) to all celebrate together—perhaps at a restaurant—on either the birthday or a date close by. The agree-

> **Better**
>
> *Some parents minimize their own birthdays and say they don't matter. Consider that celebrating your birthday is an opportunity to teach children about giving, rather than just receiving.*

ment generally clarifies that both parents can attend the child's "friend" party and that it be scheduled at a mutually convenient time.

Parent's birthday

Parents can also designate their own birthday as a "holiday" and spend the night of or the night before and the majority of the day with their children if that is their preference. Celebrating your birthday with your children is a learning opportunity for them to give rather than always receive.

Helping Your Children Cope With—and Even Enjoy—the December Holiday Season

To say that adults are distracted during the holidays is an understatement, and kids often get lost in the shuffle. For children who are coping with divorce and living in two homes, stress may reach an all-time high during the holiday season. New traditions are getting started, and their parents are beginning to learn how to co-parent.

1. Prepare your children for the logistics of the holiday.

- Talk with your children about how holidays will be handled. Kids depend upon routines. It's important for the children to have a road map about how the holidays will flow.
- Avoid asking the children what their preferences are. This may seem counter-intuitive, but they do not want to be asked to choose between parents.
- Lay out the plan for the holiday and describe who will be there so there are no surprises.
- Determine in advance how the children will transition between homes. This includes who is picking up and dropping off. Also answer the question of whether the dropping-off parent will be welcome to come in and offer holiday greetings (hopefully, yes) to the other family.

2. Reassure the children about your plans when you are not with the children.

- Make sure your children know they have your permission to have fun and enjoy their time with the other parent and family.
- Let them know that, when you are not with them, you will be fine. Describe your holiday plans.
- Create time for your children to speak with the parent not present in a quality way. Technology can help with Skype, FaceTime, and texts and emails with photos.

3. Create calm, not chaos.

- Most people try to create calm, not chaos, during the holidays. It's especially important for children to have calm when they are dealing with the loss of the nuclear family.
- Keep transitions and running from place to place at a minimum. This may not be the year to visit every relative.
- Talk with your children about what is important about the holiday and what might be hard for them.
- Create new traditions with your children that are quieter and more meaningful, such as serving in a soup kitchen or donating gifts as a family.
- Emphasize that things may be different, but that does not mean they are bad.

4. Gift-giving teaches children to nurture.

- Holidays provide a learning opportunity for the joy of giving and nurturing.
- In a positive and supportive manner, help your children select gifts or make gifts for the other parent. This gives children a sense of security and reduces stress.
- Coordinate with the other parent about shared gifts for the children and what you may have in mind about giving them yourself. Do not try to "out-Santa" each other.
- Let your children decide where to play with their gifts and whether they want to take the gift to both households.

5. Share information and events.

- Communicate with the other parent about recitals, holiday events, and religious activities. These are important to your children, and they want both parents to participate.
- Find a way to be together as Mom and Dad at these events; even sit together, if that is possible. That is the best gift of all, if you both can set aside any tension between you.
- Set the tone for family gatherings and be sure that your relatives only say kind and generous things about the other parent. Give your children the gift of love and harmony. The walls really do have ears.

Vacations

Vacation time is a wonderful opportunity to spend relaxed time with your children. Most parents designate that vacation time is reserved for when children are off from school and the parent is off from work.

> ### Better
> *Consider not designating school breaks to one parent or the other. Letting the regular schedule continue during school breaks gives both parents flexibility to schedule vacation time when it's best for everyone.*

Generally, there are two concepts regarding vacations:

- Each parent has a bank account of vacation days annually (perhaps 14 or 21 days/nights), like most employers provide.
- Each parent has "reasonable" time with the children annually.

For both vacation ideas, there is usually a tie-breaker if both parents want the same vacation days. For example, in odd years one parent has priority, and in even years the other does.

Remember that vacation time cannot trump holidays, so unless the other parent agrees, you cannot schedule your vacation on the other parent's holiday.

Vacation Bank Account Concept

Let's say that Linda and Lori agree to each have 14 days a year of vacation time with the children. Then they "cherry pick" time with the kids, choosing three days here or a week there depending upon their schedule. With agreed-upon notice to the other (five or six weeks or longer), Lori says she wants to be with the children for April break from school. Linda might say she wants to extend the Fourth of July week by 5 days.

More about the Bank Account concept:

- You have flexibility of when to take vacations.
- You can be spontaneous if something comes up three days in advance. If the other parent does not have plans, that can be fine, too.
- The five to six weeks' notice or longer is a sort of "guarantee" to have the time.
- Except in unusual circumstances, most parents limit planning vacations to the annual calendar cycle.
- You can limit the number of consecutive nights that children can be on vacation if you want to. (This usually happens when children are young.)

> ### Better
> *Remember, no one is monitoring this plan except you, so you can be flexible and you can ignore the "rules" if you both agree. These concepts are intended to avoid conflict and bring clarity.*

- How you "count" vacation days can be tricky. Generally, if you are on vacation during only your scheduled time (like your five days in a row of the 5:5:2:2 parenting plan) then those days do not "count." But if even one day falls on the other parent's scheduled time, then all of the consecutive days— whether your scheduled time or not—count as vacation. So if Lori was on vacation with the kids for eight nights and two of them were Linda's nights, it would count as eight vacation days. Whatever you choose regarding counting vacation time, it's important to be clear in the agreement.

Vacation Reasonable Time Concept

This is a very flexible and trusting vacation concept. Lori and Linda trust that they will take vacation with the kids for a reasonable time annually and provide reasonable notice. The agreement can indicate that "reasonable" is an approximate amount of vacation days and weeks of notice.

More about the reasonable time concept:

- This works best when both parents have similar annual work vacation options, and financial ability to take vacations.

- It's helpful for parents to designate summer vacation intentions by a certain spring date, like April 30. This allows for camp and child care issues to be organized.

Chapter 13

Divorce and Your Children

*"I've learned that people will forget what you said, people will forget
what you did, but people will never forget how you made them feel."*
–Maya Angelou

Without a doubt, sharing the information with your children that
Mom and Dad are ending their marriage ranks among the hardest
conversations you will ever have.

No matter what the reasons are for ending your marriage, both of you want
your children to be emotionally safe. Among the first sentences expressed by every parent client I have is: "The children are our highest priority."

One of the most important gifts of divorce mediation is its attention to the
whole family. In my practice, my parent clients and I spend a lot of time and
attention on the children. Sometimes, I put small chairs in my office to imagine
that the kids are with us. I almost always invite parents to show digital pictures
or bring a print copy to display during our mediation.

Bitter

If the air in your home is "polluted" by constant loud disagreements or tense silences, everyone is gasping for breath. Creating two homes with "clean" air is a positive outcome.

During my years as a mediator, I
have gathered information that has
become very useful to my clients
with regard to telling the children
about ending the marriage, and coping strategies for what comes next. I
provide speaking points that my clients use as a memory jog. We often
do a brief role-play in preparation for this discussion. When Mom and Dad are on
the same page and prepared, the children are more able to accept and understand
what is happening.

Ending your marriage may be sad, scary, and difficult, but staying in a loveless
or high-conflict marriage is not healthy for any of the family members. **What
causes children the most pain is when their parents have ongoing conflict.**
Ending your marriage is a learning opportunity. There are three very important
lessons for you and your children. I call these the **three-legged stool of life lessons** for you and your children.

Honesty

When discussing the divorce with your children, emphasize that Mom and Dad are being honest with each other and with them. It's honest to say, "This is not what marriage is supposed to look and feel like." With teenagers, you can add, "This is not the marriage that we would wish for you in the future."

Typically, your kids have heard you emphasize honesty for years. So when Mom and Dad model that honesty is important, even when being honest seems difficult and may hurt someone, you as parents are staying consistent with what you say and are modeling what that behavior looks like.

Courage

Another important point to make with your children is, "This is the hardest decision that we have ever made in our lives, but it is the right decision for our family. Everyone needs to be reminded that hard decisions are often the right decisions."

When parents avoid ending a marriage because it is hard and scary, they are showing kids that no decision, inaction, and paralysis are acceptable choices.

Letting your kids know that it takes courage to make a hard decision is an essential lesson that they will rely on throughout their lives. For example, you want them to make the right decisions about drugs, alcohol, sex, and bullying. It's easy for kids to assert that they would never take drugs when they are sitting at your kitchen table. It's when they are confronted with peer pressure and temptation "on the street" that they need to have the courage to make the hard decision of saying no. Your divorce process is an opportunity to "connect the dots" about how important and courageous it is to do the right thing, even when it's hard.

Resiliency (or coping for younger kids)

There will be pain and anger and sadness and confusion and sometimes even relief when children learn that their parents will live separately. These feelings are natural. The children will cycle through their emotions just like you did when you were making the decision to end your marriage. Like you, they will also experience ups and downs during the divorce process.

If you, as the parents, get stuck, your kids will get stuck. No question about it. Your children will follow your attitude and your lead.

No matter what the circumstances were that led you to divorce, how you behave and react to it will affect

Better

You and your spouse have options about how to show your children what it looks like when processing difficult and painful information and emotions. Here are your choices: You can show them dignity and respect, or you can show them shame and blame.

your children. How do you want your children to behave when they "hit a wall" in their lives? Whether it's a bad grade, a party they were not invited to, a job not offered, or a best friend who is no longer a friend, you would want them to behave with dignity and respect. Now you have to show them what that looks like.

Committing, even guaranteeing, that Mom and Dad will show dignity and respect for each other and that the kids will not hear shame and blame is a very strong predictor of a positive adjustment for your children. Protecting them from shame and blame language eliminates their need to take sides or nurture one parent over the other. The key to having resilient children is to show them how to **be better, not bitter.**

> **Better**
>
> *Modeling these three values— honesty, courage and resiliency— throughout your life will help both you and your children through many situations.*

The three-legged stool of divorce (honesty, courage, and resiliency) may be sturdy or wobbly. When you find your stool wobbling, pause and consider which leg is "shorter" and pay attention to make it sturdy again. A sturdy stool with attention to all three legs provides guidance and reassurance to your children. It lets them see this difficult process in the context of a learning opportunity.

Telling Your Children Your Marriage Is Over

One of the hardest parts of divorce is figuring out how to tell your children that their parents are ending their marriage. The way it is handled has as much impact as the news itself.

Over the years of mediating divorces, I have gathered many ideas from books and discussions with my clients on this subject. While I am not a therapist or parent specialist, many professionals I have spoken with endorse the concepts below. Of course, you know your family better than anyone, so use these ideas as a guide and customize them for your family's needs and dynamics.

Share the News Together as a Family

In my opinion, it is essential that Mom and Dad tell the children together and as a family. When one child knows something first, it is a big burden for the child to carry the secret. Also, letting Mom or Dad share the news separately leads to confusion and mixed messages and may sound like one parent is shaming or blaming the other.

- Plan where and when you will share the news and stick to it. Avoid public places and try to find a time when the family might otherwise be together, such as mealtime.

- Parents often ask when a good time to share the news is. When the air in your home is getting polluted (tense), the kids have anxiety. To be respectful and honest, sharing sooner rather than later is important and eases the anxiety. Often it is a relief for the parents as well.
- It is often helpful to have both parents in the home together for a reasonable period of time after telling the children. That way both parents can be available to answer spontaneous questions, and there is time to process the children's reactions.

How to Begin the Discussion

With very little prologue, get the children's attention by saying something like: "We have something we want to share with you."

Almost nothing matters more than preparing beforehand to be able to say the following: "Your Mother (Father) and I **both agree** that we would be a better family if we lived separately, and we are making plans to do that."

There's no question that this is the hardest sentence to say. Yet saying "We both agree" sets the stage for your kids to be reassured that you are still Mom and Dad. One parent may resist the notion of "we both agree" because he/she may not be on the same page about why the marriage is ending. You don't have to agree on "why" the marriage is ending. What is honest and true is that **you agree to live separately,** and that is what you are communicating.

> **Better**
>
> *I encourage clients to rehearse what they are going to say prior to the family meeting. The more prepared you are, the more comfortable you will feel.*

- Imagine in advance the children's reactions. If one child might run from the room, plan how you both will react. Have a shared response to avoid arguing "in the moment."
- Avoid having a child hijack the conversation or try to prevent the family from hearing the news together.
- If they ask whether you are getting a divorce, let them know that "divorce" is a legal term. What matters to the family is that you will be living separately, and that this marriage is over.
- Clarity is reassuring. While parents may think it is kinder to leave the kids with some hope that this is just a trial and you are not sure what will happen, generally that is not useful. A "maybe" message puts kids in limbo. Then they will begin to calibrate your every move and hope and wish that they had some power to influence your decision. Often they end up mad at both of you.

- Reassure the children regarding important details, if you know them. What's going to happen to the house, how are they going to see both parents, and are they staying in the same school are their top three questions. It's OK to say: "We're working on the details. Here's what we know now."

It's Not a Secret

When you tell your kids, you also need to be prepared to tell the wider world of your decision. You need to give them permission to share this decision with anyone. Like you, they need their own support system to process this information. When kids are asked to keep a secret, it may lead to shameful feelings and confusion.

If they are younger, you may ask if they want you to share it with certain parents of their friends. If they are older, they might ask "who else knows" out of fear of being embarrassed that they were not among the first to know.

It's Not Your Fault

Children, especially under the age of 10, often cannot differentiate between their world and the larger world. Younger kids see the world through a lens of magic, wishes, and power. If a dish breaks in the kitchen, they might think they influenced that.

It is quite possible that the children heard their names when you and your spouse were quarreling. Whether your words were about logistics, homework, or babysitting, younger children connect their name with the conflict, and they conclude it must be their fault. Children get a fault "virus" in their "computer"—that is, their mind. A good way to delete the virus is to say repeatedly—for months and even years, if necessary—how much they are loved by both parents.

While older children are generally more capable of understanding that the state of their parents' relationship is separate from their own actions, they also need reassurance.

Follow-Up to the Divorce Discussion

Once you have shared the news, answered most questions, avoided gory details, and have not thrown either parent "under the bus," the children will likely go their separate ways. Consider planning a family activity to occur within 20 to 30 minutes of the end of this conversation. Make sure that no one is isolating themselves. Plan an activity that involves some connection, such as going for ice cream, getting pizza, bowling, ice skating, miniature golf, pumpkin/apple picking, etc. Show your kids by your actions that you are still Mom and Dad. Let the conversation go where the kids take it, without an agenda to further explain your situation.

Avoid "Band-Aid" Answers

When kids follow up with questions, it's hard to hear sadness and grief in their voices, especially after one parent moves out.

Imagine your daughter crying and saying: "I miss Daddy, I want him to put me to bed!" Your first instinct might be to say, "Don't worry, you'll see Daddy tomorrow." While reassurance is a natural response, consider exploring her feelings by saying something else, like: "I'm guessing it's really hard not seeing Daddy every day. What's the hardest part for you?"

> **Better**
>
> Virtually all parents feel better after having this conversation. It gets rid of the "elephant in the room" and reduces the tension in the home.

This is an important moment of empathy that allows her to share more of her feelings and feel that you are connecting with her sadness. She may actually share more of her concerns. Maybe she's worried that Daddy is all alone or has no one to eat dinner with. Whatever she shares, keep building on it, and, as I often alert my clients, let her "bleed" a little. If you rush to put a Band-Aid on her feelings, those worries go inside and become stressful, and perhaps even shameful.

> **Better**
>
> This is when you have to put your pain, grief, and mourning behind you and not in front of the children. You want to make sure that your words are coming through a filter of resiliency, not a filter of pain.

I often ask clients what they think their children understand about why they are living separately. What the parents say to the children may be far different from what the children actually hear and understand.

Imagine that your child is talking to his/her best friend about the divorce. What would you hear? Often it is something like: "My Mom and Dad don't live together anymore because they fought all the time. They say everything will be OK, but it sure feels awful now."

Helping your children through the transition of living separately takes planning. It may take what feels like an Academy Award-winning performance by the parents to discuss plans with the kids.

Gratitude for the Parent Leaving the House

This is an essential and often overlooked part of separating. In order to live separately (which is now a shared goal no matter what the backstory is), some one has to leave the house.

Let's imagine it's Dad who moved out. It is very important to explain that Dad is leaving the house because you *both* decided it would be the best way to live sep-

> **Better**
>
> *Emphasize that you will always be Mom and Dad even if you are not husband and wife.*

arately. You want to show gratefulness and to have the kids appreciate how hard it is for him that he was willing to leave.

Repeat, repeat, repeat this message over the next weeks and months, especially when the kids miss Dad. This avoids making Dad feel marginalized and teaches compassion and empathy to the children. It is a very important learning opportunity about hard decisions and courage.

More about empathy

If you have not seen the movie *Inside Out*, I highly recommend it. It's not just for kids. In fact, it's probably too complicated for kids under age 10, but it sure packs a powerful message for adults.

Inside Out is an animated Disney movie that brilliantly crafts a balance between joy and sadness. The movie features a girl, Riley, and personifies five emotions in her head. With amazing creativity, the movie illustrates the tumult and conflicting emotions caused by the stresses of growing up. In Riley's case, her family moves from the Midwest to San Francisco, and it is a very challenging adjustment.

The overriding message of the movie is that there is a place for children's sadness in life. While "Joy" tries valiantly to cancel out "Sadness" and jolly Riley back to herself, in the end, Joy and Sadness realize that Riley needs both of them so she can grow through her challenges.

It seems that the same message is essential for children who are experiencing the separation of their parents. Many parents wonder, "How will I know when or if my children need professional counseling in dealing with sadness?" The road of life is filled with challenges, as we all know. Having a sounding board or a professional companion along the way is a gift to yourself and your children. Creating a counseling relationship that feels safe and accessible lets your children learn that they can use lots of resources to help themselves along the way of life.

A good way of encouraging these relationships is to discuss and be honest about how useful therapy has been to you during your own challenging times. Everything needs a tune-up occasionally; cars, household furnaces, even our trusted computers all need attention at times. People often need the same thing.

Some of the most valuable outcomes of therapy are:

- **A virus in your computer:** Difficult times can trigger previous challenges or feelings in a child. A therapist can help "delete" the connection and avoid letting it warp future experiences.

- **Pay me now or pay me later:** When things remain unresolved, future challenges (and there are always challenges) can feel two or three times more painful than necessary.
- **Shortcut to happiness:** Seeing a therapist for six-to-twelve months now may preclude a lifetime of shadowy feelings that keep cropping up.
- **Message to the kids:** Creating a therapy opportunity is a subtle message to your children that you love them and care about their well-being.

Sometimes we avoid check-ups and live with minor aches and pains. Sometimes it's hard to tell when something just needs time to heal or needs an intervention. As a parent, you have to calibrate the difference between sad and adjusting, and sad and really struggling. It's the difference between your child's 100-degree temperature when you might wait, or a 104-degree temperature when you are definitely calling the doctor.

Here are some guidelines to let you know when your child may need therapy:

- Has your child **changed his/her behavior?** For example, your quiet child becomes a chatterbox or your social child becomes withdrawn. A change in behavior may be a reaction to trauma.
- Are they **increasingly critical of their friends or siblings?** This may be a sign they do not think very well of themselves.
- Are the kids **hanging around with different kids?** A child's choice of friends often reflects their self-image.
- When kids **lash out, cry more, or try to push you away,** this can be a sign that they are looking for reassurance and need help accepting it.
- **Persistent physical complaints** may include trouble sleeping or gaining or losing weight with no medical basis.
- The onset of **lying or phobias or becoming accident-prone** is a cry for attention.
- You may see **a change in school interest or performance,** and your child wanting to do more (or less) than the usual extracurricular activities.
- Your child may show **much more curiosity and questioning about your activities,** where you are and what you are doing.
- Teachers and friends are gently **expressing concern.**
- The **child's general hygiene changes,** such as dramatically increased or decreased hand or hair washing, nail biting, or a change in care of clothes.

While getting therapy is important, the type of therapy matters also. Younger children, perhaps up to first or second grade and certainly preschoolers, might respond best to art, music, or play therapy that allows them to express themselves indirectly.

Older children can generally handle more cognitive approaches; often peer sessions are very useful. Many school districts offer in-school group sessions that might be a very good transition.

A highly recommended book to help guide parents is *Straight Talk About Your Child's Mental Health* by Stephen Faraone. As noted on the book's cover: "Parents reach for dog-eared copies of Dr. Spock when their child has a rash or the flu, but when 'moodiness' lingers or worrisome behavior problems grow, they have nowhere to turn for answers or reassurance. Now, in this compassionate resource, prominent Harvard researcher Dr. Stephen V. Faraone gives parents the tools they need to look clearly at how a child is feeling, thinking, and behaving and make wise decisions about when to call for professional help."

Some Dos and Don'ts for Children

What to <u>DO</u> to Help Your Children After the Divorce

- Reassure them often that they are not to blame for your breakup.
- Reassure them often that they are loved by both parents.
- Reassure them often that they will be taken care of.
- Answer their questions honestly and with respect for their feelings and concerns.
- Be on time when picking them up from or taking them to the other parent.
- Be responsible and prompt with child support payments.
- Establish two homes where the children feel safe and welcome.
- Continue to maintain a cooperative and workable parenting plan.
- Actively encourage them to have a loving relationship with the other parent.
- Ask other family members (grandparents, aunts, uncles, etc.) to follow these rules.

What <u>NOT TO DO</u> Concerning the Children After the Divorce

- Argue with your ex-spouse in front of your children.
- Discuss parenting issues with your ex-spouse in front of your children.
- Pump your children for information or use them as messengers.
- Ask your children to keep secrets.
- Speak negatively about the other parent in front of your children.
- Discourage their communications with the other parent while they are with you.
- Put your children in the middle or make them choose sides.
- Discuss child support issues with your children.
- Make unilateral decisions if you have shared or joint custody.

During mediation with clients who have children, I often point to an empty chair and say, "Let's imagine that your children are sitting right here and listening to every word."

Divorce presents many moments when the promises you made to your children that you will always protect them are put to the test. Often parents think about physical safety, but this test is about **emotional safety,** and it's just as important. This is the time to put your pain and justifications behind the children, not in front of them, and not have every word they hear filtered through your pain.

The following Bill of Rights for Children is a road map for adult behavior that will help your children, because it shows you respect their challenges. Many parents have posted the list right on the refrigerator. Invite your children to use the Bill of Rights to remind you and your spouse to back off or rethink your behavior. This list can be a safe way for the children to communicate difficult feelings during a very upsetting and unsettling period for them.

THE CHILDREN'S BILL OF RIGHTS WHEN PARENTS DIVORCE

- The right not to be asked to "choose sides" between their parents.
- The right not to be told the details of the legal proceedings going on between their parents.
- The right not to be told "bad things" about the other parent's personality or character.
- The right to privacy when talking to either parent on the telephone.
- The right not to be cross-examined by one parent after spending time with the other parent.
- The right not to be asked to be a messenger from one parent to the other.
- The right not to be asked by one parent to tell the other parent untruths.
- The right not to be used as a confidant regarding adult matters.
- The right to express feelings, whatever those feelings may be.
- The right to choose not to express certain feelings
- The right to be protected from parental "warfare."
- The right not to be made to feel guilty for loving both parents.

Source: *New York State Unified Court System-Tompkins County Courts. A similar version was drafted by Justice James Brands of Duchess County Family Court, New York, and Justice Ira Harkavy of Supreme Court, Kings County, New York.*

Mixing a New Romance with the Kids

Among the biggest concerns that parents have regarding their children is what happens when they are not with them. For many parents, ending a marriage and starting a formal parenting plan is the first time they have been away from their children. It is heart-wrenching, and it takes time to adjust.

> **Better**
>
> *It's useful to explore worries and concerns about new relationships and create expectations in a mediation session.*

Add the complication that Mom or Dad has a new person in his or her life, and the stakes quadruple. Images of how this new person might look like a new Mom or Dad can cause conflict and lead to competition.

If parents don't raise this issue, I always do. Clarity and the opportunity to create a pathway that will work for the children are essential.

After exploring options, most parents tend to agree on the following ground rules regarding significant others.

Waiting period. The literature is pretty clear, and most parents agree that for at least 9-12 months, from the time parents live separately, time spent with each parent should not include romantic partners. This is a time when children are adjusting to one-on-ones with parents, and that takes time. It is also a time of adjustment for each parent. The buffer of waiting helps everyone. Plan your relationship time for nights when the kids are with the other parent. Even after the children meet the new person, plan on reserving plenty of alone time with the children.

> **Bitter**
>
> *Children calibrate your facial expressions, and if they think you are upset, they will not share information with you, so it's best to be prepared and avoid surprises.*

"Are you dating?" It's helpful if both parents have a similar answer. Let each other know if the children have made this inquiry. One answer that works well is to indicate that you both are meeting new people and making new friends, both male and female. If you are dating someone, it's best to be truthful but also nonchalant.

Chances are someone may innocently report to your children that they saw you with someone, and if they have not heard that from you, your credibility is in question. You can say that you are just getting to know someone, and when or if it becomes appropriate you'll include the children.

No surprises. When you are ready to introduce your children to a potential new partner, make sure you alert your ex-spouse first. If your children announce: "I just met John/Nancy," and you are not prepared, your face will show your feelings and your children may be caught in the middle.

Introducing a new potential partner to the children

There is a fine balance regarding when to introduce children to a new partner. Too soon and you risk a "revolving door" of partners. Too late, and you'll miss the opportunity to learn how your potential partner interacts with your children. Consider dating as a laboratory, where you are figuring out what works and what does not. When the time is right, you will include the children, but you will still be willing to learn positive and negative things about this potential partner. It's not uncommon for children to feel competitive or jealous of your time. It's not realistic to expect the children to like your new partner just because you do. Go slowly and give your children time to adjust.

Some parents want to insist they meet the other person before kids are involved. It's a natural feeling to want to know who is going to interact with your children. It's hard to accept that you have little influence over this issue, so while it is sometimes difficult, it's a time when you need to trust the other parent's judgment. Ask yourself, "What will the outcome be if we meet?" You're not likely to get the measure of a person at one meeting, and if you have a negative conclusion, what are your options? If meeting works for all parties, that's fine, but avoid making it conditional.

Consider having an understanding that you and your ex-spouse will share pertinent information as a courtesy. Avoid a judgmental inquisition, and be grateful that you have been included and reassured. The main reason to share is that your children will know you have chatted and that you are supportive of each other as you meet new partners.

Reassure each other that you are sensitive to the children's needs and anxieties and that you intend to make sure the children have developed a sense of friendship and trust with the new person before they are involved in overnights.

When traveling together, consider separate rooms for each gender. It can be embarrassing and stressful to share a bedroom with Mom or Dad and a new partner.

Bitter

Be sure to prepare your children in advance for overnight guests, and alert the other parent. Avoid having surprise guests in the kitchen in the morning.

Bitter

When your new love uses the relationship with your ex-spouse as a litmus test for "love," you might consider that as a red flag. Look closely at the relationship and consider "running for the hills."

Over the years I have seen a pattern that almost always causes conflict. It's when your new partner tries to come between you and your ex-spouse by setting up rules about when you can see your ex-spouse, or that the new partner must be present at all events such as birthdays and your children's extracurricular events.

This kind of insecurity causes serious difficulty in co-parenting, and often expands into relationship trust issues. The kids are caught in the middle and have to make choices that cause stress and anxiety. With few exceptions, the best gift you can give your children is ease and respect regarding the partners of your ex-spouse. Be inclusive at parties and holidays and extra-curricular activities. Be gracious and take the high road of welcoming and forging a relationship. It's good for you, and it is essential for the kids.

Better

The biggest gift you can give your children is permission to have fun and love the other parent and, by extension, the parent's partner.

Being supportive and accepting when it might actually be difficult is a way of protecting your children. Protection is not only physical; it is emotional as well. This is a huge opportunity to help your children emotionally.

The saying "It takes a village to raise a child" includes the notion that the more people who love and support your kids, the better off they will be. Reassure your children that they do not need to "protect" you or hide their feelings from you, and that you are pleased that the children feel comfortable with a new person and that the other parent is happy.

Parental Alienation: Poisoning the Well

When a divorce brings lots of conflict to the surface between parents, this constant state of conflict can create serious issues for the children. In some cases, this results in children feeling that they must choose a side, because loving one parent means that the children are betraying the other one. Children may become very attached to one parent and disdainful—or even harbor what appears to be hatred—of the other one. The children may parrot the hostile things they hear one parent say about the other, taking those issues to heart as if the children were as deeply affected by them as the parent, and this may result in parental alienation.

Bitter

In legal terms, when one parent fosters a negative relationship with the other parent, it is called parental alienation.

What does this mean for the children's relationship with the alienated parent? The children may seek to have no relationship with that parent at all. They may be reluctant to the point of meltdown at the idea of spending time with that parent, while becoming involved in the favored parent's life at an extreme level.

The children also may make some very disturbing claims about the alienated parent that cannot be ignored. Perhaps the children say that this parent is overly strict or even abusive, while such allegations have never come up before.

In some cases, this may give the favored parent just what he or she required to drive a wedge between the alienated parent and the rest of the family. As the relationship between parents is already hostile, this parent may see the opportunity to poison the well, embracing the children's fear and anger and feeding it with his or her own.

The children's safety is paramount, of course, so allegations of abuse must be investigated, and the court may become involved in this. If true abuse is not indicated, however, the parents may have to take steps—together—to fix the fractured family unit enough to restore some kind of normal relationship between parent and children. This may involve listening carefully to the children to determine what the real problem is, reducing or eliminating the public displays of hostility between the parents, and even family counseling. The anger, fear, tantrums, and other expressions of the children's seeming hatred of one parent may mask anxiety about the entire divorce proceeding—an issue the family can address together whether or not they all live in the same house.

Sometimes the matter gets elevated to a change in custody arrangements, which must be recognized by the court.

More and more judges acknowledge the reality or concept of parental alienation, but some do not. Parental alienation is very hard to prove, and taking the case to court could backfire on a spouse who may just want the other spouse out of his/her life. Instead of getting a court order that keeps the alienated parent away from the children, the parents may come up against a skeptical judge who doesn't buy the concept of parental alienation, much less the need to change the custody agreement. Because of the adversarial process, children may need to maintain the status quo and continue in a very high-conflict situation.

Better

Because mediators are trained professionals who can provide an environment to clarify issues and resolve conflict, parents may want to try mediation before commencing a court battle.

If this is the case, the rejected parent may have to back off voluntarily for a period of time while the family gets counseling or seeks other solutions. Some relationships are so damaged by divorce that the children see one parent as the enemy until they are old enough to understand what really happened between Mom and Dad. It's a sad story, but this is the way very contentious divorces sometimes end up.

PART 5
The Emotional Divorce

Chapter 14

You're Divorced. Now What?

"Life goes by too quickly, so laugh, love, and try new things. Forgive.
Forget and don't hold grudges. Choose to be happy."
−Unknown

Let's imagine that you have finally ended your marriage. You have a signed divorce decree, and you are settling into your new independent life. The mediated agreement you created seems fair and workable, and the children are adjusting.

Before you get too comfortable, there are some additional issues to which you should pay attention. Unlike the rules within your agreement, these items are optional but just as important. I asked my colleague David B. Cook, an estate attorney in private practice in Webster, New York, to share his expertise about long-term planning in the form of wills, powers of attorney, and health care proxies.

Estate Planning

You have an estate. Just about everyone does. An estate is everything you own: your car, home, other real estate, checking and savings accounts, investments, life insurance, furniture, personal possessions, and so on. No matter how large or how modest, everyone has an estate and something else in common: You can't take it with you when you die.

When that happens—and it is a "when," not an "if"—you probably want to control how those things are given to the people or organizations you care most about. To ensure your wishes are carried out, you need to provide written instructions stating whom you want to receive something of yours, what you want them to receive, and when they are to receive it.

For example, if you have children, they cannot receive money directly from your estate (even if they are a named beneficiary) until they reach age 18. Even then, most parents would prefer some oversight of the funds until the children are older, perhaps out of college.

And, of course, you want your estate to be distributed with the least amount paid in taxes, legal fees, and court costs. It is wise to consult an attorney who specializes in estate planning to navigate your options.

The bottom line is, if you don't have a written plan for what happens after you pass away, then your state has its own long, drawn-out plan for you in probate court. But you—and your heirs—probably won't like it.

Your Estate Following Divorce

When you are married, what happens after you pass away is often much simpler. Your estate would generally pass to your spouse.

While some items have beneficiaries, such as retirement accounts or invest-ment assets, many do not. It is especially important to take care of these items.

> **Bitter**
>
> *Now that you are divorced and no longer have a spouse, you need to change the way you think about yourself, your life, and your estate.*

- **Your house.** The most important asset that does not have a beneficiary is usually your house. When you are without a spouse and own a house solely in your name, it is essential that you direct what is to be done with it when you are gone. If it is sold, how the equity in the property is to be handled should also be specified.
- **Your retirement funds.** It is very important to update the beneficiary on your retirement funds to align with your intentions. Many times this is forgotten; your ex-spouse remains on the forms and may receive the funds in the future. A popular option is to make "my estate" the beneficiary so the funds will go into your estate. Then these funds can be managed and preserved for your children according to the terms of your will.
- **Life insurance.** As part of a divorce in which children are involved, often the divorce agreement specifies that one or both spouses have a minimum amount of life insurance for which the ex-spouse is the beneficiary. The surviving parent then has direct access to funds to maintain the children's life style.
- **The rest.** You may have considerable life insurance funds in excess of the minimum obligation in the agreement. You can leave the balance to your estate by naming a certain percentage to go to your estate.

Last Will and Testament

There is an expression regarding wills: Where there's a will, there's a way; but no will, no way.

Your estate plan begins with a will. A will is a directive that records your in-tentions regarding your assets and establishes your plans for your children's care when you pass away. It is a way to collect all of your assets under one "roof," called your estate. It provides the opportunity to name a trusted person, called an executor, to manage your estate.

Almost every divorce agreement suggests, but does not require, that you each update or create your wills. If you had a will when you were married, then you

Bitter

You may have had a will when you were married, but it is no longer valid after your divorce is final.

need to modify it. If you didn't have one, you should create one as soon as possible. In either case, your will's date should be after your divorce is final.

You may have had a will when you were married, but it is no longer legal after your divorce is final.

Unless you have a will, the probate process figures out who will get the house and other assets.

Probate is the legal process proving the validity in court of an individual's Last Will and Testament. Having a will provides your instructions, but it does not avoid probate, and probate can be complicated, time-consuming, and expensive. The ins and outs of probate are complex. Again, please consult an estate planning attorney about your particular circumstances.

Power of Attorney (POA)

A power of attorney (POA) is a document that transfers your financial and legal power to another person when you are not capable of managing your finances or other legal matters. The POA gives specific and limited power to another person when you are incapacitated through medical issues or unavailable due to other reasons, such as when you are out of the country. It is prudent to have a back-up person to manage your bills, mortgage, and other obligations when you are not able.

Your spouse was the natural back-up. He or she usually had access to your joint bank accounts, both in-person, via check, or using online banking. After divorce, unless you make specific arrangements, bills may not get paid, and you will have a complicated mess to sort out when you are able to manage your finances again.

A POA can be drafted by an attorney at the same time as your will. It needs to be signed and witnessed in a very specific manner, so obtaining competent advice is prudent. The updated POA should be dated after your divorce.

Also note that your POA expires when you die. At that point, the executor of your will manages your affairs until your estate is closed. If you purchase a POA online, be sure it is valid in your state.

Health Care Proxy

As with your financial and legal affairs, you need to have a medical back-up plan called a health care proxy. When you were married, if you did not have a health care proxy, your spouse had authority to make medical decisions on your behalf. Who will make those decisions now?

After divorce, it is important to complete a health care proxy form in which you designate someone to make decisions and to honor the directions that you included in it. Your physician or attorney may provide one, or you can purchase one online. If you do purchase one online, be sure it is valid in New York State (or your state).

Note that proxies are often required prior to an in-hospital stay. Be sure all of your physicians have a copy as well as the people you named in your proxy. If you completed one on your own, it's also a good idea to give your attorney and other trusted people in your life a copy.

Have a Plan, Have Peace of Mind

There is an expression that says, "Man makes plans and God laughs." Preparing for the unexpected is always important, but often overlooked. Now that you are on your own, it is wise and thoughtful to take care of details that will make the unexpected a lot easier on those you care about.

When to Change Your Last Name

Depending on where you live, your divorce decree may contain a paragraph that gives the wife the right to return to her birth name, to a name from a previous marriage, or to use another name as she chooses. The wife can take this decree to the county clerk or other office (this varies from one jurisdiction to the next) to prove that she is no longer married and is eligible for a name change. The government office will then issue documents in the new or former name.

The wife can begin to use a different name whenever she wishes—and she is not required to change her name at all. Many women prefer to retain their married name while the children are in school, to avoid confusion or to keep from broadcasting that they are now divorced.

Chapter 15

Time to Heal

"To live in this world you must be able to do three things: To love what is mortal, To hold it against your bones knowing your own life depends on it, And, when the time comes to let it go, to let it go."
–Mary Oliver

Ask twenty divorced people about what helped them find their resiliency and healing after a divorce, and you'll probably get twenty-five answers. Over the years that I have helped clients reach a financial and practical agreement, I have also helped many clients through the emotional whitewater of divorce. Divorce is such a drastic change that my clients often are overwhelmed with the work, emotions, and challenges it brings. The process outlined below has helped many people get grounded, regain their balance, and begin healing, both during and after divorce.

To start with, give yourself permission to heal. This may mean being willing to set aside anger or bitterness. It could mean letting yourself start to believe that happiness can be yours again.

Gather a few simple materials. Start with some paper and a pen or pencil. Consider getting a separate notebook, as plain or fancy as you like, to gather and keep your thoughts together. This is your private journal, a way to focus on the opportunity for healing. Even a small shift of focus is very useful.

Set aside five minutes each day for writing. It's not a lot to ask of yourself because you are definitely worth the time. It doesn't have to be the same time every day. Add this activity to your to-do list, or set a reminder alarm on your smartphone to stop what you're doing and write.

Some ideas for possible times and places you can find to be alone:
- Before you get out of bed in the morning.
- When you drink your first cup of coffee in the morning.
- During a coffee break at work.
- During your lunch break.
- Right after the kids go to bed.
- When you climb into bed at night.

On the first day during the five-minute period you set aside, choose and read any one of the tips below. Write about how you relate to that tip. What are your thoughts? Anything that comes up is fine, even if what you write about is that you don't know what to write about. Be honest with yourself. Don't censor or edit; just keep the pen or pencil moving. If you have time and want to keep writing after the five minutes is up, by all means, keep going.

For the next nine days, work your way through the rest of the list, writing about each tip. After ten days, start over and write about the first tip again—and after another ten days, start over again with the first tip. In one month, you will have a very useful guidebook about which of these tips you are willing to incorporate into your healing.

Top Ten Things to Do During Divorce

Tips for taking care of yourself during divorce come to me from many sources. I have compiled the ones my clients find the most effective in the Top 10 list below.

1. **Take care of yourself physically.** Find a way to release stress, move your body, and clear out your mind. Yoga, exercise, and meditation are great tools.
2. **"Fair" is a matter of perspective.** What seems fair to you may not seem fair to your spouse or your children. Fair is a moving target.
3. **Wishing things or people were not the way they are is a tremendous waste of time and energy.** Instead, focus on changing what you can change.
4. **For things to change, first you must change.** That means doing something differently, especially if you cling to the idea that what you believe is the only way for things to get resolved.
5. **Your life and your divorce are different from your neighbor's, your friend's, and your brother's life and divorce.** What worked for them may or may not work for you. The decisions you are making are not subject to a "vote" from other people. Take their well-meaning advice as information only.
6. **When you forgive someone else, you are helping yourself more than you are helping him or her.** There's an old saying that is credited to the actor Malachy McCourt: "Resentment is like taking poison and waiting for the other person to die."
7. **Accept and work through your feelings.** Your emotions are your body's way of moving energy. The more you push emotions away, the more powerful and overwhelming they become. Acceptance does not mean you agree with what happened, it just means you stop the struggle with your feelings.

8. **The only thing we can really count on is change.** When things are the way you want them, be grateful, because they are going to change. When things are not the way you want them, be grateful that they will also change.
9. **Treat yourself kindly and accept kindness from others.** Allow others to do for you what you would do for them if they needed it.
10. **The right thing to do is the right thing to do,** regardless of how hard it seems or how anyone else is acting.

You will be amazed how much better you will feel after only 30 days of focused and honest journaling, and only five minutes a day at that. You may find yourself more able to:

- **Clarify your thoughts and feelings.** Do you ever seem all jumbled up inside, unsure of what you want or feel? Taking a few minutes to jot down your thoughts and emotions (no editing!) will quickly get you in touch with your internal world.
- **Know yourself better.** By writing routinely you will get to know what makes you feel happy and confident. You will also become clear about situations and people who are toxic for you—important information for your emotional well-being.
- **Reduce stress.** Writing about anger, sadness, and other painful emotions helps to release the intensity of these feelings. By doing so you will feel calmer and better able to stay in the present.
- **Solve problems more effectively.** Typically we problem solve from a left-brained, analytical perspective. But sometimes the answer can only be found by engaging right-brained creativity and intuition. Writing unlocks these other capabilities, and affords the opportunity for unexpected solutions to seemingly unsolvable problems.
- **Resolve disagreements with others.** Writing about misunderstandings rather than stewing over them will help you to understand another's point of view. You just may come up with a sensible resolution to the conflict.

The Ebb and Flow of the Seasons

Every part of the first year after your divorce will have new and special meaning. It will be the first time you face holidays and important annual events without your spouse, but each of these moments can signal an opportunity for positive change and renewal. Let's take a look at a few of these opportunities.

The start of a new year is a catalyst for many people who want to resolve to do things differently. We've all tried to set goals to make improvements. We are

going to exercise more, eat differently, stop spending frivolously; the list
goes on and on. Often the list is fueled
with negative energy, a desperate need
to change in order to "fix" all that is
"wrong" with you. The challenge is that
punishing messages such as "I am [pick
one] too fat, too lazy, too inconsiderate"
are not inspiring or motivational.

> **Better**
>
> *Carl Rogers said "The curious*
> *paradox is that when I accept myself*
> *just as I am, then I can change."*
> *Gently accepting how you are today*
> *will help you build and sustain the*
> *change you envision.*

The key to making and keeping new resolutions is to **first make a list of all
we like and honor about ourselves.** The paradox is that before we invest in the
future, we have to accept the present.

You Are What You Think

Lasting post-divorce resolutions and goals regarding the children, ex-spouse,
friends, dating, and the like need to start with an acceptance of today and a moti-
vating reason to change. That means adjusting the way you think about yourself.
One way to do that is to be aware of each "Harsh Thought" you have and replace
it with an "Accepting Thought."

Here are seven examples of typical, damaging, old thoughts and their replace-
ment, positive, new thoughts about yourself and your divorce that can support
your resolutions.

Harsh Thought: I am a failure because my marriage ended.

Accepting Thought: The end of my marriage freed me to find my
independence and courage. I look forward to discovering who I can be in this
next chapter of my life.

Harsh Thought: I am jealous of my ex's relationship to the children. It feels like
a win-lose competition, and I feel as if I'm losing.

Accepting Thought: My kids need a safe and wonderful relationship with
their other parent. I will support their relationship by saying only positive
things about my ex.

Harsh Thought: No one will ever want to love or be with me again. My
romantic life is over.

Accepting Thought: I am an interesting and lovable person. A broken heart
is an open heart. I will keep my heart open to the possibilities of loving again.

Harsh Thought: The kids are never going to be happy. They are angry and
upset all the time.

Accepting Thought: This is a difficult time for everyone. I will focus on the children and create a calm and attentive environment. I will set the tone of coping and resiliency. It will start with me.

Harsh Thought: I have no time to exercise, eat healthy, or get enough sleep. Single parenting is so exhausting.

Accepting Thought: Yes, my life is exhausting. I will feel better if I do one thing for myself for 20 minutes everyday. I will find 20 minutes to call my own. I can take a bath or a walk, meditate, work out to an exercise video, write in a journal, or choose another soothing, restoring activity.

Harsh Thought: It is so hard for me to stay within my budget. I just can't seem to control the spending.

Accepting Thought: Managing money is complicated. I will find ways to help myself create and manage a budget by reading books (available at the library for free) and doing Internet research.

Harsh Thought: I never imagined that my life would be this difficult and challenging. Sometimes it feels overwhelming.

Accepting Thought: Yes, life is challenging. Whether married or single, raising kids and working can feel overwhelming. I will start a gratitude journal. Every single day for 365 days, I will write down one new thing I am grateful for. That will keep me balanced and centered.

Most people want to find ways to sustain changes that they think will make them happier. You may think, "If I were thinner, healthier, richer or in love, then I would be happy." The core reason for New Year's resolutions in general is the pursuit of happiness. According to Deepak Chopra, in his book, *What Are You Hungry For?:The Chopra Solution to Permanent Weight Loss, Well-Being, and Lightness of Soul*, permanent happiness is an illusion. What we should aim for is a state of steady contentment. Acceptance means not struggling or resisting, and it especially means not speaking harshly to yourself.

> **Better**
>
> *Happiness and unhappiness happen to us all. Being happy all the time is not the goal. It's accepting where you are in the present moment.*

The New Year's resolution I recommend for you—and always set for myself—is to speak gently and kindly to yourself, regardless of the circumstances. Speak to yourself as if you were supporting a beloved friend or young child going through a difficult time. Just as it does for them, supporting yourself opens the door for the positive changes coming your way in the New Year.

Summer Solstice and Healing

Just about halfway through the year, summer solstice is the longest day of light and has become the symbol of renewal and new beginnings. It is nature's way of telling us that the long, dark days of winter do end. This timeless, natural cycle is an enduring message of which we often need to be reminded.

Ending a marriage is among life's darkest journeys. There is emotional and financial havoc. Other people distract our thoughts and hijack our feelings. Children, parents, other family, and friends are also experiencing dark moments about your divorce. It's not only hard to see the light, but carrying it to others feels almost impossible. But nature is a good teacher. The shortest, darkest day in December is followed every day by adding just a few minutes of daylight. By June, there are 15 hours of daylight rather than only eight in December. It happens gradually but steadily, and so it is with healing.

There are several ways to help your healing during divorce that act like sunlamps in the middle of the winter. Unlike sunlamps, this inner healing requires only your willingness to choose healing and go forward. Here are some tips that will move you into the sunlight and longer and happier days.

Tip 1: Self-Talk

Most people agree that we are our own harshest judge. We rarely speak to others as we speak to ourselves. If we trip, we call ourselves "clumsy." If we forget to pick up milk at the store, we mutter about being "stupid." While going through a divorce, we can be very hard on ourselves.

Divorce is a fragile, highly emotional time; you need to *be your own best friend.* There is a difference between self-reflection and accountability versus harsh self-talk. You may want to reflect on your actions and gently soothe yourself by admitting you are scared or grieving or angry. These are not excuses, but feelings. Feelings are not right or wrong; they just are.

Speak to yourself as you would to your child sobbing about a friend who hurt her. Think about how you support your best friend who lost a job and needs empathy, not criticism. Most people do not have skills to sit with someone else's pain, and even less with our own. Rather, we are taught to comfort others, fix their problems, or insist they get over it.

I often suggest to clients to get and nurture a plant. Water it, clip it, and care for it as a symbolic reminder to pause and take care of yourself. If you can interrupt the critical voice, even a couple of times a day, and replace it with understanding and gentle soothing, you will move out of the darkness into lighter days.

Tip 2: Release Resentment

Resentments are toxic and not only distort your thinking, but they can also affect your health. They show up in the body as a bad feeling in the pit of your stomach, clenched teeth, or shoulder pain. They can even make it hard to breathe. As your spouse (or ex-spouse) is living the life of his/her choice, your resentments simmer and even boil over. Your resentment will not influence someone else's behavior; it will only harm you.

> **Better**
>
> Mark Nepo said "You do not have to hold on to your pain to hold on to your truth." Focus on reframing depleting thoughts to replenishing thoughts and thriving.

Tip 3: Forgiveness

Many people don't realize that when you forgive someone else, you are helping yourself more than you are helping them. Forgiveness is not reconciliation, forgetting, or agreeing with someone else's actions. Forgiveness is a shift away from revenge and harmful wishes toward the person who wronged you.

One outstanding resource on forgiveness is *Mediating Dangerously: The Frontiers of Conflict Resolution* by Kenneth Cloke. He writes: "Forgiveness is not something we do for someone else, but to free ourselves from unhealthy pain, anger and shame. Forgiveness is a gift to our own peace of mind and self-esteem. It may appear weak, but it actually makes you stronger and less vulnerable to others."

You may hear people say they "survived" their divorce. But the goal here is not surviving, but thriving. The tips above may seem like an overwhelming assignment, but they are the Rx of healing. It may help to have a sounding board or therapist who can help guide you through healing.

As you come out of your personal season of darkness, it is essential to give yourself permission to feel the warmth of the sun and the comfort of support in this next season of light. Permission to laugh, enjoy life, and find happiness is not meant to eclipse or block out your pain; it is a crucial tactic for healing.

> **Better**
>
> "The supreme act of forgiveness is when you can forgive yourself for all the wounds you've created in your own life. Forgiveness is an act of self-love. When you forgive yourself, self-acceptance begins and self-love grows."
>
> –Don Miguel Ruiz

The Autumnal Equinox

In the midst of fall, we come upon the notion of changing who we are with a mask or a costume. This often starts when we are children preparing for the annual Halloween trick-or-treat outing. The adults around us ask, "Who are you going to be for Halloween this year?" The question supports the idea that we can "try on" other identities and choose to become someone else.

Most of us actually wear a mask and a costume all year long—sometimes more than one. Every day we decide what face we will present to the world. For some, the choice is reactive; it feels out of control and not a choice at all. For others, it is a planned persona that is constructive for dealing with the realities.

We all know that different people deal with challenges in different ways. On the positive side, we hear stories of courage: for example, the athlete who loses a limb by accident or disease, and yet goes on to run a marathon. Adults who have overcome childhood challenges show others the way to conquer theirs and transform their lives.

Then there are negative stories that some construct to justify wallowing in despair, place blame, or avoid personal responsibility. Many of us have had a friend or acquaintance who has made being miserable a part of who they are. This may be the result of the "Why me?" sense that they are victims of circumstances beyond their control, or they may nurse angry feelings about the person who "done them wrong."

In both cases, the story becomes the mask through which the person views life, and through which others view the person.

Ending your marriage is high on the list of life's most challenging events. The pain involved in losing this key relationship is as real as that felt by people who have lost a limb. For many, divorce feels like a part of you has been amputated, and it takes time to learn to "walk" again. It takes great effort to put on a positive face and meet the responsibilities of children, work, and family.

Doing right actions helps you heal, and it has the added benefit of inspiring your children and family. Divorce is a learning opportunity, and you are the teacher, even though you may not think of yourself as one.

Your children are sponges when it comes to your behavior. They know when you are wearing your angry, punishing mask or your sad but respectful mask. They take their cues from your masks about how to behave when they are angry or sad. Kids model your behavior and feel as justified about it as you may feel when you behave that way.

As you go through life after your divorce, choose to wear a mask of dignity and respect. While it may feel uncomfortable to wear at first, over time this mask will attract more "treats" for you and your children.

Better

Whatever the name, when you embrace loving kindness for yourself and give it to others, it has magic that helps you change the course of your life.

Pathway to Self-Care

Clients often say, "If I look and behave OK, he/she will think everything is fine. Then he/she gets a free pass after really ruining my life." However, letting go of the pain, anger, and even your mindset to punish the person who hurt you does not take away your truth.

> **Better**
>
> *There is an expression in twelve-step recovery programs: "Actions first, and then beliefs."*

What truly ruins your life is letting someone else's actions diminish even a minute of your "quota of days." Generally, your pain does not influence the other person to change his/her behaviors. The more ignored you feel, the more intensely you may ratchet up your painful, angry and punishing behaviors. The irony is that those feelings boomerang, and you end up feeling worse. Healthy healing recognizes the painful feelings, honors the challenges, and allows the light in.

By now you may be saying: "Easy to say but very hard to do." And I agree with you that it is something that does not come naturally to most of us. Turning the other cheek is very hard to live by when you feel you have been wronged, betrayed, and treated poorly. When we are hurt, our inclination is to punish. Here's the paradox: The more you punish someone else, the harder it is for you to see the light and accept the sunshine. These thoughts keep you in a prison of pain.

There are two keys to your freedom:

• Kindness to yourself.
• Kindness to others.

These two paths of kindness can be cultivated through the Buddhist practice of metta (see note below). Metta is a Pali word that has two meanings, "gentle" and "friend." Metta is a daily affirmation that wishes yourself and others well. The magic happens when you repeat the affirmation four times, each time with a focus on one of four people. With the exception of yourself, you can change the people daily.

• Yourself
• A loved one (child, parent, friend)
• A neutral person (Starbucks barista, mail carrier, teacher)
• Someone you have strong negative feelings toward (perhaps your ex-spouse)

Here is one version of the Metta Meditation:

May I be safe, physically, spiritually and emotionally.
May I be balanced and have peace.
May I be healthy and make good choices.
May I have ease.

Repeat the affirmation four times, each time focusing on one of the four people you are holding in your mind each day.

With a focused intention to absorb the metta affirmations of self-acceptance, love, and kindness, there is a shift in how we

> **Better**
>
> *It is the fire of the kiln that makes the pottery shine. This is your chance to shine and to consider the question poet Mary Oliver asks: "Tell me, what is it you plan to do with your one wild and precious life?"*

feel and behave towards others. People call this shift compassion or forgiveness or acceptance.

There are many resources, articles, and books on metta practice. A good start would be *The Sacred Art of Lovingkindness: Preparing to Practice (The Art of Spiritual Living)* by Rami Shapiro. Consider trying this practice for thirty days and see what happens.

Must Love Dogs: A Relationship Plan

"He doesn't love me." "I cannot trust her." "There's just no respect between us anymore."

These are the sentiments clients often express in my office when trying to explain why their marriage is ending. Sadly, these words—love, trust, respect, and many other relationship words—are rarely defined and are often a moving target. These words mean different things to different people. It's no wonder that a husband or wife might not measure up to a definition that is rarely defined and is often difficult to articulate.

Consider someone telling you, "You can't sing." It's very likely that you really can sing; virtually everyone can sing. It's clear the accuser has a specific definition of "sing" in mind, and, in his opinion, you don't measure up. The ongoing conversation often turns into a barrage of, "Yes, I can sing" and "No, you can't sing." Rarely is there a pause to understand what "sing" means to each other.

I have found that when clients are struggling to let each other go, it helps when they can separate loving each other versus loving the marriage. In Chapter 2 of this book, I offered insights about how often people cling to the marriage because they are scared of change or loss, not because the spouse's qualities bring great things to the relationship.

The notion of what qualities you want in a partner is the key to relationship success. Sometimes the qualities that seemed endearing during your courtship are annoying now. Some of my clients remember the spontaneity and adventure that sparked their romance. Now they view that as a negative, wishing instead for the other to grow up and take responsibility. It is natural for individuals to change priorities as life's challenges emerge. The key to long relationships is finding ways to change together.

What I have learned is that individuals have rarely given thought to what qualities they want in a partner. Short of completing the profile on Match.com or other online dating sites, very few people take the time to accurately describe what kind of partner they are looking for.

I have invited many clients over the years to consider the following exercise. Most are not only intrigued, but grateful. Here's what I suggest.

1. **Over a period of 2-3 weeks, jot down the qualities that you might want in a partner.** The list must have at least 30 qualities. You want to get past the usual loving, respectful, trusting, kind, sort of qualities and dig deeper to other important qualities.

2. **When you're driving in the car, exercising, or doing the dishes, words like "sense of humor," "energetic," or "healthy" will emerge.** Jot them down.

3. **Keep your list positive.** For instance, replace the quality "not selfish" with a word like "generous."

4. **Do not think of your current partner, and do not share this with your partner.** This is your heart's yearning, your magic wand; any quality you choose is acceptable.

5. **Once you have a list (and the longer, the better), the next step is to define what the qualities mean to you.** Again, this may take a couple of weeks. Take your time. This is an essential step. Write three or four sentences about what each quality means to you. For example:
   - **The quality:** Sense of humor. *That might mean:* I think the morning comics are very funny. I laugh out loud every morning when I read them.
   - **The quality:** Energetic. *That might mean:* I get up early (what's "early" to you?) every day and just keep going all day with gusto and without complaining.

6. **Review the qualities and find the top four or five that are not negotiable.** I imagine that every person has all of the qualities on your list at some level. However, they likely do not define them the same way you do. Or a quality's strength or definition or order is different from what is important to you. Remember: everyone can sing, but it matters what your definition of "sing" is. For example, consider the quality of a sense of humor. Your idea is laughing at the morning comics. Your current partner's idea is teasing other people. You both have a sense of humor; you each define it differently.

7. **It is likely that your spouse has all the qualities (in one way or another) that you listed.** But the ones you have as non-negotiable are not his/her strong suit. Your spouse has good and fine qualities, but not the ones you need to sustain an adult relationship.

Now you have a relationship roadmap

What you have developed is a roadmap that will guide you through life regarding the notion of partnership. It is not intended to be a criticism of a specific person. It is your private guidebook about what is important to you.

I have actually done this exercise for myself several times. Of course, the order and even my definition of the qualities changed over time. My list when I was married at age 21 would have looked quite different from my list today. Then I might have said financial security or physical attractiveness; today my #2 non-negotiable quality I want in a partner is, "Must love dogs." That was definitely not on my list when I was younger. Today, I would not choose a partner who does not love, embrace, adore, and want to have dogs. Yes, that's right—I might love someone, trust and respect that person, but if they do not share my love and passion for dogs, it would be a deal-breaker, because that is essential to me. You may be surprised but certainly enlightened to understand what you really need from a partner.

> **Better**
>
> *There is an expression: "Any road will work if you don't know where you are going." On the relationship road, you need to know how to read the signs and understand what they mean for your journey. Only then can you change roads when needed or return to journeying together.*

When a Friend Goes Through a Divorce

Eight years. That's the average length of a first marriage that ends in divorce.

The actual 2012 U. S. Census Bureau statistics—the last year they were surveyed—are that 41 percent of first marriages, 60 percent of second marriages, and 73 percent of third marriages end in divorce. So, chances are, you have co-workers, friends, or family members going through a divorce.

Divorce is a traumatic time for people, and it is natural to turn to friends for support. As the friend, you may already know that providing that support can be overwhelming emotionally, sometimes very time-consuming, and even frustrating for you. It also can bring up all the feelings that you had when you were going through your own divorce—feelings you have long since resolved and have no need to revisit.

Donna Roberts said, "A friend is someone who knows the song in your heart, and can sing it back to you when you have forgotten the words." You want to be a good friend, but you also need to protect your own emotions as well. Here are my tips for striking a healthy balance:

1. Avoid Giving Advice.

One way to help is to minimize or avoid giving tangible advice. Most individuals who are in deep distress are actually not looking for solutions, but rather to vent and to be heard. Listen carefully to your friend. When Mary says, "How am I going to have enough money when I am on my own?" you might consider reflecting her worry by saying something like: "It must be scary to worry about how to make ends meet."

Offering suggestions like getting a job, or asking for more money, and other well-intentioned problem-solving ideas can promote despair rather than support. And you'll likely hear "yes-but" detailed reasons about why each of those suggestions will not work.

On the other hand, you might connect her with someone you know who has "made it" financially after a divorce and whom you know would be willing to share her story and serve as an inspiration.

2. Be Inclusive.

The transition from being a full-time spouse and parent to sharing time with the children is huge. Your friend may be very lonely and anxious when the children are away. Arrange some friend time and include her as often as possible in social gatherings. One comment I hear repeatedly is "It's a couples world," and it does seem that way. Inviting your friend to a movie or dinner date with several other couples lets her know that she is still a valued friend and an important person as an individual, not just as part of a couple.

3. Set Boundaries.

Maintaining a relationship with both parties of a divorce can be dicey. Not being a messenger or mediator is essential. Be clear that you intend to be supportive to both of your friends. If your friend wants you to choose, then be honest and let him know that you care about both people, and you are not going to judge or choose sides. Then it's up to your friend. He may choose his anger (at his wife) over his friendship with you.

This is particularly evident when people or family host a gathering and are asked about who is invited, implying that if they invited the other party in the divorce, "Then I'm not coming." The best response is to explain that each invitee needs to make his or her own decision, and that you do not want to choose among friends.

4. When Friends Are Also Relatives

For many people, friends are relatives. The divorce may affect a sister- or brother-in-law who has been in your life for years, often attending your school or even working at the same place you do. It is very hard to be forced to choose between family and friends.

The adage that "I am not divorcing you" is wise, and at the same time it is hard to pay attention to everyone's feelings.

The first step in maintaining both relationships is not to collude or agree with either party's "story" about why the marriage is ending. Remind them that you are not taking sides, and that you do not want to be part of the collateral "damage."

If there are children, they need to feel safe to be with their cousins, grandparents, and other family members on both sides without worrying that the other parent is not allowed to be present.

5. Support Systems

Finally, it is helpful to understand how your friend is connected with support systems. Is she seeing a therapist? Is he getting good information from a mediator or attorney regarding navigating the divorce process? Is she aware of the peer support groups in town? Does he have a financial planner or tax accountant to help with finances? Has she read any books about divorce?

Understanding her support team will help you defer to their expertise when you talk. As her friend, your main role is to be as good a listener as you can be.

Epilogue

My Parting Gift

When we finish the mediation process, I give each of my clients a special gift: a single ceramic tile with this message on it: *"You need both rain and sunshine to make a rainbow."*

I encourage my clients to put a potted plant on their tile, and nurture the plant as a symbol of the way they need to care for themselves. I encourage them to be gentle to themselves, and end the harsh words and trash self-talk. Taking care of the plant may be a way to interrupt some of the harsh words they use so freely about themselves.

The tile serves as a symbol of hope and inspiration during what can be one of the most difficult transitional times in their lives. If I can help them—and you—understand that the good and the bad, the exciting and the painful, the bright spots and the darkness are all part of the healing, then I have succeeded in my work.

This is what I find so rewarding about guiding people through all of the questions—big and small—in the mediation process. I see so many people come out on the other side and find new hope, energy, inspiration, and yes, even new love. We work together to find the way to be *better, not bitter,* when the divorce is behind them.

It may be helpful for you to know that I have been right where you're standing today, looking at twenty-five years of marriage that ended rather suddenly. I was devastated and referred to myself as a puddle on the floor.

What stands out during the first year or two of ending a marriage is the roller coaster of feelings: the awareness, the disbelief, the hoping and the praying. I realize how important my support system of friends and family were to me. I remember how hard it was to accept help and how overwhelming it seemed to manage the house on my own. I even had to learn to pay bills, as that was not my job in the marriage.

For a while I was just really off balance. Being divorced felt like a stigma and saying it out loud was devastating. I did not want to be in that club any more than you do. I felt like I was wearing a different skin, like I had to be someone else for a while. In those years I was just surviving, not thriving. Like you, I had to go through the mourning and grieving stage to let go of the life I thought I had.

Gradually, I realized I could not grieve for the rest of my life and when I came out of the process, I reinvented myself. I found a new spirituality apart from my religion, and—most importantly—I began to trust in curiosity rather than certainty. I was comfortable not knowing what would happen from day to day.

Of course, I worried about my children, who were then ages 15, 13 and 10. The end of my marriage was pretty sudden for all of us. The kids went through ups and downs, and it's hard watching your children be sad and confused. Their trajectory surely changed from where it might have been, but they all landed in safe and successful places. They found their grit and their resiliency, and today they have a very good relationship with both Mom and Dad.

Before my divorce I was a corporate executive, I had my children, I was active in the community, and I believed that I had a marriage that would go the distance. In the years of transformation following my divorce, I found out that curiosity serves me better than certainty. I learned how to embrace change and the belief that good things and bad things happen, but the struggle is optional. I am fine not knowing "everything" and appreciate the potential that comes with curiosity. My personal journey led me to become a divorce mediator. When I realized that divorce can be viewed through a compassionate, peace-making lens, I knew I had to make this my life's work and purpose.

Now, 22 years after my own divorce, I understand that divorce is a badge of courage (not failure as so many people feel initially), and that hard decisions—like the decision to divorce—can be the right decisions for you and your life. I feel that my own divorce was a sort of divine intervention, that I was guided in some universal way to find my new life, a new husband, a new spirituality, to have dogs in my life, and to flourish in my career as a mediator. And it's important to mention that my former husband and I have been very good friends for years. We joyously share our children, grandchildren, holidays, and celebrations together. That's the vision I hold for my clients and their children.

It comes back to the three-legged stool I describe in Chapter 13: honesty, courage and resiliency are the important lessons you and your children take away from the process of divorce. If you can be honest with yourself and your children, and have the courage to face the monumental challenges of going through a divorce, you will find resiliency on the other side. I know I did, and I have helped thousands of people find their way through this process as well.

I hope that you will find your way to put the dark days behind you and build a *better, not bitter* life. Stop waiting for Friday, for summer, for someone to fall in love with you, for life. Happiness is achieved when you stop waiting for it and make the most of the moment you are in now.

Acknowledgements

I want to acknowledge the many people who have helped and supported me in writing this book.

First and foremost, thank you to my Mom, Hope Mann, who is my biggest fan and has said for as long as I can remember, "You have a book in you!" Here it is, Mom. And to my children, Dave (Tory), Emily, and Juli (Paul), who are the finest examples of resiliency, courage, and support "then" and "now." Thank you for your steadfast love. I am blessed. And, of course to Turk, my husband, who may actually nudge my Mom out for "biggest fan." Turk is my muse and my love. He has provided loving and practical support for my book, my mediation practice, and for me.

To my precious dogs Kayla, Cody, and Spirit (all now passed) and Grace, whose constant companionship gave/give me comfort, daily exercise, and inspiration (dogs do not hold grudges).

To my dear friends Lori and Jim Gelbort, who have been with me on every step of my journey from college to mediator. Your ever-present love and wisdom are a blessing.

Heartfelt thanks to Mary Anne Shew, who has been my webmaster and blog editor for 14 years. Her business and Internet expertise and devotion have enhanced my mediation practice and provided the foundation for this book. And to Michelle Arbore who guided every aspect of my social media presence with her savvy and professional expertise.

To my editor, Randi Minetor, who "sewed" my blog posts together to create the essence of this book. I am very grateful for her keen sense of organization and writing expertise and her initial and unwavering support of this project.

My awe and loving thanks go to Lori Capron Galan, a dear friend, and the creative inspiration for the design and layout of this book.

I would not be the mediator I am today without the support, encouragement and mentoring of so many colleagues. I am especially grateful to Mara Fain, my first mediator teacher, then mentor and forever my dear friend. To Michael Hagelberg, who graciously wrote the Foreword for this book and has been a mentor and collaborator during my career. Thank you also to Seema Ali Rizzo, Patricia Gibbons, and Michelle Cimino (three well-regarded matrimonial attorneys) who have provided legal perspective and editing guidance during my book writing and for my practice.

I am very grateful to attorney Sharon DiMuro, who has been an essential resource to me and my clients for virtually my entire mediation practice, and for the friendship that we have developed along the way.

Thanks too for the collegial encouragement, support, and now friendship of mediators Gail Ferraioli, Bobbie Dillon, and Beth Danehey. Our shared passion for peacemaking and conflict resolution has enriched our lives and our careers. Thanks also to Linda Joffe and Lowell Lakritz, the loving duo, who added creative insight and wisdom to this process. And very special thanks to Nina Alvarez and Carolyn Birrittella, the marketing team that launched this book from my desk to the marketplace.

To the many colleagues who provided unique expertise in writing certain portions of this book (which were originally web blogs) and who also extend that same expertise to my clients as valuable resources. Thank you to David Cook, real estate attorney; Jamie Block, CPA; Kristen Jenks, CFA; Brenda Piazza, college planning consultant; Deborah Schaal, bankruptcy attorney; and Mark Shannon, senior marketplace analyst.

And finally, a sincere thank you to **my clients,** who have trusted me with the privilege of helping them cross the bridge from marriage to independence. You have inspired me with your courage and dignity in your most challenging moments. Your willingness to mediate and share your fears and your hopes is a daily affirmation that, when people have the opportunity to be valued, respected and heard, solutions emerge.

Resources

Note: **Appendices A-F** *are New York State guidelines and will vary from state to state. The information is current as of 2017. Please check the New York State websites for updates to this information.*

Appendix A

GUIDELINES FOR CHILD SUPPORT

Both parties acknowledge that they understand that New York State Guidelines for Child Support mandates the following unless the parties agree otherwise:

- Child support is to be paid in an amount equal to the following percentages of combined gross income up to the first $143,000 (adjusted 1/16) adjusted every two years for the CPI:

    17% one child
    25% two children
    29% three children
    31% four children
    35% five or more children

- The non-custodial parent pays the appropriate support percentage in proportion to each party's percentage of the gross income of the two parties. Additional expenses (in the same proportion) are to be paid by the non-custodial parent for health insurance coverage, day-care and uninsured health care of the child(ren);

- The parent's incomes for the purposes of the guidelines include gross income from all sources less spousal maintenance actually paid, less child support paid for other children, public assistance, supplemental security income, and

- Other factors that can be considered:

    a. The financial resources of the child(ren)
    b. The earning ability and financial resources of each parent
    c. The standard of living the child(ren) would have enjoyed had the marriage not been dissolved, reduced by the impact that maintaining two households rather than one may have upon the standards of living of the parties
    d. The physical and emotional condition of the child(ren) and his/her educational needs; the non-monetary contributions that the parents shall make toward the care and well-being of the child(ren); financial need as determined by budget-estimating process.

Appendix B

WHEN YOU DEVIATE FROM THE CHILD SUPPORT GUIDELINES

New York State child support law allows parents to deviate from the Child Support Standards Act (CSSA) guidelines, provided that they have indicated what their child support obligations would be had they followed the guidelines, have affirmed their CSSA obligations to be presumptively correct, and have justified the proposed deviation to the satisfaction of the Court.

When agreeing to a deviation, the parties must show that the CSSA guidelines would result in an "inappropriate or unjust" award, based on one or more of the following factors, per DRL Section 240 (1-b)f:

- The financial resources of the parents and those of the child;
- The physical and emotional health of the child and his/her special needs or aptitudes;
- The standard of living the child would have enjoyed had the marriage or household not been dissolved;
- The tax consequences to the parties;
- The non-monetary contributions that the parents shall make toward the care and well being of the child;
- The educational needs of either parent;
- A determination that the gross income of one parent is substantially less than the other parent's gross income;
- The needs of other children of the non-custodial parent
- Provided that the child is not on public assistance, extraordinary expenses incurred by the non-custodial parent in extended visitation provided that the custodial parent's expenses are substantially reduced as a result thereof;
- "Any other factors the court determines are relevant in each case...."

Marital misconduct of either parent is not to be considered.

Appendix C

EMANCIPATION EVENTS

In New York State, a parent must financially support a child until the child turns 21 years old or becomes emancipated.

When a child is emancipated, it means that the child no longer lives with the parents and is self-supporting.

If the child is financially dependent on a parent, that child is not emancipated. A child who was once emancipated can become dependent again on the parents before turning 21 years of age.

In general, a child under 21 is emancipated if:
- The child is married.
- The child is in the military.
- The child finished 4 years of college from high school graduation.
- The child is 18 years old and working full-time (summer or vacation jobs do not count).
- The child permanently leaves home and ended the relationship with both parents for his/her own reasons (except if the child left home because of abuse by a parent or a similar reason).

Appendix D

TEMPORARY AND POST DIVORCE SPOUSAL MAINTENANCE

The Calculation of Spousal Maintenance (SM): Two Formulas
There are two different formulas for determining the guideline amount of spousal maintenance. One is used when *child support is being paid* by the potential spousal maintenance payor; and the second is used when *no child support is being paid* by the maintenance payor.

Note: Income is gross income, (from all sources with some exceptions) adjusted for Social Security and Medicare taxes. The same income definition is used to calculate child support income.
Note: These are the same two formulas used to calculate Temporary Spousal Maintenance.
Note: The decision of whether child support will be paid must be made first, as it affects which formula is used to calculate the guideline amount for post-divorce spousal maintenance. Then the maintenance amount (temporary or post-divorce) will be calculated prior to the child support amount. This is because the amount of maintenance is used in the child support calculation.

When Child Support is Being Paid by the Maintenance Payor:
This formula is used to calculate SM to a spouse when there are child support-eligible children.

   Step 1: 20% of Payor's income up to $178,000, MINUS 25% of Payee's income.
   Step 2: Payor's income up to $178,000, PLUS Payee's income x 40%, MINUS Payee's income.
   Step 3: The lower of the two amounts above is the guideline figure.

Where No Child Support Is Being Paid By the Maintenance Payor to the Recipient Spouse:
This formula is used when there are NO child support-eligible children or the maintenance payor is also the custodial parent for child support purposes or for Temporary Spousal Maintenance.

   Step 1: 30% of Payor's income up to $178,000, MINUS 20% of Payee's income.
   Step 2: Payor's income up to $178,000, PLUS Payee's income x 40%, MINUS Payee's income.
   Step 3: The lower of the two amounts above is the guideline figure.

Factors Used to Consider Adjusting Spousal Maintenance
Above or Below the Guideline Calculation

When considering spousal maintenance, courts in New York State consider the following (a, b, and c) as well as the 15 factors listed below. With the exception of Factors 14 and 15, these same factors apply to Temporary Spousal Maintenance.

a. The spouse lacks sufficient property, including marital property apportioned to him/her, to provide for his/her reasonable needs.

b. The spouse is fully or partially unable to support himself/herself through appropriate employment, or is the custodian of a child whose condition or circumstances make it appropriate that the custodian not be required to seek employment outside the home.

c. Maintenance shall be in such amounts and for such periods of time as is just, without regard to marital misconduct and after considering all relevant factors. In determining the amount and duration of maintenance, the Courts in New York State consider:

1. The age and health of the parties;

2. The equitable distribution of marital property and the income or imputed income on the assets so distributed;

3. The present and future earning capacity of both parties, including a history of limited participation in the workforce;

4. The need of one party to incur education or training expenses;

5. The termination of a child support award before the termination of the maintenance award when the calculation of maintenance was based upon child support being awarded which resulted in a maintenance award lower than it would have been had child support not been awarded;

6. The existence and duration of a pre-marital joint household or a pre-divorce separate household;

7. Acts by one party against another that may have inhibited or continue to inhibit a party's earning capacity or ability to obtain meaningful employment. Such acts include but are not limited to acts of domestic violence as provided in section 459-A of the Social Services Law;

8. The reduced or lost lifetime earning capacity of the payee as a result of having foregone or delayed education, training, employment, or career opportunities during the marriage;

9. The care of the children or stepchildren, disabled adult children or stepchildren, elderly parents or in-laws provided during the marriage that has inhibited or continues to inhibit a party's earning capacity;

10. The tax consequences to each party;

11. The standard of living of the parties established during the marriage;

12. The contributions and services of the payee as a spouse, parent, wage earner and homemaker, and to the career or career potential of the other party;

13. The wasteful dissipation of marital property, including by either spouse transfers or encumbrances made in contemplation of matrimonial action without fair consideration;

14. The availability and cost of medical insurance for the parties;

15. Any other factor which the court shall expressly find to be just and proper.

Duration (Length of Time) Spousal Maintenance Will Be Paid

The new laws established the following advisory schedule for post-divorce maintenance in New York. In mediation, couples may create agreements that differ from the guidelines. The courts retain the option of awarding "non-durational" meaning no end of SM if appropriate.

Length of the Marriage	% Guideline for Duration of SM Payment
0 to 15 Years	15% to 30%
More than 15 to 20 years	30% to 40%
More than 20 years	35% to 50%

Income Cap $178,000 for Temporary and Post Divorce

The income cap for temporary maintenance is **$178,000** of the payor's income. The $178,000 cap also applies to post-divorce maintenance and spousal support. There is a COLA provision that adjusts the cap every 2 years beginning January 31, 2016. Child Support Income Guidelines take into consideration "combined parental income;" the new maintenance guidelines only apply to the payor's income up to the $178,000 cap.

Appendix E

FACTORS IN DETERMINING POST DIVORCE
SPOUSAL MAINTENANCE

- **The income and property of each spouse,** including each spouse's share of the marital property as divided by the court.
- **The length of the marriage.** Spouses who are married for a long time are more likely to get more spousal maintenance, especially if the spouse who wishes to receive maintenance raised the children at home, or if he or she earned significantly less than the other.
- **The age and health of the parties.** The SM may be larger for an older spouse or one in failing health.
- **The present and future earning capacity of both spouses.** The court will look at the spouse's future ability to support himself or herself. If a spouse can return to school or find higher paying employment, he or she may receive more maintenance on a temporary basis.
- **Educational expenses.** The maintenance may cover the time needed for a spouse to pursue an advanced education, with the goal of becoming financially independent in the future.
- **The duration of a joint household before marriage, or separate households before divorce.** This helps the court determine the length of the dependent relationship between the spouses.
- **One spouse's acts against the other to prohibit the spouse from getting a job.** This takes domestic abuse into account.
- **One spouse's ability to become self-supporting, and what this will entail.** If a spouse has the ability to support him or herself, he or she may receive temporary maintenance until he or she can secure a job. Some spouses will never be able to support themselves because of an illness or other factors, so they may receive lifetime maintenance.
- **The impact of one spouse laying aside career aspirations to stay home with children.** After a long period out of the workforce, the spouse who cared for children at home may not be able to resume his or her original career choice. This loss of lifetime earnings can have significant impact on his or her financial security in divorce.
- **Where the children live.** If one parent must be home with a child or children after divorce (if a child is very young or has an illness or lifetime disability, for

example), child support alone may not be enough to support this arrangement. Spousal maintenance may be required in this case.

- **Ongoing care for children, stepchildren, adults with disabilities, or elderly family members.** If a spouse will have to forego employment to remain at home as a full-time caregiver, SM is necessary to support this arrangement.

- **Spouse's age and length of absence from the workforce.** It may be difficult for the spouse who has been at home for a long time to find any kind of job. In this case, a larger maintenance award may be indicated.

- **Exceptional child-raising expenses.** School, day care, and medical expenses are larger for some children than for others. The custodial parent may need more maintenance in addition to child support.

- **Taxes.** SM is income, so the spouse receiving it will have to pay income taxes on it, while the person paying support can deduct this on the annual tax return. The court takes these amounts into consideration.

- **Distribution of property.** One spouse may need to pay maintenance to the other to pay off equity in a home or as another way to satisfy the requirement for equitable distribution.

- **The contributions of each spouse as parent, homemaker, or wage earner during the marriage.** This recognizes the non-financial contributions of each spouse, and the impact these contributions of time and effort on the other's career.

- **The wasteful dissipation of marital property.** If one spouse has essentially squandered an asset—through frivolous purchases, reckless damage, gambling, or some other method—the court may require that this spouse compensate the other by paying an equitable share to the other spouse.

- **Transfers or encumbrances made in anticipation of the divorce.** If one spouse has attempted to disguise or hide assets or deny the other spouse access to these assets because he or she intended to file for divorce, the court still will take these assets into consideration in determining SM.

- **Health insurance.** A spouse who was covered by the other spouse's health insurance plan may now have to pay for his or her own insurance. The court will look at this cost when assigning SM.

- **Other factors.** The couple must consider things that are unique to their specific situation when determining the SM amount. Every divorce is different, so there may be additional circumstances that are not listed here.

Appendix F

DIVISION OF PROPERTY: GUIDELINES FOR
EQUITABLE DISPOSITION

Both parties acknowledge and understand that when considering the equitable disposition of property, the Courts in the State of New York consider:

- The income and property of each party at the time of marriage, and at the time of the commencement of the action
- The duration of the marriage and the age and health of all parties
- The need of a custodial parent to occupy or own real property in the future, and to use or own its household effects
- The loss of inheritance and pension rights upon dissolution of the marriage as of the date of dissolution
- Any award of maintenance under this contract
- Any equitable claim to, interest in, or direct or indirect contribution made to the acquisition of such marital property by the party not having title, including joint efforts or expenditures and contributions and services as a spouse, parent, wage earner and homemaker, and to the career or career potential of the other party.
  The court shall not consider as marital property subject to distribution the value of a spouse's enhanced earning capacity arising from a license, degree, celebrity good will, or career enhancement. However, in arriving at an equitable division of marital property, the court shall consider the direct or indirect contributions to the development during the marriage of the enhanced earning capacity of the other spouse
- The liquid or non-liquid character of all marital property
- The probable future financial circumstances of each party
- The impossibility or difficulty of evaluating any component asset or any interest in a business, corporation or profession, and the economic desirability of retaining such asset or interest intact and free from any claim or interference by the other party
- The tax consequences to each party
- The wasteful dissipation of assets by either spouse
- Any transfer or encumbrance made in contemplation of a matrimonial action without a fair consideration
- Any other factor that the Court shall expressly find to be just and proper.

Appendix G

BUDGET TEMPLATE

EXPENSE	Monthly	Annually
HOUSING		
Rent		
Mortgage		
Property Taxes		
Other		
Total		
UTILITIES		
Fuel Oil		
Gas		
Electricity		
Cable		
Telephone		
Internet		
Cell Phones		
Water		
Trash		
Other		
Total		
FOOD/ENTERTAINMENT		
Groceries		
School Lunches		
Entertainment		
Subscriptions		
Dining Out		
Total		
CLOTHING		
Self		
Children		
Total		
EDUCATION		
Child Care		
Preschool		
Private School		
Religious		
College		
Other		
Total		
COLUMN A TOTAL		

EXPENSE	Monthly	Annually
INSURANCE		
Life		
Homeowners/Renters		
Health/Dental		
Auto		
Umbrella		
Optical		
Disability		
Uninsured Medical		
Other		
Total		
NOT REIMBURSED		
Medical		
Dental		
Optical		
Pharmacy		
Total		
HOUSEHOLD/HELP		
Repairs/Appliances		
Painting/Gardening		
Snow Plow		
Other		
Total		
AUTOMOBILE		
Car Payments		
Gas/Oil		
Parking		
Maintenance/Repairs		
Other		
Total		
SUPPORT		
Vet/Pet		
Child Support prior		
Alimony prior		
Other		
Total		
COLUMN B TOTAL		

Expense	Monthly	Annually
RECREATIONAL		
Extracurricular		
Country Club		
Vacation		
Sr. HS Expenses		
Allowances		
Health		
Sports		
Club/gym		
Birthdays		
Summer Camp		
Total		
MISCELLANEOUS		
Hair/Barber		
Nail Salon		
Massage		
Gifts		
Charitable Contributions		
Union/Org. Dues		
Total		
TAXES		
Federal Taxes		
State Taxes		
Village/Town Taxes		
SS/Medicare		
Total		
DEBTS		
Credit Cards		
School Loans		
401K-PensionLoans		
Other		
Total		
RETIREMENT		
Other		
Total		
COLUMN C TOTAL		
+ Column A TOTAL		
+ Column B TOTAL		
GRAND TOTAL		

Appendix H

RESOURCES

http://bjmediationservices.com/divorceresource/
This section of BJ Mann's website provides the following resources to help you with your divorce journey:

- The links to all the sites mentioned in this book (current as of this book's publication) as well as links to other excellent online resources concerning divorce.
- Recommendations for books covering a range of topics about divorce.

Chapter 2: Moving Off Square One
http://www.cnvc.org/
The Center for Nonviolent Communication is a global organization that supports the learning and sharing of Nonviolent Communication (NVC), and helps people peacefully and effectively resolve conflicts in personal, organizational, and political settings.

Chapter 6: Putting a Price Tag on Emotions
http://www.myfico.com/loan-center/refinance/calculators/home-refinance-calculator/
myFICO is a company that helps you understand your FICO score, how it relates to your credit record, and much more. This link takes you directly to a calculator for determining the cost to refinance your house.

Chapter 7: Health Insurance, Taxes, and Other Inevitables
https://nystateofhealth.ny.gov/
The New York State of Health (NYSOH) Official Health Plan Marketplace.

http://info.nystateofhealth.ny.gov/IPANavigatorSiteLocations
The New York State of Health (NYSOH) Official Health Plan In-Person Assistors / Navigators locator.

https://nystateofhealth.ny.gov/agent/hx_brokerSearch
The New York State of Health (NYSOH) Official Health Plan Broker locator. A Broker or Navigator can assist you or your employees to get health insurance through NY Health Exchange. You can authorize a Broker/ Navigator to work on your behalf.

https://www.ssa.gov/planners/survivors/onyourown3.html
Social Security Administration (SSA) "Survivors Planner: Benefits for Your Surviving Divorced Spouse." If you have a surviving divorced spouse, they could get the same benefits as your widow or widower provided that your marriage lasted 10 years or more.

https://www.ssa.gov/planners/retire/yourdivspouse.html
Social Security Administration (SSA) "Retirement Planner: Benefits for Your Divorced Spouse." If you are divorced, your ex-spouse can receive benefits based on your record (even if you have remarried).

https://www.ssa.gov/planners/retire/divspouse.html
Social Security Administration (SSA) "Retirement Planner: If You Are Divorced." If you are divorced, but your marriage lasted 10 years or longer, you can receive benefits on your ex-spouse's record.

https://www.irs.gov/help/ita/what-is- my-filing- status
The Internal Revenue Service (IRS) tool to determine your federal tax filing status.

Chapter 8: Child Support

http://www.ncsl.org/research/human-services/guideline-models-by-state.aspx
National Conference of State Legislatures. Child support guideline models by state.

https://www.childsupport.ny.gov/dcse/pdfs/LDSS-4882W.pdf
If your spouse stops making child support payments, you can apply for New York State intervention by filling out the application at the link above.

Chapter 9: Spousal Maintenance

http://www.nycourts.gov/divorce/calculator.pdf
New York State Temporary Spousal Maintenance Guidelines Calculator.

https://www.irs.gov/pub/irs-pdf/p504.pdf
IRS Publication 504: Divorced or Separated Individuals

Chapter 11: Co-Parenting

https://www.cbp.gov/
United States Customs and Border Protection

http://www2.monroecounty.gov/health-vitalrecords.php
Monroe County (NY) Vital Records

Index

Made in the USA
Monee, IL
10 December 2019